Eleña

a novel of intrigue and romance

By

JERRY M. YOUNG

Library of Congress Catalog Number 92–070078
Covenant Communications, Inc.
Eleña
First Printing April 1992
ISBN 1–55503–388–1

To my family and friends
who have made this project possible.

CHAPTER 1

News Briefs
Friday, January 11, 1991

WASHINGTON, D.C.—Congressional backers of President Bush's Persian Gulf policy today unveiled a resolution that would authorize him to take the United States to war against Iraq, and predicted it would pass over the weekend.

Anti-war rallies have increased across the country. Participants speak of a new sense of urgency in the wake of the failed talks. Senator David Pryor, D-Ark., says he is concerned that support for the war is building in the wake of the failed talks between Secretary of State James A. Baker III and Iraqi Foreign Minister Tariq Aziz.

U.N. HEADQUARTERS, NEW YORK—U.N. Chief Javier Perez de Cuellar leaves for Geneva today to meet with European Community foreign ministers before his conference with Iraqi President Saddam Hussein on Saturday, just three days short of the U.N.-mandated deadline for Iraq to quit Kuwait or face possible attack.

ROCKVILLE, MD —

A SINGLE LIGHT HANGING IN THE MIDDLE OF THE ROOM CAST ominous shadows on the far wall of the one-bay industrial unit. Two men huddled beside a work bench. Reflections around them sparkled from a wide assortment of glassware—flasks and beakers of all kinds and sizes. Chemicals packaged in bottles and tins crowded the work area. One of the men wore a long, white laboratory smock. The other man stood slightly behind the chemist as if by doing so he could protect his expensive business suit from being soiled or even melted by strange elements.

The chemist spoke with a thick German accent. "There are three compartments in each bottle," the chemist said. "On the bottom of this bottle is where the explosives are. Ja? Just enough to spray the gas in a big cloud. Too much will burn off the gas and you won't kill as effectively. Ja? Then in one compartment of the bottle you put this chemical. You see? Alone it is harmless. You cannot smell it. You cannot taste it. It is like water. And now you put this chemical on the other side. It also is harmless alone. And you can only smell it a little bit. But it is like sour water. Now you must be careful not to let the chemicals touch when you arm the bomb. Ja? Together they make the gas.

"Then you take this tube. It snaps in place like this. But you do not want to put it in the top until you are ready. If something happens, it could be a problem. Ja? But when you are ready, it fits right in a hole between the other two. And the bottle looks like a two-liter bottle of soda pop.

"To start the bomb you twist the cap on top like this. I hold this one outside so you can see. And this chemical drips onto the plastic. Here. Watch how it dissolves through this piece of plastic. It makes a bit of smoke but it acts too quickly to be a problem to you. If you want it to dissolve the plastic more slowly you use more water. Ja? Here, I give you a chart.

"Then the chemicals flow through the holes in their compartments. They come together. And this chemical keeps going to the explosive. And the bomb goes off. The effective killing range is about twenty meters all around. But the gas will continue to kill for twenty minutes. Then it is gone. Kaput! And nobody can tell what happened.

"So what you think? You like it, ja?"

The man standing beside the chemist nodded his head.

"It is perfect, Voelkel. That is, if the gas works. Will it work? Will it kill?"

"Hah! Will it work? Will it kill? Judge for yourself." The German produced several before and after photographs. "These were taken in your own country, Kassim. In the north."

"The Kurds?"

"Ja. You can see that inside it is most effective. That is where you want to put the bombs. Ja?"

"Ja," the customer replied. "I need six bombs for inside."

"Vunderbar," the chemist exclaimed, throwing a kiss into the air with both hands. "I will get you the bulk chemicals. See? Five gallons of each. You can make other bombs as you need to make them. One chemical is in the dark bottle. The other is in the clear bottle. They both look like punch. The fuse tubes are in the empty soda bottles."

"And the explosives—for the bottom?" asked the customer.

"They are already loaded inside the empty soda bottles. So, your whole order is ready: five gallons of each chemical in the large bottles; six empty soda bottles with fuse tube inside and explosive in the bottom. It looks like a party, ja?"

"A great party," the customer laughed thinking about the various locations he would put them—at least three in the rotunda of the Capitol Building—at the busiest hour of the day.

"And look," the chemist added. "If you change your plan and want to make a larger bomb—ja?—just take one cap from the small bottle—with its tube. Fit it inside the tube from the large bottle. You have to do this so the chemical from the fuse will drip right onto the plastic and not into the other chemical. It just snaps in place like the small bottle, like this. Twist the cap the same and let them drip the same. But you will need to find some way to spread the fumes once the chemicals mix together. A fan would be best."

"An alternate bomb for an alternate plan?" the customer looked at the chemist and sneered. "I do not believe I will need an alternative. My plan is foolproof."

WASHINGTON, D.C. —

Aside from a few tourists who slipped into the pleasant but functional congressional office buildings, everyone else had business there. These would notice Nephi Nicholes as he walked among them. They had to. Theirs was a world structured in power. And basic rules of survival called for noticing anyone with clout. Nephi didn't have much. He just looked like he did. He moved so quickly through the halls they would wonder what business he had. In a crowd people would pick him out because he carried an aura they couldn't quite identify. And his smile suggested he knew something they should.

But unlike those who sought to create the illusion of power by artificial means, Nephi always had walked with purpose and confidence. His eyes always had reflected a complex system of knowledge and understanding. And he smiled because he wanted to smile. Why shouldn't he? He actually was getting paid for working here—here in Congress—the U.S. House of Representatives. Mainly he served as Congressman Ron Hersch's press secretary. But he carried legislative responsibilities too. And that put him inside—inside where the clash of wills could happen anytime, anywhere.

He had been here a little over six months and he was learning quickly the lessons of power. Members of Congress argued in front of the public. But long before anyone saw them struggle between themselves, their personal staff members fought greater battles. They took their Member's side in preliminary meetings and private conversations. They thrashed out concepts and details—often shaping major legislation themselves—more frequently injecting major concepts and preferences into minor legislation where they hoped no one would notice what they had done.

Nephi had become one of them. And he loved it. He loved being thrown into the front lines of all this verbal warfare. He held strong beliefs about his country and how it should operate. He had a burning desire to make things better than they had been. Quickly he had learned something he had never before realized: the President didn't run this country, Congress did; and Congress didn't run the country, the majority party did; and the majority party didn't run the country, the power brokers for special interest groups did. So being here with a particular sense of values that ran contrary to the interests of controlling power brokers was an honor, a challenge, stressful to the extreme, and highly satisfying. That's why he smiled.

He was smiling on his way into work that Friday morning. Rounding the corner of the hall just before stepping into the reception area of his office, there was no reason for him to suspect anything different from the day before. Surely the neutral beige walls, covered halfway down and all around by deep, rich browns of stained, wooden paneling, cabinets, desks and shelves, would be the same as they always had been.

But on this day, all that well-established veneer had become simple background for a splendid, overwhelming display of color—flowers—of every kind and every shape. In the midst of them, holding a bulky bouquet of roses, stood the office receptionist as if the display had been planned around her. It had. Her face betrayed the story. Traces of tears stained her full, spontaneous smile.

"Who died?" Nephi asked.

"No one died," chided a senior staff member from the legislative side of the office. "Sariah's engaged."

Nephi smiled, suspecting as much. But why should he lose a perfect opportunity to tease a friend?

"So, you finally got Yussef to believe he couldn't live without you?"

Sariah recognized what he was doing. She had brothers who loved her enough to tease her. And she knew exactly how to deal with their kind. She just turned her shoulder slightly, to emphasize an air of haughtiness, and answered.

"No. He figured that out for himself, thank you."

"My gosh, Sariah," Nephi continued in his teasing mode. "Are you sure you want to get hooked up with that guy? I mean, he's only at the top of his class. Doesn't he get his Ph.D. with honors this summer? Can you really live with all that?"

She giggled. "I can live with that." She tightened her arms around the roses and caressed them with her cheek.

"Then can he live with you?" Nephi couldn't hold back the laughter that had been building up within him.

"He'd better," she straightened her back and looked just a bit demanding.

Two senior staff members from the legislative side of the office stood nearby, witnessing the exchange, their faces set in open disapproval of Nephi's behavior. To them, Nephi had committed a serious offense against their fellow woman. And the offense—his prejudice—obviously was greater since Sariah was

Arabian. His gross deportment proved again their belief that the Congressman had made a major error in bringing Nephi onto the full-time staff.

One of them had wanted his job. Both of them knew she was far more suited for it than Nephi ever could be.

So they tightened their grouping around Sariah to protect her, blocking the intruder's access to her. This occasion was best appreciated by women only. To restrict his participation surely would enhance their own.

But their subtle maneuver caused Sariah more problems than it did for Nephi. She deliberately took a step forward and leaned so she could talk with her friend.

"Can you believe all these flowers? Yussef sent every one of them. Two men were waiting at the door when I arrived this morning."

"There probably isn't another blossom in all of Washington," Nephi said, shaking his head.

She giggled.

"And he's probably the brokest student in all of Washington," he added.

That made her blush. She knew how extravagant it was for her fiancé to buy so many flowers. But she knew also that he came from a wealthy family and that this first expression of opulence was but a beginning. Allah had been good to her.

Last June Nephi Nicholes had slipped quietly into Washington. He left Springville the day after graduation and had driven the southern route from Utah as fast as he could. He didn't even take time to visit Mormon historical sites scattered along the way. His dean had allowed him to graduate on condition he complete this internship that summer. Not only was it a matter of integrity, it also was a great opportunity for Nephi. And he wanted to get on with it. The rest of his life beckoned.

By taking the southern route from Utah he approached Washington on Interstate 81, running up the Shenandoah Valley, near the border of West Virginia. To a kid who grew up in Utah where things seemed to grow only when water was diverted to them, the plush fields of rural Virginia not only pleased his eye but promised an abundant future. But these vistas gradually gave way to a highly populated Northern Virginia. Major real estate developers offered homes and condominiums as far out as Manassas, roughly 50 miles south of Washington. From there it just got worse—more densely populated. Before long the view of his surroundings became hidden behind well-groomed and thickly planted parkway forests.

Frequent signs along Highway 66 announced off-ramps and intersections. Mileage to Washington got smaller and smaller until he reached Rosslyn. *Just a few miles ahead,* he thought as he headed into a tunnel with huge buildings towering on each side. But the tunnel was short and curved to the right. Just after he emerged he could see bridges and a river. Beyond the river, peeking above and through the trees—his first glimpse of Washington.

Increased traffic escorted him across the Potomac. But shortly after crossing the bridge the heavy traffic slowed then stopped. Because of the congestion, the highway had turned into a virtual parking lot on Constitution Avenue.

Around him now were the scenes he had seen in pictures others had taken. Washington Monument really did stick straight up over the trees. And what were all these other buildings? The traffic was beginning to move again, and as he passed the Ellipse he stole a fast glance of the White House.

"Stupid traffic! How's a person to see all this without having an accident!" he mumbled.

And there was the Smithsonian. Good grief! There was another one, and a third. He thought there was only one Smithsonian. But he had just passed three—and now a fourth. And didn't one of the signs on the other side of the street say the Department of Commerce? What else was he missing?

"Where can I stop?" he shouted at his windshield. "I'm missing everything."

At the far end of a grassy, tree-lined area—it had to be the Mall—stood the Capitol Building. Magnificent! All that white against so much green, and powerful even against the faded blue of the sky.

He actually would be working there, or near there. His specific destination could not be far from there. But how could he get there from here? For a moment, about all he could recall from directions given him was that the House offices were south of the Capitol.

"Great," he mumbled to himself. "If I only knew which way was south, I'd be all right." Somewhere after Manassas his inner compass had begun to spin and neither north nor any other direction had settled clearly within him. By all rights the Mall should have been running north and south. Obviously, it was not. In his mind north was that way. But that's not the way it was on the map. Nothing around him remotely resembled a constant, well-fixed landmark.

They certainly could use a good Utah mountain out here, he thought.

The Capitol was supposed to be the highest point in Washington. But often it was not high enough to see because of the trees and buildings. And the Washington Monument wasn't much better. The longer he drifted with the flow of traffic the more his newcomer frustrations intensified. He didn't like being lost.

Then he remembered pictures he had seen. House office buildings were on the right side of pictures taken from this angle. He turned right, headed across the Mall, then turned left. That put him on Independence Avenue. And there were more Smithsonians, and all kinds of government buildings.

Driving a few blocks with the Capitol closing on the left, he discovered the Rayburn Building on his right. It was a name he recognized—one of the House Office Buildings. What a huge thing, he thought. White marble with ivy growing prolifically on its walls.

A small, older building came next. Nephi almost missed it because of the narrow street dividing the two. That would have to be his building, the Longworth Building—where he would be spending the next 10 weeks of his life. Not as glamorous as the Rayburn Building. Oh, well. It still was part of Washington.

He turned right as soon as he could and began searching for a place to park. That proved more difficult than finding the neighborhood in the first place. Over half an hour later he locked his car and began walking toward his future.

Roy Ivars served as Administrative Assistant to Congressman Hersch. He hired everyone—subject to the Congressman's approval. This was the first time Nephi had met the AA although they had spoken by phone several times.

"I hope you don't mind," Nephi explained. "I figured I could hit town early and get acquainted with the staff sooner."

"No problem," the AA said. "But Fridays are a bit casual around here," Roy Ivars admitted after introducing himself to his new intern. "Generally Congress is not in session on Fridays. Members go back to their districts. You'll have your BYU seminar sessions on Friday, so most of the time you won't be here on Fridays either. For the rest of us, Fridays are a time to clear up loose ends and get ready for next week."

After chatting for a few minutes Roy invited Nephi for a tour of the office. He began by introducing the Congressman's press secretary, Ed Bennett. Their desks were separated in the narrow room by a standing divider with file cabinets and shelves squaring off work space around them.

On Bennett's side was one of two Hewlett Packard LaserJet printers they had in the office as well as the office fax machine. Also he had rigged some recording equipment beside his telephone to process actualities—that is, freshly recorded comments by the Congressman—to radio stations in the district. This production setup intrigued Nephi more than anything. He enjoyed tinkering with these kinds of things. Noticing his interest, Ed invited him to help some time.

To get to the rest of the staff, Roy led Nephi through a narrow hall around the Congressman's office. Normal space in the hall had given way to the office mail boxes, a refrigerator with a small microwave on top of it, coat racks, and one end of a photocopy machine that partially blocked an exit from the Congressman's office.

Once in the next room, Nephi met two more members of what Roy called "our team"—the Senior Legislative Assistant and an outgoing intern.

"This is his last day," Janice Fielding announced.

"And this is my last project," Jim Preston boasted. Then,

when he was certain his boss had turned her head, he frowned, rolled his eyes and pointed to the stack of letters and envelopes he had been folding and stuffing. "Constituent mail."

"We answer every letter that constituents send us," Janice explained, making sure she hadn't caught her worker saying something derogatory.

"*We* answer *every* letter," Jim repeated, glancing quickly at Janice and forcing himself to smile at her.

She chose to ignore the outgoing intern's tone of voice and the emphasis he put on "we" and "every." "You'll be doing a lot of this, Nephi. We get letters on every possible issue. I have one rule, you never send out any letter without my approval or the approval of one of the senior staff members. Is that clear?"

Nephi nodded. The procedure sounded simple enough and very logical. He wondered why she barked the instruction with the voice of a drill sergeant.

Roy Ivars excused himself, leaving Nephi in his future office with his new boss. And it surprised her when the new kid asked if he could help his outgoing comrade.

"Of course," she said smiling warmly now that the AA had left. "But you really don't have to start until Monday."

With the two interns working, Janice knew the mailing would get out and she began wondering how soon she could arrange to be gone for the afternoon. Two quick private calls was all it took. She instructed Jim to take messages. He was to tell callers she had a meeting on the Senate side and would not be back.

The interns kept working as if she had been there. But her absence allowed them to loosen their conversation. Jim seemed anxious to reveal how he felt about his assignment.

"It could be so interesting," he observed. "But I haven't enjoyed it much—the way things are. I just don't feel like I learned as much as I could have. Best thing has been Fridays. They take us on special tours. Dr. Adams arranges them with different agencies. I kind of envy the students that work in those places. They always seem to be doing interesting things during the week. All we do is write letters."

Nephi shook his head wondering what he had gotten into.

Then he wondered what a typical letter looked like. He stopped stuffing to read.

It had to do with the Central Utah Project.

"I thought Congressman Hersch supported the CUP."

"He does," the outgoing intern stated.

"But this letter gives the impression he does not."

"I know."

"How can it go out this way?"

"Because Janice Fielding approved it and ordered me to get it out—today."

"But this isn't right. How can she do this?"

"She does what she wants. And we do what she wants. That's the way things are around here."

"But this letter will hurt the Congressman's image."

"After today that isn't any of my business."

"Maybe I'd better show this to Mr. Ivars."

"Go ahead. But I don't want anything to do with going over to the enemy."

"The enemy?"

"Yeh. You know. The enemy—the other side—over there where Roy Ivars works."

"Other side? What do you mean? Why not? This letter is flawed. Even I can see that. One word. All we need to do is change one word." Nephi stood up and started toward the connecting hall.

"Wait a minute, Nephi. You don't know what you're doing."

"All I'm doing is what she insisted on—letting someone approve a letter."

"Boy, you've got a lot to learn. Look, you asked why not? You really meant why don't I take it over there? Well, I'll give you an honest answer: because Janice Fielding will be giving me a grade for my work here. And if she knows I had a part in taking this letter over there—showing it to Ivars—I won't get a passing grade."

"Sure you will. She's tough, but she seemed like a nice person."

"Don't count on it, friend. You'll be threatening her little world here. She won't like it at all."

"Well, I'm going to show it to him anyway."
"It's your funeral."
But it wasn't a funeral at all.
What it amounted to was war.

Roy Ivars realized immediately that Nephi had caught a major error that could have embarrassed the Congressman right out of office. Fluke though it was, the new intern got the credit for discovering it—and the condemnation.

Janice Fielding's embarrassment surfaced in both active and passive vindictiveness against Nephi. Her friends allied themselves against the intruder. Words spoken around him carried barbs, booby traps and insults. Massive, tedious jobs turned up on his desk once or twice each day. Excellent form letters he wrote had to be rewritten to satisfy the whims of his immediate superiors. Changing "happy" for "glad" became a routine procedure he learned to endure.

The length of his ten-week internship would have seemed impossible had it not been for Nephi's ability to retreat into himself from time to time and receive spiritual relief. In the quiet of his third Sunday night in Washington, a strong impression filled his soul. It startled him, disturbed him. And for awhile he rebelled against it. He couldn't help himself. It seemed so unfair. Why should he be required to ask Janice Fielding and the others to forgive him? They had offended *him*. The Spirit should have been instructing him on how to accept their apologies—how to be noble in forgiving *them*. He asked for confirmation and forced a reaction, anxious to discover the original instruction to be something carnal or evil. For a few minutes he had himself convinced that what he had received had been some kind of counterfeit. It just seemed so contradictory to his understanding of justice in the situation.

But the Spirit withdrew when he did that. And its withdrawal left him a clear message through vivid contrast. Once he had been warmed and strengthened. His mind had been opened and filled with understanding. Now there was a void and his mind constricted. He knew he had been wrong. It took most of the night but finally he purged himself of his ego-driven ideas. He fully accepted the message. He would obey. The instant he submitted, let go of his personal inclinations, he came to realize a greater truth. He had reached a major turning point—not in his relationship with the senior staff—but rather within himself. Having won that battle, saying the words to the senior staff became a simple matter of conversation.

In public they accepted his apology. But they left early that afternoon to celebrate with dinner and a movie. By the time they got to the office in the morning they began working their plan to prove Nephi unfit to serve in a Congressional office. His apology clearly showed him too weak for what they did here. Janice gathered statements from the other legislative assistants and met with the Congressman. She regretted to report that Nephi Nicholes was making too many mistakes, did not comprehend the work and was not carrying his weight. She recommended he be terminated.

Roy Ivars took pride in his interns. Careful interviews reaped the best crop available each term. Though he had little control over their day-to-day activities, he monitored their work from a distance. That also gave him a slim line on what was happening on the other side—the legislative side. But when Congressman Hersch called Roy into his office to reveal what Janice Fielding had reported, it shocked the administrative assistant.

He interviewed the intern. But Nephi was reluctant to talk about what had happened. Roy even asked if this had anything to do with the letter he had intercepted on his first day. Nephi still said nothing. Then the skilled attorney cross-examined his intern as if he were a hostile witness. Nephi wasn't hostile. He just found it difficult to explain what had happened. And he still wasn't certain where to place his loyalties.

It didn't take Roy long to extract from Nephi what he had suspected. And he made his own report and recommendation to his boss.

"I can't fire Janice," Ron Hersch told his administrative assistant. "She's too good at her job. Who would replace her? I need her expertise in my committee assignment. You've got to find some other way to get this staff working together, Roy. And I want you to do it as quickly as you can."

It was Roy who told Janice that Nephi was not going to be fired. When she objected, he had no alternative than to reassign Nephi to work with him and Ed Bennett. And inter-office relationships returned to the cold war strategies that existed before Nephi arrived.

Once emancipated, Nephi responded to Roy Ivars' leadership. He plunged into his assignments—not merely handling constituent mail but working with legislation and sometimes writing press releases as well. From Nephi's first day in new surroundings, Roy could see that Nephi possessed a real talent for this work. The intern could quickly burrow to the heart of any bill or issue he was assigned to analyze.

Before long the Congressman also came to notice and appreciate Nephi's talent. He especially liked the way Nephi could summarize bills or issues into talking points. That allowed him to speak as a Congressman should, appearing knowledgeable about an issue when his real knowledge was limited.

Then, near the end of Nephi's internship, Ed Bennett resigned.

The scramble for his job reopened inter-office conflicts and wounds. First to apply was a Janice Fielding protegé. Two applications came in from other offices. But it took some urging from Roy Ivars before Nephi submitted his application. With a strong recommendation from his administrative assistant, Congressman Hersch brought Nephi onto the full-time staff.

Roy took Nephi to lunch the day the announcement was made and issued a challenge.

"This assignment is not going to be easy for you, Nephi. In order to write about what the Congressman's doing, you've got to work closely with the girls on the legislative side of the office. The boss insists on it. He won't tolerate any hard feelings to interfere with your work. That's a condition of your employment. Is that clear?"

"Yes."

Roy accepted his answer with a nod. "I'm sure you're aware that some serious grudges against you still linger over there."

"Yes."

"Somehow you've got to work around them—work with those who have them. You've got to get those people to set aside those grudges—get rid of them, and cooperate with you. That's imperative. Understood?"

Nephi nodded.

"The more you can get them to cooperate with you, the easier it will be to shape this staff into a real team. Nephi, we've got so much talent in this office, it scares me. On our side, on the legislative side, back in the district—we could easily have the strongest, most effective staff on the Hill. All we have to do is work together—let go of this nonsense of protecting petty domains and territories and work together. We've got to make that happen! Will you help me do that?"

Roy's eyes drilled into Nephi's mind. This man had dedicated himself to Congressman Hersch. He had been responsible for salvaging Nephi's internship and had opened to him this opportunity. Now he had given this challenge. How could he deny such a request?

"Of course," he pledged.

"Great!"

With the commitment made, Roy moved on to Nephi's responsibilities. Procedures became very specific. When a press release was called for, Nephi would interview the Congressman. He would get a briefing from the appropriate legislative assistant before writing the release. After he wrote the release he would show it to the LA, make whatever changes were required; then show it to Roy and finally get the Congressman's approval. Roy became a bit more general in his instructions on how to interact with the LAs. He simply made it quite clear that Nephi was to exercise courteous and professional businesslike protocols and language at all times.

Nephi let the procedures be etched deeply into his mind. Nothing seemed out of place or unreasonable. But even he could see that this whole situation would be more work than it needed to be. He didn't mind work. Not even that kind of work. He just didn't like the idea of having to please so many people. The same LAs who took turns changing "happy" for "glad" still would be editing his material for publication. To that limited degree they still had control over him—and his future.

"This is nothing but a foot in the door, Nephi. You're in the system now. What you make of this opportunity is up to you," Roy said, challenging his ally.

Nephi spent as much time as he could with Ed Bennett. Mostly they talked while the outgoing press secretary chucked his possessions into boxes for shipping home.

"You'll do real well," Ed kept telling Nephi. "You've got a talent for this work."

But Nephi couldn't help wonder why he kept saying it.

"Could I ask you a question, Ed?"

"Sure." He continued thinning his files—boxing some, leaving some and throwing some away.

"How come you're doing this? I mean, you're good at your job. How come you're leaving now?"

The press secretary studied his replacement. He smiled. But his expression didn't convey pleasure.

"I'm leaving 'cause you're here," came the flippant answer.

"Come on. You can't mean that. I wasn't looking for your job."

"I know," Ed said with a toss of his hand as if to wave off the previous thought.

Then he let his frame settle against the filing cabinet. "But in a way it was you. I mean it, Nephi. You really do have a talent for all this business. It needs to be cultivated. But it's there. And with you and your potential here I saw my chance to get out while I could."

Ed's eyes looked straight ahead at nothing. The tone of his voice slipped as his words slowed.

"I guess maybe I'm just tired. You know what I mean?"

Nephi nodded his head. Burnout. He'd heard of it. It had never happened to him. He couldn't understand how anyone could become burned out from work, especially this kind of work.

"It's like I don't even want to try anymore," Ed confessed. "I mean, when I got here I really believed I could make a difference. You know? I came in here with big ideas that my presence here would be the one ingredient needed to turn this country around—get it back to some basic principles that made it such a great country.

"But it's all over for me now. And look how much I did. Nothing's changed—except to get worse. There's been a socialist wall building up in this country for over fifty years now. And I'm just tired of beating my head against it. That's all."

He pointed his finger at Nephi and continued.

"Now it's up to you."

Nephi shrugged. "If you couldn't do anything, what will I be able to do?"

Ed smiled. "Go through the motions, kid. Everyone else does. Hang on. Maybe you'll get lucky."

Nephi had no idea what more he could say. But he felt he had to say something. So he dribbled a bit of etherial idealism.

"I'll do my best."

That brought a laugh out of the retiring press secretary.

"You sure have a lot to learn, Nephi. And I hope you can survive this place long enough to catch on."

"What do you mean?"

"I mean that doing your best simply isn't good enough. Doing your best will drive you as mad as it has driven me. Look! I know you're a good, conservative thinker. And you'll write good, conservative copy. But who will ever see it? Huh? Nobody. And do you know why?"

Nephi moved his head for a "no."

"You just wait. You'll see. You'll find out that the gatekeepers out there—the editors and news directors you have to deal with every day are more of an enemy to this country than the liberals in Congress. And one day you're going to be every bit as frustrated and angry about how they deal with you as I am with the way they have dealt with me. Just don't count on your stories getting into print the way you want them to be. They'll cut them apart. They'll turn them inside out—whichever way they want—to suit their own whims. You don't have a chance."

Nephi stared at Ed. There had never been a hint of such feelings. Clearly they had built up in the man over the years. Nephi had to wonder how much truth they held—how much of a warning they really were to him.

Ed continued his monologue, emotions raising the strength and fury of his words. When he realized how loud his voice had become he sat down with his knees close to Nephi's knees and he lowered his volume. At the same time he adjusted his expression to compensate.

"I hate to tell you this, Nephi. But this country's going down the tubes. And I'm going home before it gets so bad that we all get squashed by it."

He stood up again, grabbed a fat file from the top drawer and held it out for Nephi to take.

"This is just one example of what you're going to be dealing with. Look what they did last year. They passed the Americans with Disabilities Act. I still can't believe the President signed it. I handled this stupid issue. And it made me sick. I don't have anything against crippled people or anyone else with a disability—a true disability. But the movers and shakers knew they'd never be able to get it passed without support from a lot more special interest groups. So they loosened up the definitions to include millions more people—not just the ones with real disabilities. And what did they end up with? Do you know this bill is the first piece of legislation that gives civil rights status to homosexuals?"

Nephi looked at him in shock.

"It's right there in the bill." Ed pounded his finger on the file Nephi held in his lap. Then he opened the file, shuffled some pages and took out the bill itself. He thumbed through the well-used document to a page with many passages highlighted with yellow.

"Look at that! By definition a person with a disability is anyone who can be considered to be disabled—AND anyone with a special relationship to a disabled person.

"The promoters kept saying that provision just protected family members from getting fired from their jobs because they might have a handicapped person in their family. I'm telling you that's not why they shoved that definition down our throats. This bill—now a law of the land—protects a lot more than the real disabled and their real families."

He moved in his chair and pointed his finger at the file again.

"Did you know that everyone with the HIV virus has already been declared by the courts to be 'disabled?'

"Look, the largest block of people with AIDS got the stupid disease by some immoral or illegal act—either in some homosexual relationship or by sharing contaminated needles in some sleazy, back alley drug orgy.

"We did everything we could do to get that definition limited to people with real disabilities. But the liberals threw their weight around and got what they wanted. Now we're left with a civil rights act that says not only do the contaminated sodomites get civil rights protection but their partners get civil rights protection as well. And the law forbids straight people from saying anything about it because just expressing an opinion would be in violation of the civil rights of the contaminated person. And the act allows people protected in this act to sue anyone who complains about how unfair it is. They could make off with automatic awards of tens of thousands of dollars."

Ed took a deep breath and sat back in his chair.

Nephi looked at the man, studied him. Something new had emerged in the man's face.

"It's just not right," Ed continued. "I love my country. But I'm fed up with this kind of garbage."

For a moment Nephi could see tears in his eyes. Ed's lips tightened and the muscles in his chin quivered.

"The ADA, the budget fiasco, the clean air act—any one of those things has the potential of destroying this country. All of them in force assure it," Ed's voice forced itself through strong emotions. He took a deep breath and continued.

"I can't take it any more. It's all yours."

They held a party for Ed and everyone wished him well. But what he said lingered in Nephi's mind. For the first time he wondered if his own efforts could possibly make a difference. How long would *he* last—batting his own head against that same wall Ed spoke about—before he would be burned out? And what about all this madness with Saddam Hussein? Was the Iraqi invasion of Kuwait simply the beginning of a conflict that would end with Armageddon? A lot of people thought it might—including Ed Bennett.

But sometime between the hour Ed left and the hour Nephi came to work the next morning his concerns had been dismissed. A deep assurance had come to the new Congressional staff member. He was in the right place, doing the right thing. Nothing else mattered.

And one man's poison began generating into another man's full-course meal. A week or so later, Nephi thought of that while listening to the one-minute special order speeches. Already he had identified a number of Congressmen he considered his favorites. The Honorable Robert S. Walker for one. He was great. And Congressman Henry J. Hyde, perhaps the most eloquent orator of the bunch. And Representatives Bill Dannemeyer, Newt Gingrich, Bill Archer—they weren't going home. They remained in the fight. Good men. Dedicated to speaking out against going in the wrong direction. No. This country was not as close to self-destruction as Ed Bennett had portrayed. As a matter of fact, without dedicated people sustaining the fight, self-destruction would be assured—perhaps accelerated.

And there still were things to be done—things he could do.

"I'm giving you this press assignment, Nephi, because someone has to do it," the Congressman told him on his first day as a senior staff member. "But I don't want you to get bogged down with it. You're too valuable as a legislative analyst to let this get in your way here. So just keep me afloat in the media. Okay? I want a presence, not domination. I won't have you competing with our press-happy neighbor from the Fourth District. Okay?"

Nephi came to learn this was perhaps the greatest of all contradictions and potential liabilities that he faced. It was a typical approach for the Congressman to say such a thing—even to one of his most trusted employees. Yet Hersch really enjoyed seeing his name in the newspaper. When he made headlines it carried him into a state of near euphoria. Still he insisted to everyone that he didn't care—that he had seen his name in print so often that it didn't affect him any more.

But it did.

And Nephi had to learn such things in a short, short period of time.

Ron Hersch wasn't unbalanced in this regard. Egos dominate politics. Washington exists as a conglomerate of egos and super egos stretched to extreme. Hersch had suppressed this in himself as many do in the showcase of political action. He had fashioned his dominant image with hard work. He jealously guarded that image even to the refusal of accepting the appearance of seeking recognition for recognition's sake—except, of course, when he earned the right to it.

Nephi's problem became clear when he observed that natural recognition by the press worked most naturally when the press was reminded of what was happening and why it was so important. He had to do this without becoming terribly obvious in his efforts. In other words, he had to extend himself beyond his boss's instructions without his boss becoming too aware of what he was doing.

After all his education—interrupted by a Mormon mission where some of his education had been intensified—he now was learning extraordinary lessons in life. Washington, D.C., is the gathering place for every political and economic philosophy and movement in the world. As the most powerful seat of government, it is where those collective elements of power assemble. It is the place where conflicts between determined minds take place. Through generations a strict code had emerged to protect expression within boundaries mandated by both constitutional and congressional rules. Practical survival as well as success demanded those rules be kept. Sometimes they were.

In this atmosphere, it was not enough to express truth; one had to express it in an acceptable way. Meanings frequently became hidden in rhetoric that confused and obscured real intent.

Survival within this context requires basic skills at reading and writing between the lines. Motives and intent have to be dissected every bit as much as—perhaps more than—actual words and deeds. Diplomacy and tact seem to justify a pattern of lies and cordial subterfuge in the world beside the river Potomac. It was this contradiction and liability that Nephi had the greatest difficulty understanding, dealing with, and adjusting to.

In the relative quiet of his cramped workstation, with many of the flowers in view, Nephi thought of the young couple who had just announced their engagement: Yussef Makal and Sariah Khaldun. What a strange situation—in light of the conflict building in the Persian Gulf and the imminent efforts to settle the dispute by military means.

She was from Iraq and he from Kuwait. They both had come to America as students. Both had proven themselves brilliant. They made a charming couple.

Sariah was beautiful. Her long, black hair fell in gentle curls to frame a face with skin that looked much like expensive porcelain. She had dark eyes that dominated her expression. Even the fullness of her lips—when they were moistened with ruby coloring—could not distract from the quality of her eyes. They exposed her intelligence, her vivaciousness, the mysterious quality about her, and a number of other things any man would be fortunate to possess.

Yussef's bearing brought more attention to him than his appearance. He was almost as light as Sariah. But many hours in the sun had tanned him more deeply than her, and the heavy ghost of his beard added density to his coloring. Yussef also had a strong nose. But he, too, had expressive eyes—intense windows for the soul of a man in serious quest of life and its mysteries.

It seemed only natural they would be drawn together. Nephi had made it possible. He had met Yussef at a seminar on Middle East issues. Within an hour they were solid friends. Two days later Sariah showed up to work in the congressman's office as an intern. She charmed Nephi with her warmth and intelligence. Immediately he thought of Yussef. It only took two phone calls and the three of them had a date for dinner—on Nephi. That was a month ago. Only a month. Now an engagement bound Yussef and Sariah together and generated pure satisfaction within the Utahn. Family is all-important to Arabs. Nephi had learned that several years before in a religion class at Brigham Young University. The betrothal established Yussef as Sariah's protector. In this far land they had become family to each other.

"I really am happy for you," Nephi approached her shortly after things in the office had quieted down that Friday. "I hope you didn't mind my joking with you."

"I knew what you were doing. And I was honored you would consider me friend enough to do so. My brothers and my cousin would have teased me the same way. You made me feel as if I had been with them."

"That is most kind of you, Sariah. I am honored by your expression," he said, a little embarrassed to hear it. The way she was looking at him made him anxious to change the subject.

"It is true. You are like them. I think you are a nice man. And you know what? I am surprised you have not become a true believer. You act like one."

"I am a follower of The Book, as you say—a follower of Jesus Christ. He taught us to love one another."

"As we learn from the Koran," she injected.

"It is easy to show brotherly love and kindness to people like you and Yussef," Nephi said before he continued hesitantly. "That is why I am concerned for you."

"Why are you concerned, my American cousin?"

That unexpected expression lifted a smile onto Nephi's face.

"Well, it's the times, Sariah," he said. "You did not pick the best of times to fall in love."

"You mean, with a Kuwaiti?"

"Yes," he said. "And he with an Iraqi."

"Oh, Nephi," she began. "You are so perceptive. I am very worried. This war has brought nothing but grief and anxiety into my life. And confusion."

"I can understand grief and anxiety, Sariah. But confusion?"

"Yes," she admitted and reluctantly continued. "You see, it's my family—my father and my brothers."

"You once told me they had been arrested."

"Yes. And they were fortunate because they were released. It took a great deal of money to get them released. But we managed."

"That should be good. Why is it confusing?"

"It is confusing because we are still watched closely by Saddam's secret police. The last I heard, my father, my brothers and two of my uncles were forced into the army. And it is feared they have been sent to the most front lines. Oh, Nephi. I have heard what they do there. The men are there just to be killed—to take the first attack. They are expected to be killed. They are given little or no training. The real army waits to counter attack. No one cares about the men in the front lines. It was that way in the war with Iran. It will be the same when America attacks.

"And my mother—all the women in the family. They will be used as hostages. Wait and see. They will be placed in shelters where military equipment is hidden. If America attacks and bombs the installation, the hostages—women and old men, my mother and sisters—will be killed."

Nephi listened, shocked by what he heard this very young, very frightened woman saying. The war had placed her family in jeopardy. No. Saddam Hussein had placed her family in jeopardy.

"Isn't there anything we can do?"

She shook her head. Tears began to form and she bowed her head to hide her emotion.

"And Yussef. I could lose Yussef, too."

"How, Sariah? How would you lose Yussef? He loves you. I don't think this war will change that."

"You don't understand. And I'm so confused."

"Confused? What do you mean?"

"I'm not sure I can talk about it."

Nephi kneeled beside her and touched her face, leading it to look at him.

"Sariah. What's the matter? What is there about Yussef that is confusing you?"

"He wants to go back to Kuwait. He wants to become a freedom fighter. If he goes back, I know he will be killed. Oh, Nephi. Everyone around me is being killed." She began to sob.

"Now wait a minute. Sariah, no one's been killed yet. Right? And it could be that your family will survive. You have to hold on. You can't let your family down."

She straightened her back and worked at forcing herself to stop crying. "I know. Thank you. But I'm still worried about Yussef."

"Okay, what's to worry? He's not going anywhere. Believe me. I can tell you they did recruit some Kuwaiti volunteers not long ago. But that's over. They aren't recruiting anymore volunteers. I suppose they will train those guys and send them into Kuwait as freedom fighters. But I doubt they will do that again. Too many civilians with guns would simply get in the way of the real fighting. So I think you can stop worrying about Yussef leaving for Kuwait."

"But that's not all. He's doing something very dangerous right here—right now. I know it. But he won't talk about it."

"What do you mean, Sariah? I don't understand."

"Neither do I. Yussef has been acting very strange. I'm afraid. Will you talk with him? Oh, please talk with him. Maybe you can stop him. I know he's doing something awful."

"Wait a minute. I still don't know what you're talking about."

"Well, you know how he feels. He wants to fight the war—free his country."

"Yes."

"Then why is he making friends with bad men?"

"What bad men?"

"Men from the Middle East. Everyone knows they are evil men."

"Evil men?"

"Yes. Evil. Terrorists."

"Terrorists?"

She nodded and wept.

"I know he will be killed. And I will be left a widow as well as an orphan."

"Whoa. Wait a minute," Nephi said, his voice racing to head off her increasing anxiety. "Let's go back over that one more time. Only this time let's fill in a few gaps."

She nodded.

"You say that Yussef has been spending time with terrorists?"

She nodded again.

"How do you know this?"

"The people involved in such things are well known in our community. There are the mean ones, the dangerous ones. Then there are the stupid ones who follow just because they are impressed by what the mean ones say. Intimidated. Yes, they are intimidated. And they look to the ones with bold talk. The ones who speak of violence. Such men promise them that if they die they will have died in Jihad—a holy war —protecting Islam. It is their chance to be carried directly to the bosom of Allah and special privileges in the Gardens of Paradise."

"And Yussef is friends with them?"

"He has been spending more and more time with them. He even has given up his studies."

"Has he given up his time with you?"

"No. Not all. But enough to make me question him. When I do, he gets mad at me. He says it is his business. Not mine. That a wife should not interfere with a husband's duty."

"Wife? I thought you were just engaged."

"He said that before we were engaged. I told him I was not his wife and he just told me that I would be soon."

"And that's how you became engaged?"

She tilted her head away. It was not the Islamic way and she was embarrassed to admit it.

"Yes," she said timidly.

"Well, if that doesn't beat all! Yussef does have a way about him—for such an intelligent guy. But you're sure he's spending time with real terrorists?"

"Yes," she admitted again. Her face was filled with a measure of fear—and a touch of shame.

*   *   *   *

It had finally reached midmorning and Yussef's hunger increased his interest in the doughnut shop around the corner. But he fought against the temptation. If he left his position even for a moment, that was certain to be the time when the pig would go somewhere.

He had been following Kassim al-Jarwi through the night. He had managed to follow him to an industrial park in Rockville. He had taken pride in the thought that he had not been seen by the terrorist. And his reward was to learn of one more important contact the Iraqi pig had made. Surely they were doing something evil inside that building. At that time of night it was a certainty. He had no idea what it was. All he knew was that Kassim drove out of the building after being inside for an hour. Yussef suspected whatever Kassim had gotten was in the trunk of the car. He would break in if he was given the chance. Chances were that it was some kind of bomb.

With hunger and fatigue crowding him, Yussef became more and more convinced that Kassim was inside his apartment resting from the night's activities. He waited another half hour and decided to make his report to the agency. Also, they would know best what he should do.

As he switched on the ignition to his car he wondered if they had delivered the flowers to Sariah as he had ordered. Surely such a gesture would ease her concern for him. He loved her very much. But he had a man's work to do here. He had found the best way to fight against the enemies of his country. It was important that he stay in the fight until they had destroyed the satanic force that had started it all.

Also, he thought of his family. He had not heard from any of them in weeks and he was concerned. The last time he had spoken with his father, he had learned that most of the family fortune had been transferred to a numbered account in Switzerland. Because of his situation outside Kuwait, Yussef had been given the account number. It was a grave responsibility. He knew he would only use it in an emergency or if his family was killed. At least the fortune was safe. Rebuilding the family once all this was over was assured. With Sariah beside him, he could accomplish all things.

He gave one more glance at the entrance to Kassim's apartment and then drove away. He would make his call to the FBI from a pay phone, then he would retire.

* * * *

Inside the 14-story apartment building, Kassim al-Jarwi carefully reviewed the evening's work. Recognizing his success produced an excitement within him that had denied him the sleep he knew he should take. Except for one moment when he thought he was being followed, he had accomplished everything necessary. He had made his report, as usual, through the Iraqi embassy in Paris. He knew they would be pleased with his progress.

And they were.

"The best way for us to destabilize the movement against us will be terrorist attacks," Kassim's control told him. "Saddam himself has ordered it. And it is good news that you are ready to perform your assignment."

"Thank you," Kassim responded.

"Are you certain you can rely on the people you have chosen?"

"Yes."

"You mentioned the Khaldun girl?"

"Yes. She is in a perfect position. She works for a Congress-man and has access to the Capitol."

"Will you be able to use her?"

"I will need to know precisely what you have done with her family. I am certain she will be willing to do exactly what I want in order to save them."

"That is good. I will send you the latest report. It will be at your office in the Yemani Embassy tomorrow morning, your time. Now, what about the American girl? Can you really trust her? She has no ties to our country."

"Her ties are in me."

The controller's voice laughed. He understood perfectly well what his operative meant.

"But will she take this step, even against her own country? Her own family?"

"Of course," the operative responded with customary brag-gadocio. "I have decided that her usefulness is not in carrying secrets. She will carry the ultimate message."

"And make the ultimate sacrifice, I presume?"

"Of course," the terrorist said as if he were bored.

CHAPTER 2

News Briefs
Saturday, January 12, 1991

WASHINGTON, D.C.—Congress is expected to vote today on the resolution that would give President Bush the authority to use military force against Iraq if Saddam Hussein does not withdraw from Kuwait. A close vote is expected in the Senate, but the House is expected to pass the same resolution without difficulty.

In a last-minute communiqué to the Senate today, President Bush said that the last, best chance for Saddam Hussein to get the message that America was united and prepared to enforce all 12 U.N. resolutions against the Iraqi occupation of Kuwait "was in your hands."

TAIF, SAUDI ARABIA—Secretary of State James A. Baker III Friday told pilots and crew members of the 48th Tactical Fighter Wing that "we pass the brink" of war with Iraq precisely at midnight next Tuesday. The deadline "is real," Baker said. "Efforts to extend it or postpone it will not succeed. Saddam can believe that or not, but if he doesn't he will have made his most tragic miscalculation."

VILNIUS, U.S.S.R.—Soviet troops stormed Lithuania's main printing plant and national guard headquarters Friday, pushing the 10-month-old Lithuanian confrontation with the Kremlin to the boiling point and leaving seven injured.

ALEXANDRIA, VA —

HE DREAMED OF HER AGAIN. AND THE DREAM LINGERED—every detail of the final scene etched clearly in his mind's eye. Even after he had opened his eyes he could still see her standing there in that spacious room—the delicate fountain beside her—and a woman, an older woman nearby, almost as beautiful as his Elena. Elegance dominated the complex scene with its many details. Even all the people in the background seemed important. One of them could have been his boss, Roy Ivars. What was he doing in a dream with her?

Nephi eased his legs off the bed. Lights from the parking lot allowed him to see in this pre-dawn hour. Even without light Nephi knew where the chair was—and the dresser—and the path leading out of the bedroom. He slipped into his slacks and ducked into a sweatshirt before retrieving the fat, old-style briefcase from his closet and moving into the living room. The same intrusion of exterior light that constantly illuminated the bedroom at night filled the living room with subdued halftones.

In renting his apartment, Nephi had settled for a one-bedroom deal. He would have preferred an efficiency apartment. But none were available when he needed to move in. Also, even though it cost more, he had taken the furnished package. He had no other choice. He planned to save enough money so he could purchase furniture. He could decide then whether it was worth it. Those kind of possessions always had to be moved somewhere else, eventually. For now, he felt comfortable in his temporary surroundings. He had the basics. And a bit more. The place was big enough for a party. Also, if he wanted to, he could invite a roommate to share expenses. But he decided to be very selective in that choice. Privacy meant a great deal to him. At least it allowed him to finish his dreams in a proper way.

He sat on the well-worn couch and turned on the lamp. He took a soft, chisel point pencil and a kneaded eraser from the briefcase, and finally a sketch pad. He spent a moment scratching the edge of the pencil's lead against a bit of fine sandpaper. On approving the shape and surface of the pencil's tip, he opened the sketch pad to a fresh page and began to draw.

As usual, his preparations had disturbed details of his dream very little; at least no details from that final scene had been lost. So his hand quickly blocked in the shapes and relationships of the objects he would be working with: the fountain, the people in the background.

But most important of all was the girl—Elena—that auburn hair falling in gentle swirls about the soft fair tones of her skin. From the beginning of this sketch he struggled getting her features right. Something about them troubled him. He had seen lines on her forehead in this dream. They never had been there before. Her lips were closer together, tighter—and her soft cheeks more angular. Darkness shaded her eyes. He didn't like drawing her face with the features as he had seen them.

He tried changing her expression to make it more pleasant, if not happy. But deviations never turned out very well. He reminded himself that if he wanted to complete an accurate drawing he had to draw it as he had seen it.

Anxiety rushed his hand, and details that might have produced a magnificent scene were left out. But with each line he drew, feelings of foreboding increased. He muttered to himself the questions that had persisted since these dreams had come into his life.

Was she real?

Who was she? If she was real, then where was she?

He began leafing back through the sketch pad to find drawings of happier times. She certainly had seen the world. There she was under the cherry blossoms. But a Pagoda had been built among those trees, not a tidal basin nor a Jefferson Memorial. How happy she looked then. He wondered if he would be as happy when the cherry blossoms burst out this spring in Washington.

He stopped at another page in a different sketch pad—the first of three pads he had filled. She seemed happy there. She was younger and happened to be standing underneath a Shinto shrine. He figured she had to have been visiting Japan again.

He let the pictures pass before him as quickly as he could thumb through them. Each had its own character. The earliest ones had been crude. The features of the girl were not always well drawn. Nor were the objects which had been drawn around her. But each succeeding sketch showed improved skill and eventually each picture clearly reflected an image of the same person.

It made sense for her to have been the daughter of a serviceman or perhaps a diplomat. She had been taken too many places to have been the daughter of home-bound American parents—even if they had been wealthy. Nephi always had thought well of her parents. Until recently, she had seemed secure, well adjusted and loved.

There was one sketch of her in a bed—a hospital bed. He recalled that when he drew it he had developed a severe pain in his lower abdomen. When he was willing to admit his pain was not real, it went away. He had to wonder if Elena had really had her appendix out.

Elena. Was that her real name? He stared ahead at nothing, in the direction of the makeshift bookshelf against the wall across from his place on the couch. His mind tried again to sense her reality and the reality of that name. He had no way of knowing who she was. Actually, he had no empirical proof that she existed. Faith alone had become his proof. Consistency had marked his dreams, consistency of her features, consistency in watching her growth to womanhood, and most importantly of all, consistency in repeated assurance by the still, small voice. Many times he had been told by that voice that she was real, and that one day soon they would meet.

Soon. That word had become a nightmare to him. What "soon" meant to people on the other side of the veil had to be radically different than what that word meant on this side.

This ongoing experience began shortly after he turned twelve. In his first dream he saw her in the corner of what had to be a classroom. He had never seen one quite like that one. He had a feeling it was in a foreign country. She was working at an easel. But others around her were seated at tables, reading or writing.

He remembered how pretty she was. As important as he felt his dream to be he dared not tell anyone. Twelve-year-old boys were not supposed to be dreaming of ten-year-old girls. How did he know she was 10? Again, he just knew. There was no way to prove it. He just knew it.

That was the same way he came to believe her name was Elena. Until three years ago he had no idea what her name was. Then in the process of drawing another sketch the name Elena slipped into his mind. It came to him as clearly as if someone near him had spoken it, and he quickly wrote the name in one corner of the sketch. But the sound hadn't come through his ears. It just took shape in his mind. Yet it had been a voice, formed into a sound that he could recognize as plainly as he could identify any other voice. It had a distinct quality about it, totally unlike listening to his own thoughts.

That's how Nephi learned about the still, small voice. And that's how he learned Elena's name. At least that's what her name seemed to be—what he thought it was. He felt comfortable enough with the way he had written it. Still it didn't seem right. Something seemed to be missing. But it was a name—a start. He considered it a blessing just having something to call her. If there was more to it he would just have to be patient for the rest. For now, whenever Nephi thought about her, there continued within him a strong assurance her name would be something like Elena. Elena. His Elena.

In reviewing the series of sketches—three books nearly filled with them—he liked the ones where she seemed to be happy. Aside from the technical fact that it had been easier for him to draw her when she was happy, it was uncanny how much happier he felt when he knew she was.

He stopped at one sketch he had done shortly after he had arrived in Washington. The temporary sense of relief that he had sought by reviewing happier times vanished, and a powerful sense of concern for her returned.

That had been the most morbid drawing he had done of her. She stood as the central figure in a darkened room. A single source of light washed out the faces of those around her. Very few half-tones existed in this sketch. There was light and there was dark. She did not appear to be in any immediate danger, merely in a very sinister place, with sinister people. He recalled the singular thought that had pressed upon him as he had drawn that sketch: "Get out of there!" And he muttered it again as he sat on his apartment sofa.

He glanced at the sketch he had just finished and felt a sense of depression from it—much like what he had felt with the sinister sketch. If he could only help her, he thought. But how?

Especially now.

He could spend no more time with her. And he could not afford to let the discouragement he felt distract him too long. He had to go to work.

Before he locked the sketches away he had to look once more at the picture he had just drawn.

Frustrations swelled within him again.

Who was she?

Where was she?

If she was in trouble, why was he forced to share her burden? Especially since he had no way of knowing how to help her?

Nephi stepped carefully down the steep, grassy slope and crossed Reynolds Street to the nearest bus stop. He stood waiting for the bus under a dormant shade tree along with a very round black woman and a skinny Latin American. Rarely did he ride the bus to work. He preferred driving. But as he completed his prayers before leaving for work, he felt the strongest impression that he should ride the Metro system to work rather than drive his car. It came with such force that he asked for confirmation. When that came with as much intensity as it did, he simply started walking toward the bus stop.

This would be an historic day at work. Congress rarely voted to authorize the President to go to war. And he would see it happen from the vantage point of being inside the system.

It would be more work for him. Normally he didn't mind. But today he knew he would be tired. Dreaming of Elena generally left him drained of energy. He could not afford such lethargy this day. Perhaps that was why he had been instructed to ride the bus. Perhaps it was meant for him to rest while someone else drove. Perhaps if he had driven, he would have had an accident.

At least it gave him a chance to think about something other than traffic. He could plan his day. He could structure what he would write in his news release.

He could think about Elena.

And he could try to stay alert.

The bus meandered around the Landmark district before moving onto I-395. Heading north, the bus made an exit at King Street to pick up more passengers. It would do the same thing once more before leaving the freeway a final time for the Pentagon.

With all the distractions around him, concentrating on work netted him nothing but increased sluggishness. The natural thing for him to do was submit to thoughts of the girl. Where was she right now? What was she doing? What was she thinking? Who was she with?

It made him smile to think that in her lifetime she virtually had taken him around the world—and he had not spent a nickel on airfare. Not a bad record for a kid named Nephi Nicholes who had never ventured more than 250 miles from that booming metropolis of Springville, Utah—until he was called to serve his LDS mission in Seattle, Washington.

Nephi adjusted himself in his window seat so a broad, middle-aged man could sit beside him.

What if they actually voted against the President today? The House would pass the resolution. With the Jewish members in coalition with Republicans the vote would be overwhelming. But in the Senate it would be close. Nephi tried to think of a good lead sentence for either circumstance. What would he write if the Senate vote failed?

His concentration ebbed and in his mind's eye he saw Elena's face again. Had she not been so worried he might have felt better. Yes! That was it! She was worried! Something serious worried her. Something—or someone. It wasn't something small. He could sense that. It had to be something big. It sobered him to think that what bothered her could be life-threatening, especially if it meant her life.

The man beside him reached overhead and pulled the cord. He wanted off at the next stop.

Nephi forced himself to ignore feeling the weight of the man pressing against his shoulder. He forced his thoughts back to his work. What would he write if the vote in the House failed? No. Failure looked impossible.

He studied the people around him. They all had the same look on their faces. It was the look of boredom. No. It was the look of endurance. Perhaps both—endured boredom.

He wondered again why he had been so strongly impressed to ride the Metro system today? He had a car. And he loved to drive it. It had plenty of power; it got decent mileage in town and great mileage on the highway. He had a parking space in the House parking system—underground and secured. It would have been a lot easier to just drive to work this morning. Surely he would not have had trouble staying awake in traffic.

The bus left the freeway for its final stop at the Pentagon. It slipped down the ramp, turned into the I-395 underpass and turned right onto the road skirting the huge parking lots that surrounded the Pentagon. Finally the driver turned, angling toward the Pentagon and headed slowly for a long, concrete island designed as a Metro-Bus terminal. A roofed shelter with glass partitions served as a waiting and staging area for patrons. It also sheltered the escalators located near both ends of the island. Designers had installed banks of three escalators in order to have an extra one hauling passengers during peak hours, either up or down depending on the time of day.

Nephi stepped from the bus, shoving on the doors so they wouldn't close on him. He wondered again if his instructions had been accurate. On his way down he began questioning the validity of his impression. If it wasn't a true message, then how did he foul up? What had gone wrong? Where was the clue to discerning the counterfeit—if it had been a counterfeit?

Always there was a least one way to distinguish true messages from counterfeits—deceptions by the adversary designed to distract, dissuade and destroy. Back in his apartment there hadn't been the slightest indication the instruction might have been false. Actually, the contrary had been true. Three of the four spiritual tests he had learned to apply in such circumstances had been present. The most valid had been the feeling of peace that had come over him when he received the message. That had to have been his strongest assurance. But along with that he could recall how his mind seemed to open—to be filled with pure intelligence when the message had come. It had not been given him to see a fullness of what was ahead. But the experience had filled him with complete confidence that in time he would know all the Lord wanted him to know. Finally, even though it had been slight, there had been a burning in his bosom he could not deny.

Nephi shook his head and tightened his lips. He had done the right thing even though he still didn't understand why. There had been no other choice for him. Once assured of the instruction's source he had to do it—he had to take the bus.

Still it troubled him to be buffeted with so many questions and doubts. It felt a little better when he realized that the feelings of anxiety and confusion had not entered his soul until after he had boarded the bus. Since that moment they seemed to be attacking him from all sides.

Now even as he walked, he found no pleasure anticipating the fatigue that would catch up with him—soon. He definitely would have trouble writing his news releases. Always it took longer for him to write a press release when he was tired. The toughest part would be listening to all those speeches. How could he stay awake through all of them?

"My gosh," he mumbled to himself as he joined the crowd flowing into the bowels of the Metro system. "If she's so worried about something so serious, and I'm being told about it, how come I don't know who she is, or where she is, or exactly what her problem is?"

He moved with the crowd through the doors that opened directly onto the Metro platform. Sleep. He was beginning to feel drowsy. Over the years he had conditioned himself to believe he was in trouble when he didn't get eight full hours. At least that was what he blamed when things bogged down on the day following one of his dreams.

The more sorry he felt for himself, the more he wished he had driven. At least he wouldn't have run the risk of having to stand through the whole trip—or part of it. He stepped onto the Yellow Line train and managed to get a seat—next to a window even. And he stared through the glass—the dirty glass—and became mesmerized watching the blurred walls of the tunnel slip past.

Then the dark tunnel was left behind and the train flashed out into the daylight. In place of the tunnel walls was a view of the Potomac and the 14th Street Bridge carrying traffic across it. The train crossed the river and then nosed back into a hole that ran underneath Washington, D.C.

At the next station, L'Enfant Plaza, Nephi got off and headed through the massive, domed cavern toward the escalator leading down to the next level. There seemed to be a lot more noise echoing through cement catacombs than there should have been. At the top of the escalator he could see why—the platform below was jammed. A lot of the people were carrying signs which read "No blood for oil!" and "Not another Vietnam!"

"Great," he muttered, visualizing the obstacle this protest would play in his attempt to get to work.

About half way down the escalator, he began to study the structure of the crowd. It didn't completely fill the platform, but it was large enough to make him wonder if one train would be able to carry them all.

But wait!

Nephi noticed a girl standing on a bench about half-way along the platform. She was waving her arms and shouting to the crowd. She looked familiar.

Very familiar.

It was her.

Elena!

He shouted out her name but she was too far away and the noise made by the crowd was too great.

He pushed through the crowd. But the sluggish crowd refused to let him through.

A train came—not his train—one going in the opposite direction. He watched her disappear into the mass of bodies and signs. She was going to board that train.

So would he. He had to get on it. In a desperate lunge he made it into the closest car before the doors closed. The car was loaded to the limit and he found himself jammed against the door. But he had made it aboard. He wasn't in Elena's car, but that was all right. He was on the same train with her. He would find her at the next stop.

It came up quickly. Smithsonian. He was pushed from the train as soon as the doors opened. He was surprised at how many were getting off at the Smithsonian; he thought more would be going to the White House. So many people to fight through, he thought, so many people to check. Was she getting off here or down the line? Panic seized him as he ducked between and through the mob on the platform looking for her face. At the same time he had to check the windows of each car. She had to be on the train. He had to find her, see her, know which car she was on.

Again, he barely made it back on board before the doors closed. He would do the same thing at Metro Center. He anticipated an even bigger problem there. Metro Center was a major connecting station.

But his fears were unfounded. There were less people milling about there than had been moving around at Smithsonian. He scanned the faces and shapes of the people leaving the train and peered through the windows at those remaining on the train. It was hard to tell where she was. So many people were standing up, he couldn't really see who was on the far side of each car.

Then he saw her. She was standing—actually leaning down in a conversation with a man seated beside her. Nephi plunged into the train again.

Finally he was in her car. He maneuvered so he had a direct view of her. That was the best he was able to do. He knew he could not reach her. He would bide his time until they were out in the world again and then he would make his approach.

"My gosh!" he muttered so loud that a black woman next to him turned and looked.

Nephi shrugged and smiled, not able to think of anything to say and then turned his attention to Elena again. He still had to figure out a way to meet her. He couldn't just go up to her and say, "Pardon me, lady. But I've been dreaming about you since I was twelve. What's your name? And how about marrying me?"

Marrying him?

Actually, he had never thought of it so directly. He had been so obsessed with just finding her that he had simply ignored what might come of being acquainted—of being friends—of being more than friends.

But since she did exist—since he could see her and since she was saying real words and laughing real laughs—all his options were open. And suddenly courage mingled with his fears and excitement.

Before allowing himself to plunge ahead with his thoughts, he paused for a moment and silently gave thanks to the Lord for this great blessing.

When he looked up and saw her again, he marveled at how precise had been the features he had seen of her—her slightly turned-up nose, the curves and points of her lips, the soft delicate curve of her cheeks, her feminine though athletic looking body, and the blend of her auburn hair against that lovely skin.

Wow!

There wasn't anything he could see about her in real life that was not exactly as he had seen about her so many times before. He even bet himself that she would have that little mole on the back of her shoulder that he had seen when she had worn summer clothes.

In order for him to see that mole in real life, he would have to be around when she started wearing summer things this year.

He would.

Somehow he would.

At the next stop, McPherson Square, the crowd she was with began moving off the car. He had to move out of the way or get crushed in the rush. He kept looking over his shoulder to see if she was coming. She was. He would just move slowly and let her catch up with him.

But the crowd wouldn't cooperate. And neither would she. The crowd was pressing him toward one escalator while she headed for another. He could see her make it to her escalator before he could reach his. Once she got to the top she would be ahead of him. He fought off panic thinking that he could make up whatever distance he needed to by running, or at least walking up the fast lane of the escalator. But that, too, was blocked. Demonstrators wanted to demonstrate—they didn't care that they were obstructing what could be a beautiful relationship.

He closed the distance between himself and Elena when he got off the first escalator. But the crowd still had her blocked off as if they had devised a plot to protect her from him. He wanted to beat them off with a stick. He didn't have a stick. They had all the sticks—sticks with signs on them—signs that were getting in his way.

At the turnstiles he knew he had lost any ground he had gained. But he pressed on. He wanted to run up the long escalator to the surface, but it was blocked by more demonstrators. At least this was the last time they could block him. Once he made it to the street he would be rid of them.

He was wrong. At the top he still had to press through more crowds of people. He barely managed to avoid collisions with two different panhandlers at the congested entry of the station. They yelled at him, claiming they had a right to be there and he couldn't push them around. He shrugged, smiled, and hustled away toward the street. But the mob filled the sidewalk, too, forcing him to step into the street, outside the parked cars, to search for her.

There she was, at the head of a pack of demonstrators just half a block away. If everything went right he could reach her before she crossed H Street. Nephi slipped through the crowd as best he could. But the light turned and he watched her continue along the side of Lafayette Park toward the White House. She was just crossing Pennsylvania Avenue when Nephi got the green light. He began to run, jogging at first, then increasing his speed until he was almost sprinting. But the light stopped him again. He would have ignored it except for the number of policemen wandering around.

By this time Elena had crossed Pennsylvania Avenue and had disappeared into the pedestrian area between the White House and the Treasury Building. Nephi kept fudging into the intersection, anxious to move on. But an officer spotted him and pointed back at the curb. Noting the size of the officer and the threatening look in his eyes Nephi felt obliged to return.

He could no longer see Elena. But he knew where she was headed. All he had to do was sprint across the street and hurry down the walk that separated the White House from the Treasury Building, then cross the next street and locate her on the Ellipse.

Yep. That was all. But it was a long light.

The White House stands within a large plot of land, protruding as a kind of spur north from the lower or western end of the Mall. The carefully secured area on which that famous house sits is called President's Park. The White House itself fronts onto Pennsylvania Avenue. Most of the park extends as a massive back yard which can be seen from the President's Oval Office. The south boundary of the park is expressed in a pleasing curve, bulging toward the top of the Ellipse. A wrought iron fence secures that boundary. Many tourists and demonstrators walk the narrow, curved sidewalk just beyond the fence. A two-lane road runs beside the sidewalk and on the other side of that is the Ellipse. That is where serious demonstrations regularly form. And this one looked like it was going to be serious.

As soon as the light turned green, Nephi's long legs reached out. Halfway across the street he increased his speed by shortening his stride and raising the tempo. Before he hit the curb he was running. Every security guard on duty that day noticed the weird guy in a business suit sprinting where people normally walk.

Nephi noticed their glances but he didn't care. He purposely did not make any threatening gestures in the direction of the White House and applied his best manners as he slipped between groups clustered around the visitor's entrance.

There was only a two-lane street left to cross, but on the other side were hundreds of protestors that would make Elena difficult to find.

Across the narrow street, police maintained a fence, of sorts, to keep demonstrators from pressing into traffic. Nephi made his way through a makeshift opening and began a methodical search.

He discovered that people stood or sat in groups. There were signs of all sizes. Without the signs he might have been able to spot her right away. But she was probably on the inside of a group hidden from his view by a sign.

She had become the needle in this haystack of humanity. He felt like an alien walking among them. Most were wearing what Roy Ivars had termed once as "the uniform of non-conformity." But in addition to military fatigue styles, many well-dressed citizens had joined the ranks.

Nephi could only recall that Elena was wearing something simple. It would have been suitable anywhere—even in the Capitol. But he had no recollection of the colors. He would when he saw it again—if he saw it.

A wave of anxiety surged through his body. He had to find her. Although only appearing in his dreams, she had become a major part of his life. And now, since he knew she existed, he was more convinced than ever that she was about to play an even greater part in his future.

To calm his panic, he told himself she was not lost—just misplaced for the moment.

He started around to the right and meandered so he could search a fairly wide swath of the crowd. On his return from the far side, he spotted her. Had he started out to the left he would have seen her in a couple of minutes.

She stood within a medium-sized clique. Most of the people she was with were well groomed. Most of them appeared to be Arabs.

Four of them had formed a close-knit group. They seemed especially friendly with each other: two men and another woman. The woman was beautiful—not as beautiful as Elena, but beautiful in her own way. One of the men stood with an air of defiance or perhaps arrogance. The other seemed quiet, almost asleep. Both men had mustaches. All of them, including Elena, appeared to be enjoying the day.

Now that he was so close, he suddenly wondered what he would say to her?

What would she say to him?

If he ever needed help from the Spirit, it was now.

But while the anxiety he felt focused on the need for the Spirit, it destroyed the discipline and skill required to qualify for receiving answers. And distractions from the crowd, its movements and its noise, prevented him from thinking clearly as well. Nothing came to him—from the Spirit or from his own mind.

Still, somehow he knew he could not allow this opportunity to pass. At least he needed to learn who she was. He didn't have the foggiest idea how he was going to do that. All he could do was look at her, stare at her, hope something would happen to bring their lives together.

He knew she talked with people about the demonstration. If he had to do that he would. Then maybe he would dazzle her by telling her he worked for a Congressman. That seemed to impress other people. Why not her?

On the other hand, maybe he could start by asking her to explain her reasons for being against the war. Yes. That was it. He would get her talking. He would keep asking questions until he found out everything he needed to know.

Carefully, he began his final approach. Indecision had slowed his pace. But she soon would be in range. All he needed now was a little luck and a little timing. He needed to reach her when no one else would bother them. Great! He was down to his last six steps separating them.

Suddenly, from behind her, came another man. As soon as she was aware he was there, she whirled and threw herself into his arms.

Nothing could have sabotaged Nephi's composure more completely. He reached for her but caught himself and let the weight of his body as well as his dreams fall back on his heels.

His mind seriously considered attacking the interloper. Who was that guy? What right did he have in pressing himself on her in such a way? What had he done to her?

What had she let him do to her?

Whoa! He slowed himself in an effort to drive these emotional thoughts from his conscious mind. She had no way of knowing what she was doing and who she should have been looking for. Surely one day she would come to recognize him—to know what she needed to know about their relationship. She had to be given a fair chance to learn about that relationship. But there was nothing at all fair about what had just happened. It hurt deeply.

Before he could fully recover, he watched the man lead Elena from the group. They walked through the crowd, across the grass toward the trees that lined the lane curving around the east side of the Ellipse. Cars lined that street, parked "by permit only" that various agencies in the area would issue.

Double-parked there was a limousine. The man opened the door and helped Elena inside.

Nephi had followed without any thought to his position and how exposed he was to their view. It didn't matter. They didn't seem to notice him. When they drove away he found himself alone in the street. He wanted to run after them, but all he did was watch—watch as a strange man drove away with a woman he still didn't know, even though she held the key to his heart and his future.

CHAPTER 3

NEPHI STOOD IN THE NARROW STREET STARING AT THE intersection where the limousine had disappeared. Within seconds the frustration he felt reduced itself to hostility toward a man he had never met. A little slopped over onto Elena—condemning her judgement, her choice of friends. He wasn't ready to admit she had chosen a lover.

How could such a nice girl get tangled up with such an obvious sleazebucket? He had arrogantly flaunted his money and status. The man's clothes had to have been tailored just for him. The limo was luxurious and the license plates indicated that the limo's occupants had diplomatic immunity. And Elena had fallen for the whole scam.

That guy was responsible. Well, he would not be immune from the wrath of Nephi Nicholes! No, sir! He pounded his right fist against the palm of his left hand. His mind jumped forward, aching for the moment that same fist would make contact with the creep's nose. Yes! He would pound that jerk into the ground. How dare he touch his beloved Elena!

Whoa! He caught himself. The intense emotions multiplying within his soul triggered thoughts and feelings quite foreign to Nephi's nature. He became aware of the source these feelings came from and was a little frightened as he sensed how self-destructive they were. What he had to do was resist those kinds of thoughts—gain control of himself—fight off all the dark feelings of revenge and retaliation. For they had carried him far from the commitment he had made some time ago—to love his enemy.

It took a shout from a patrolman to make him stop thinking and start moving.

"Get out of the road!"

Embarrassed, he glanced behind him. He had only been lost in his reverie a few seconds. Even so, three cars waited in line for him to move. "Sorry," he mumbled, giving a wave of his hand at the drivers. Then he noticed they were just tourists. "What's all the rush?" he thought. "They're not late for work."

"Work!" he shouted. "I'm late for work."

It was no time for the Metro. He turned and headed across the grass, away from the Ellipse. He moved under the spreading trees lining the park and on reaching 15th Street, he raised his arm for a taxi.

Once settled in the back seat of the taxi, Nephi tried to prepare his mind for the tasks ahead. But focusing beyond his emotions proved difficult. He had spoken with his boss enough to know how Congressman Hersch felt about the war. It was the actual language Nephi would use that was not yet established.

Why hadn't she waited for him?

Of course, she had no idea he existed. While he had been blessed—or cursed—with a knowledge about her, it was highly unlikely she knew a thing about him.

Wait a minute. Stop it!

So how am I going to decide what to write? He dreaded the thought of watching all those speeches on CNN.

But that guy. How could she go for a guy like that? I mean, it was so obvious he was just after her for her body. He had to be a real jerk.

Love thine enemy.

Well, that creep certainly qualified.

Nothing was working to get his mind off Elena and her dark-eyed companion. But one thing would. He hesitated only because the last vestiges of emotion still clouded his soul. Even so, he forced himself to bow his head.

"Father," he said clearly in his mind. "I need some help here.

I've got some harsh feelings toward one of Thy sons whom I don't know. Help me to control myself, Father. Let Thy will be done in this as in all things. And grant unto me peace, even the peace of the Spirit. In the name of Jesus Christ. Amen."

After that he felt better. But he knew it would be a long siege. Even though his prayer had restored a measure of peaceful strength within his soul, he could still feel the emotional strife lingering there on the periphery of his battered defenses searching for a weak spot for the next assault.

The whole episode had been highly traumatic. To see her. To get so close to her. Then to lose her. . . . and to lose her like that. He had to relax. The Spirit would not help him if he was going to feed those kinds of thoughts.

The cab pushed its way through the unusually heavy Saturday morning crowds—people not caring what the cars wanted to do. Saturday tourists would have been bad enough. Now there were demonstrators, too. Cars would have to give way to their political demands.

Following Nephi's orders, the driver headed to the little horseshoe on the west side of the Longworth Building. Nephi knew that door was open. Perhaps he should have altered his plan and gone to the front entrance. No. This was better. He could see there were too many people outside the front entrance.

Traffic at the little horseshoe was much better. Even so, they ended up in a line of cars. In front of them was another cab. Directly under the portico there was a big, gray limousine.

A limo?

No! Not just *a* limo—*the* limo!

It couldn't be. But it was. He could tell by the license plate. It was the same gray limo that had driven off with Elena.

"Now what was a guy like that doing in a nice place like this?" Nephi thought.

Nephi paid the driver and walked under the ivy covered portico before pushing his way through the revolving door. And there they were. Right there. They had not yet gone through the magnetic detector. She stood not three short steps from him—waiting beside the desk at his left. The guard was running his finger down the list of Congressional offices.

"You say Hersch?" the guard asked.

"Yes, officer," the Arab acknowledged. "Congressman Ronald Hersch's office."

It took Nephi by surprise. But he adjusted quickly. What a break!

"Could I help you? I'm on Congressman Hersch's staff."

"Well, what a perfect coincidence," the man fawned with practiced ease, his English showing only a trace of an accent. "Yes, I believe you could, thank you. We are looking for a young woman who works there, I believe. Her name is Sariah Khaldun. Are you acquainted with her?"

Sariah, Nephi thought. The man acted as if he didn't know her. Who could have given him her name? Had Yussef sent them here? Was this guy one of the legitimate members of the Arabian community in Washington? Or was he one of Yussef's new friends? The ones Sariah feared? Nephi's thoughts moved so quickly they only caused him to hesitate for a second.

"Yes, Sariah works with us. But she may not be working today. Even though Congress is in session, it's Saturday and there's only a skeleton crew here. If you would like to come up we could find out if she's scheduled to come in."

"May we?" the man said with a silky smile. "We would appreciate that very much."

"Of course," Nephi answered, forcing himself to display a courteous manner.

The officer had stopped looking for a number to call. Instead he moved into position to process the two of them through the magnetic security station.

The woman—Nephi just knew her name would turn out to be Elena—placed a plastic grocery bag with three bottles of soda pop on the counter and walked through the detector. Why she was carrying soda pop with her he could not understand. She didn't have them with her on the Ellipse. He would have thought her friend would have preferred some kind of wine with his lunch. On the other hand, if this had been a gift for Sariah it would have been much more appropriate than alcohol, which Muslims avoid.

The guard hardly looked at the bottles—just two-liter bottles of soda. Standard brands. He placed the bag at the far end of the table.

"My name is Nephi Nicholes. Are you friends of Sariah?"

"A friend of a friend," replied the man as he walked through the detector. It did not ring as Nephi had hoped it would. It would have been great if the guy had been carrying a concealed weapon.

"But allow me to introduce myself. I am Kassim al-Jarwi. I am cultural attaché with the Embassy of Yemen."

"How do you do, sir," Nephi forced a smile and took hold of the man's extended hand.

It was soft. Totally without character. Nephi wondered if the lack of strength was a cultural thing like an American Indian's handshake. They are so conscious of their space and of honoring the space of others that Indians serve up a limp hand for shaking. Such customs had been confusing to Nephi who had been raised to believe that the strength of a handshake reflected the basic strength—or lack of strength—of one's character. Then he remembered the first time he took hold of Yussef's hand. It had been solid.

But this al-Jarwi guy's hand was not. Somehow Nephi was not at all surprised to sense its weakness.

"May I present to you Miss Maria Moore? She is providing me with a most valuable service, at the moment, in an urgent project."

Nephi turned and looked directly into her face for the first time. It took him only a second to plow through the disappointment he felt at learning she was not an Elena. Without doubt, as a Maria she was every bit as beautiful as she would have been as an Elena. And with her standing so close, looking into his eyes, her name somehow seemed unimportant.

"I am very happy to meet you," Nephi said automatically. His heart pounded and he felt clumsy.

Her lips curved into a spontaneous, friendly smile as she extended her hand.

Nephi touched her for the first time.

He took her hand. Nice—it definitely had the softness of a woman yet her grip was firm. "A woman with character," Nephi thought. Of course, maybe the handshake test was not so conclusive as he had thought. If Maria had any character at all she would not be running around with this slimeball—not even if she *was* "involved" with one of his projects.

Then she spoke.

"Nephi, is it?" she said smiling. "What an interesting name."

Such a nice voice, Nephi thought. A voice he could live with. No question about it.

"Yes," he responded to her. "That's what people tell me. I guess my parents thought I might need something interesting to carry with me—sort of as an ice breaker."

She smiled again.

Her smile made him feel warmer than before—probably much warmer than Maria had intended. Of course, she could not control what went on inside his head. All she intended was to acknowledge his release from the potentially embarrassing reference to his strange name.

"Shall we go upstairs?" Nephi asked, leading the way out of the entry and into the basement hall. "We'll see if Sariah's here."

"Thank you," al-Jarwi said. "As I mentioned, we were given her name by a mutual friend. We were hoping she could help us tour the Capitol and perhaps look in on the debates today. It would be extremely useful to our project."

"Oh, well," Nephi turned as they passed the Longworth Building's post office. "If that's all you need and she's not in, perhaps someone else could help you. As a matter of fact, I'd be happy to conduct a tour for you myself." He gave a strong look in Maria's direction.

She didn't notice. But al-Jarwi did.

"We would be extremely in your debt if you would do us that immense service," al-Jarwi said too cordially.

Overacting, Nephi judged. He hated overactors.

Kassim measured the young man, a mere boy. Clearly an accommodating sort. Naive in a bureaucratic way. Also, obviously struck by the beauty of his companion. Well, he was right. She was a beautiful woman. Why else would he have spent so much time with her? The thought made him smile. There had been plenty of others he could have chosen. Some had been far more committed than Maria was. But Maria had many more advantages. He was teaching her the rest. Studying the stride of the young man in front of him he could tell that this one could be taught as well. If he had the time he was sure he could turn him.

That Sariah was not in the office was confirmed when Nephi had to unlock the door. Had she been there the door would have been open. However, he quickly found that someone else had arrived earlier because the lights were on and the mail had been sorted—a task Roy Ivars normally did on weekends. No matter who had been there, he or she was not there now. Nephi was on his own.

Kassim concluded this as well. But he could not decide how to turn it to his advantage. With more information he just might be able to compensate for the Khaldun woman's absence. Unfortunately, Maria was useless in this kind of situation. She had not been trained well enough to react to such circumstances—to improvise and to take the implied direction of her team leader. Besides, Maria was not fully aware of why they had come. It would have been a mistake to brief her completely.

It would have been so much better had the girl, Sariah, been there. It would have taken him less than five minutes to convince her to do what needed to be done. Intimate details of her family's circumstances would have been enough to convince her to carry the bottles through the security stations into the Capitol.

Then they would place the bottles in three locations, twist the caps and be gone long before the bottles conveyed their fatal message from Saddam Hussein to the American Congress. The war had not started. But the imperialist pigs debated the issue and would vote on it soon. This would be a message to them to keep out of matters that did not involve them. What fools. If they only knew how close they were to a war—a war they could never win.

"That is so disappointing that Sariah is not here," al-Jarwi said. "I was hoping to find her. She was highly recommended to me and I was so anxious to meet her. Also, I have messages from her family in Iraq."

"You do?"

"Oh, yes."

"I'd be happy to give them to her. She's most anxious to hear from them," Nephi offered.

"Oh, how nice of you, Mr. Nicholes. But you must understand, they are very personal. I am obligated to give them to her myself, you see. I was just hoping to reach her very soon because I know she is anxious to receive them."

"Yes. She has been very worried about her family."

"To be sure," al-Jarwi reflected. "These are troubled times. But perhaps you will be good enough to help me with her address or her telephone number. I could contact her this afternoon and give them to her."

Nephi looked at the man, watching the smile behind the well-trimmed goatee. He was showing a bit too much teeth to satisfy the Congressional aide. He used a moment to quickly seek guidance and was rewarded with an instant, strong, negative answer.

"I'm sorry, Mr. al-Jarwi. But we have a firm policy to not give out home telephone numbers or addresses. However, I would be more than happy to contact her and give her your number. I'm sure she will be anxious to speak with you."

Nephi perceived irritation in the man's face. It amounted to a slight twitch in a facial muscle that caused one eye to nearly blink. Subtle, but revealing, it provided Nephi with a modest share of satisfaction.

Not only did Kassim feel irritated at the boy's reluctance to reveal Sariah's telephone number, he felt irritated also at the boy's obvious enjoyment in blocking the way. For an instant he thought of simply knocking this weakling out of his path. Sariah's number would be on someone's Roladex. He could find it, entice the woman to come and take care of everything as he had originally planned. They could be finished inside an hour. He would leave Maria to watch Sariah. And he would be on his way home. But, of course, at this point, force would not be appropriate. He should at least try to find another way. After all, it seemed to involve a simple adjustment.

He would use this boy to help them carry the bombs inside the Capitol. Sariah had been his first option. She would have been the best because she was the most vulnerable person on his list. He knew he could persuade her. He never had trouble with women—especially vulnerable women. But she was not available. Now he would use this boy. And to use him he would not want to antagonize him—at least not now.

"Well, perhaps you would be kind enough to take us on a tour, and perhaps show us where to sit and listen to the debates."

"I would be happy to."

"Wonderful. Shall we go? I mean, is it convenient for you to go right now?"

"Of course," Nephi said. "I just need to leave a note for my boss. It will only take a minute."

What great fortune, Nephi thought to himself. He was going to spend some time with her. To heck with this guy. Somehow, he knew he would be able to find a way to learn more about this Maria Moore.

Al-Jarwi and the girl stood by the door waiting for Nephi. Maria held the bag with the bottles in it.

"Would you like to leave that here?" Nephi asked.

"That is kind of you," al-Jarwi said. "But no thank you. We will take it with us. Then we will not have to come back for it."

Nephi nodded. "Well, you can leave it at the door with the guards."

"What?" al-Jarwi exclaimed.

Nephi thought it was great to see this guy lose his composure. But what a strange thing to be upset about. Why should this guy lose his cool over a couple of bottles of pop?

"They are very strict about letting people carry objects inside the Capitol Building," he said.

Al-Jarwi looked at the little, insignificant bureaucrat. As fast as he normally thought and calculated, he found it difficult to think at the moment. This son of a pig farmer had become more than an irritation to him. But he could not allow his emotions to interfere. He had to fall back on his training.

Relax. Smile. Adjust. Never place your enemy on guard. Be patient. Another time will present itself. Well, he thought, it was the will of Allah. And he would now need to find some advantage in his present situation.

Of course! He would have to turn him. Use him. It would not take much. Time gave him an advantage. With both the boy and Sariah in place, he might even be able to plant more bombs—as many as five or six. But how should he turn the boy?

Of course! Maria! As inexperienced as she was in such things, there was one thing she excelled in already. And that would be all the boy would require. She had become the object of this boy's attention since they met him in the lobby downstairs. Yes. Maria would turn him. Then he would have both of them—all three of them—to use in the ultimate assault against the Great Satan.

"Well," al-Jarwi finally said. "I am sorry. But I just was thinking of my schedule today. So long as Sariah cannot give me a tour today, it would be best if I wait until Monday. And unfortunately I will not be where Sariah would be able to reach me today. No. I will have to call her on Monday. She will be working on Monday, will she not?"

"Oh, yes," Nephi said. He was glad he had not tried to call her right then. And another thing, he didn't like the idea of this big shot al-Jarwi not presenting some kind of card. A legitimate diplomat would have presented a card. This guy obviously didn't have a card to give. That's why he wouldn't give his phone number. There probably was no phone number to give. Yes, Nephi assured himself. He had done the right thing.

"What a shame," al-Jarwi said in his over-acting way. "I was so looking forward to Sariah taking us on a tour. It would have been good to hear her tell us about it in Arabic—our own tongue."

"But you speak perfect English," Nephi wanted to catch the man in whatever game he was playing. "You certainly do not need an interpreter."

"It is kind of you to say that. I do take pride in my English. But it is a working language for me. On the other hand, Arabic is so poetic and so restful to the ear. I was looking forward to the experience."

Then the alleged diplomat leaned back and raised his arms as if he had been surprised by an idea.

"Ah, but what am I thinking about. Maria. You do not speak our tongue, do you? I had forgotten about that. You would not enjoy the tour if Sariah gave it to me in Arabic, would you?"

Nephi noticed that Maria looked at al-Jarwi. Her face played on the uncertain side of neutral.

"No," she said weakly, with a shrug of her shoulder.

"But of course you would not and it is unfair of me to expect you to do so," the swarthy man said, obviously with another thought waiting to be revealed. "And since we both must take this very important tour, perhaps it would be best for you to take it today—in English—with Mr. Nicholes here. That would allow me to take it next week some time—when Sariah is working."

Nephi could have cheered when his rival said that.

"If only Mr. Nicholes would be so kind as to accommodate you."

Nephi had to hold himself in some kind of reserve. He didn't want to look that anxious.

"Of course. I'd be delighted to extend this courtesy."

"But, Kassim," Maria said in a slightly insistent voice, "we have to meet those people—together." She placed great emphasis on the word "together."

"Oh, my dear. They are of no importance. Certainly not nearly as important as this. Especially if you can listen to the debates."

"The debates?" she asked.

"Yes. You know. The debates. We need to get information from the debates."

She said nothing. She just scowled at al-Jarwi. Nephi could see she was beyond irritation. This was a full-blown mad.

"Then it is settled. Maria, you will go with this kind man who has so graciously offered his services to us. And I will take the tour on Monday when Sariah returns to work or whenever is most convenient to her. Of course, that will not be as good as today because the debates will be over. That means you must pay attention to everything that is said."

"Kassim," she spoke in a firm voice. "Could I see you a minute?"

They walked to the doorway leading to the hall. It was far enough for her to whisper to her companion.

"Kassim, I don't want to listen to any speeches. I want to be with you today. Do you understand?" Anger forced the words between her tightly clamped teeth.

"And I with you, my love. But this is important. We cannot accomplish today what we came here to do. But there is a way we can accomplish even more. Can you not see how attracted that man is to you? I want you to turn him. It will be easy. All you have to do is make yourself appealing to him. Listen to him. Make him think you like him. Be nice to him. He is in a singular position to do everything we need to do. Between him and Sariah we will accomplish our objective. Do you understand?"

She nodded.

"That is good. Now go to him. Make him happy."

"Kassim. I am not interested in making him happy. I want to make you happy."

He took hold of her chin. "It is the same thing, my love. For without him we might not be able to accomplish our goals. And if we do not accomplish our goals—I will be very unhappy."

Nephi stepped into the hall, gladly bidding farewell to al-Jarwi, and making sure he wouldn't lose his way. What a contrast the diplomat had been. At one time there had been a distinguished look to him. There had been the soft handshake. There had been the irritations. Always there had been the recoveries, rebounding from obstacles. Now there was something new—a well-dressed, sophisticated diplomat walking down the corridor of the Longworth Building carrying a common grocery bag filled with bottles of soda pop. The man carried them so awkwardly—almost as if he had never carried such a thing before in his life.

Nephi turned and stepped back into his office. For the first time he was alone with Elena—his Elena. Only she wasn't his Elena. She was a Maria. And she was not his at all. In fact, it was pretty obvious she didn't even want to be there with him for the tour. But that was all right. She was there. And she was making an effort to be cordial to him. He would accept cordiality for now. He simply would need to turn that cordiality into something more.

"Would you be seated, Miss Moore. I just need to put something away in my desk. Then we'll be on our way."

She smiled at him and took one of the chairs. She noticed the picture of Saddam Hussein on the cover of *Newsweek*. She picked it up but didn't do too much with it. She preferred just looking around, seeing what a Congressman's office was like—the statuettes and plaques, the pictures and books, and flowers all around. She wondered if they always kept this many flowers in the office. Pretty extravagant, she thought.

Nephi wrote quickly. He would not be giving the normal tour. And he wanted Roy Ivars to know he would not be back until the vote was taken. He would meet the Congressman in the Speaker's Lounge. He would then escort their boss to the various press sites.

Then he paused for a moment to thank the Lord for having brought Elena—Maria—into his life—for real. He asked for help in making an impression on her that would last. Then he acquiesced to the Lord's desires. But that was the hardest thought for him to express.

"Okay," he announced. "Let's get out of here."

CHAPTER 4

THEY LEFT THE LONGWORTH BUILDING AND ANGLED TO THE corner. They had to wait for the light before crossing Independence Avenue. A few demonstrators had gathered around the south entrance, but most of them were clustered around the stairs at the east side of the Capitol. They hoped to intimidate members who would have to walk through their ranks. But most members knew enough to enter the Capitol Building through the network of tunnels connecting with the office buildings. Tunnels permitted work to continue in spite of foul weather or demonstrations. Nephi wondered if he might have been better off taking Maria through the tunnel system. He felt a need to avoid controversy in this initial contact with Maria.

"How long have you been in Washington?" he asked as they walked toward the Capitol beside the half-wall that held back the massive growth of shrubs and foliage.

"About two months," she answered. "Dad was assigned to the Pentagon."

"Come from overseas?" Nephi asked. He knew they had. He just wanted to hear her say it.

She told him they came from Germany. Her father was in the Air Force.

"Were you going to school over there?"

"I took a class or two. Mostly I just visited the people."

Her answers seemed kind of cold. He sensed the need to find some way to get her talking about herself.

"You glad to be back in the States?"

She just shrugged.

"Going to school here?"

"Couple of classes. Night school."

"Working, I guess."

Another nod. Boy, this was painful. Nephi knew he would never be able to break through whatever barrier she had erected around herself if he didn't get some help. So he spent the rest of the walk across the grounds silently asking the Lord to help him with what he should say and how he should say it.

This time he received an answer. A feeling of peace assured him that things would be okay. Unfortunately, nothing in the way of actual language had accompanied the assurance. He would have preferred being told what to say—even just a few words with which to start his conversation. He gestured for her to step into the revolving door at the public entrance at the south end of the building. He gave it a bit of a shove to help her get the heavy glass moving. Once through he waited while she moved through the magnetic metal detector. Still he had no idea how to begin.

"Well, here we are," he said. Not very creative but enough for a start.

They stood on the first floor at the south end of the Hall of Columns.

"If you're into architecture you already know the Capitol was built along neo-classical lines," his words flowed with ease. It quite surprised and pleased him. Thoughts simply appeared in his mind and he articulated them much more intelligently than he had expected. "Somewhere in the building you will find all three kinds of columns—Doric, Ionic and Corinthian. We're standing at the end of the Hall of Columns and the ones you see here are Corinthian. Notice the cornices at the top. Those flourishes up there represent tobacco leaves. All through the building you will see tobacco leaves immortalized. It seems kind of strange from our vantage point today, what with all the lung cancer we enjoy in this country and all. But tobacco really had a stabilizing impact on the economy of those struggling colonies. If we hadn't developed the tobacco industry back then, chances are pretty good we would be speaking a different language right now—Spanish probably, maybe French."

Walking through the Hall of Columns, Nephi explained that the statues between each column were a part of the overall program on the House side of the Capitol. On approval, each state could place two statues in the Capitol. They had to be representations of citizens worthy of national recognition.

"Upstairs there's a statue of Oklahoma's favorite son, Will Rogers; also Hawaii's King Kamahamaha, among many others. For years, Utah only had one statue—Brigham Young. But just last year a second statue was installed. It still stands in the rotunda. Philo Farnsworth, the father of television. We'll see him, too, when we get up there."

They entered an area dominated by short, stout pillars and arches, and Nephi explained it was the Crypt. Around the walls and between the pillars were sculptures, artifacts, and displays of various things. Most of the units around the walls were carvings. Some once adorned the Capitol but had been replaced in remodeling projects. There were pictures and drawings of the Capitol in its various stages of construction and expansion.

Nephi pointed to one block of white marble that remained partially carved. Above the rough, solid mass the figures of several women dressed in 19th century clothes could be seen.

"I think it's too bad this was never finished any farther than you can see it," he said. "It reminds me of a group of pioneer women heading for Utah. It's not. I'm not sure who it represents, but every time I look at it I can't help thinking of my ancestors crossing the plains to reach the sanctuary of the Great Salt Lake."

"You're a Mormon?" she asked.

He noticed a warmer tone in her voice. "Yes, as a matter of fact, I am," he answered automatically. Then he followed up with a question of his own. "You seemed to ask that with a little enthusiasm. Do you know much about the Mormon church?"

"Not much. I had a girlfriend while I was in Japan who was a Mormon. Our fathers flew in the same squadron. We went to school together. We had a ball."

At last! The ice had broken. It was the first indication that she was willing to not just go through the motions of this tour.

She had caught up with him. No longer were her thoughts with that al-Jarwi guy.

"What happened to her? You still keep in touch with her?" he asked.

"No. I haven't written her for a couple of years. Last I heard she went to Brigham Young University and got married."

"That's where I went to school. Great place to meet people. She's probably busy with her new family," Nephi offered with a bit of a chuckle. He didn't like the idea of having to cover for a neglectful friend.

"No," Maria explained. "She's written me twice since her marriage. I'm the one who hasn't written."

"I see," Nephi added, his voice trailing off.

"I mean, she's so different now. We've just gone our separate ways," Maria said.

"Sure," Nephi said, trying to get off the subject. Obviously Maria seemed to feel guilty for losing contact.

"She sent me a picture of her baby. Beautiful little girl," Maria persisted.

"Aren't all little girls beautiful?"

She smiled at him. It was a warm smile. And she began walking closer to him.

"But things have changed for me, you know? I don't have time for keeping up with the past."

"I can relate to that."

"I mean, she's the one that hung around. I know we promised to write to each other forever. But I just don't have time to keep track of her. I wouldn't even know where to write."

"I understand." Nephi said. Then he thought of something important to say—something that just might help him maintain contact with her if everything else failed. "But if you ever change your mind I'm sure I could find her address." He was bluffing a little. But he knew it was possible to find members of the Church through the Church Office Building.

"Eleanor."

"What?"

"Eleanor was her name. Eleanor Jameson. I think her married name is Blake."

"You want me to try and find her?"

"No. It would be too much trouble. I couldn't impose on your time like that. I know you're busy."

"That wouldn't be any trouble. I'd be happy to try."

"Oh," she hesitated. "No. It's been so long. She probably has forgotten about me."

"I doubt that. It sounds like you two were close friends."

"We were. I mean, we did everything together. We were like sisters."

"She take you to church?"

"No. Mom wouldn't let me."

"Too bad."

"Why?"

"Oh, I think you'd make a good Mormon. You look like you would have done well crossing the plains."

Maria gave him a curious look.

He stopped her and pointed to a plate in the floor.

"Ever wonder who or what's to blame for the screwed up way this town is laid out?"

"You mean with the roads going every which way?"

"Yep."

"Wasn't it some Frenchman?"

"Yep. President Washington picked a Frenchman. Major Pierre Charles L'Enfant was the one to blame for all this. The best thing he did was pick this site for the Capitol Building. Jenkin's Hill. Everything went downhill from there."

She looked at him and tried not to acknowledge or encourage the pun.

"So he drew out a city with everything emanating from here. They say he drew the map on a handkerchief. Others say he dropped a plate of spaghetti on it and when he shook the spaghetti off, there was the design of Washington—with all its diagonal streets and its crossing streets. I think it looks more like the spokes of a wheel than anything."

"I know. I really have trouble finding my way around in this city. It's horrible."

"They thought so, too. By the time they were ready to move the seat of government here, he was gone. Fired. But they were stuck with the design, I guess.

"Anyway. Here is the very spot from which the whole city emanates."

They continued through the hall and found a display on the Senate, which they glanced at briefly and moved on.

"I'm not all that up on what's over on this side—the Senate side, Maria. But as we are walking around you'll notice busts of men in various places. They are of those who served as Presidents of the Senate."

"You mean Vice Presidents?"

"Yes. They are both. And you will probably spot, as we wander around here, many who later became Presidents—Nixon, Truman, Bush, among others."

"Oh, yeh. Bush was Vice President, too, wasn't he?"

"Yep. Now, while we're here, before we go upstairs, would you like to ride the tram over to the Senate Offices, or would you like to go up to the gallery where they're debating the war."

She looked at him. Kassim would be mad at her for not tending to business. But it would be more fun to ride the tram. Kassim wouldn't need to know about it.

"Could we do both?"

"Sure."

He led her to the elevators and took one to the basement. Stepping off, an officer directed them to their right. They walked through a doorway and went down a short escalator to the tram landing. They waited for the one marked "Dirksen" and rode it past the stop for the Russell Building. On their return trip, Senator Jake Garn got on board.

"You're working for Ron Hersch, aren't you?"

"Yes, sir."

"Aren't you the one with the good old Mormon name?" He held out his hand to greet the staff member.

"Yes, sir. Nephi Nicholes."

"I thought so."

"And this is a friend of mine, Maria Moore."

"Miss Moore," the politician shook her hand too. "You visiting Washington?"

"No, sir," she said and wondered why she added the sir part. "My father's in the Air Force. He's working out of the Pentagon."

"You Arnie Moore's daughter?"

"Yes, I am."

"I know him very well. We've flown together a couple of times. He's a good man."

It embarrassed her to hear him say it. But she thanked him anyway. Come to think of it, why did this Nicholes guy call her a friend? She wasn't his friend—yet. Kassim had ordered her to make him like her. He hadn't said anything about her having to like him. Kassim planned to use him to complete his project—to send a message to these politicians to stay out of the Middle East. But he seemed so nice—this guy Nicholes—naive but nice. Given the right circumstances—well, why should she speculate? Her lot had been cast with Kassim. She was his woman. Not his only woman—but he was nice too, in a foreign sort of way. Different kind of nice than this Nephi fellow. Would she ever be able to trust Kassim? No. Would she ever be able to trust Nephi? It was too early to tell. But she felt warm around him. He was different. She liked that.

"We're just taking a bit of a tour here today. You going over to vote?" Nephi asked the Senator.

"Yes. They've called for a vote. And this one is going to be close. Would you like to go up and watch?"

"Yes, sir," Nephi quickly responded and then looked at Maria to see if she wanted to.

Of course she did. Kassim would be excited to hear that she actually had been inside when the vote was taken.

Senator Garn escorted them to the gallery and made sure they had seats before he left. A few minutes later they saw him walk onto the floor and shortly after that Vice President Dan Quayle, acting as President of the Senate, called for the vote.

The droning voice of the clerk called each Senator by name and the roll call proceeded until Senator Wirth's name completed the process.

Mr. Quayle announced the vote—52 for and 47 against the resolution to empower President Bush to "use United States armed forces" to expel Iraq from Kuwait. The resolution passed.

"How can they do that?" Maria asked in a voice much louder than the rules allowed.

Her reaction brought the gavel banging against the desk. "There will be no reaction from the gallery, please," Vice President Quayle ordered.

Nephi had been watching her as the vote progressed. Changes in trends caused her to smile or agonize. By the time the final vote was taken and she could see the result, it proved too much for her to deny herself some kind of expression.

Nephi looked at her. "Let's get out of here."

That seemed to agree with her. She willingly walked up the few steep steps to the door and outside. Nephi took her by the arm and led her across the hall to the corridor that ran on the east side of the building and would connect them with the House gallery without going through the masses.

"Maria," he said firmly as they walked along. "I know you feel strongly about the war."

"You can say that again. I don't know why we have to get into another Vietnam. Haven't the fools learned anything?"

He held up his hand with the palm down and advised her to speak quietly. He needed to say something to her. It was his responsibility. Before they entered the House, she had to know what the rules were. It would not be easy. He still had to lock in on something that would attract her, not alienate her. So far things had gone well, he thought. But a feeling nagged him to say something soon to help her think of him as a friend. Becoming more than a friend could come later. Still, he had no idea what those initial words might be.

"Do you think the House will show more sense?" she asked in a softer voice, but with a determination. "They said they had enough votes to pass this stupid resolution."

She was angry. And she seemed to be filled with increased anger at each step. He caught up with her and took her by the arm. They were standing at the end of the hall, before it turned to lead into the hyphen that connected the old part of the building with the new wing on the House side.

"Maria," he began. "We have the honor to be standing in the very place where history is being made. This is the most powerful legislative body in the world. And we're watching that legislature do something that will affect the lives of hundreds of thousands of people."

"Millions of people," she said in her ire.

"That's probably more like it—millions," he continued. "But we're going to do ourselves no good if we can't keep our emotions under control. They'll actually throw us out. Only the Congressmen and Senators can express themselves and their feelings. The rest of us have to take it as it comes. Do you know how many times I've had to sit and listen to people who make me sick with their rhetoric?"

"I'll bet," she agreed. "I know just what you mean."

"My problem is that I still have to work here. I do what I can within the limits of my job. And I believe that contribution is valid and important. I don't want anything to jeopardize that, do you understand?"

She looked up at him. She didn't care what he thought. Yes, she did. All this wasn't his fault. He was a nice guy. And she didn't want to do anything that might cause him problems.

At first Nephi saw nothing but the rebelliousness that had built up inside her. Then he saw something soften. While she held her lips tight and had flexed her cheeks so they strengthed her position, there was something in her eyes that changed, softened. And in a moment she simply let out a big breath and relaxed.

"Yes. I understand."

"Maria," he continued. "I've only known you just a little while," he lied. He knew her better than any stranger ever could. "But I've come to like you. And I'd really like to get to know you a lot better."

The softened version of her rebelliousness moved even farther into a smile. Her eyes held firmly in a study of his face.

It was a pleasant face, she thought. Except for his obvious political faults he seemed to be a good man. Would anything come of this contact with him? She had no idea. But it didn't seem to her to be such a bad idea. His gentle way had taken her by surprise. Then she remembered Kassim had told her to make friends with him. She could allow herself to do that. But for the sake of her relationship with Kassim, that's as far as she was prepared to go at the moment. She refused herself the luxury of envisioning anything further—one way or another. She had forgotten Kassim had ordered her to make him happy. She would reserve for herself that option.

"Could I ask you to keep your thoughts and emotions to yourself while we're in here?" he asked softly.

She nodded.

"Have you ever played poker?" he asked.

"Yes. But I always lose," she almost laughed.

He smiled. "So do I. But I have learned how to keep a neutral poker face. Can you do that for me?"

She nodded. "I'll try."

"Thanks," he said and took hold of her arm to lead her around the series of turns through the corridor.

They emerged into another crowded hall. Officers directed the people waiting to get into the gallery. Nephi's ID cleared the way and placed them in a short line. Before long there was room for them in the gallery and she looked down at the proceedings.

The room below them was virtually empty. There were several people at the complex dais where the Speaker—or in this case, Chairman—was seated. The House was not in session. It was the Committee of the Whole. And the Committee had a Chairman, not a Speaker. In front of the Chairman were places for clerical workers. Only a few Members could be seen on the floor. A small group clustered around a table on one side of the aisle and another small group circled a table on the other side of the aisle. One man stood in front of the speaker's dais. He was the only one talking.

Nephi leaned as close as he could to Maria. Oh, she was soft. He fought against the distraction. He began to whisper in her ear and she leaned toward him so she could hear more clearly. Her hair fell gently against his cheek.

"Where that man is standing is traditionally called the well. I have no idea where the term came from, but if you read testimony where a member of Congress says he's speaking from the well, then you will know where it is."

She smiled and nodded.

"On each side of the aisle there is a member in charge of the floor debate for his party. Democrats on the left and Republicans on the right. Each side is allocated so much time and the floor leader has to manage it so everyone who is supposed to speak is given the chance. But this is an open debate. Time limits are not as important as they are when they get down to the end of a session, and they still have to pass the budget and a hundred other bills. Then they squeeze everyone down to 30 seconds instead of one, two or five minutes or half an hour."

She nodded again.

The speaker finished saying, "With that I yield back the remainder of my time."

The Chairman pro-tem whopped the big gavel down and said, "The time of the gentleman has expired. The Chair recognizes the gentleman from New York."

Nephi put his arm around Maria and pulled her close to him. It wasn't an attempt to get fresh. He just wanted to say a lot of things—quietly. On the other hand, he didn't deny enjoying the action either. Nor did he deny himself pleasure in her reaction. She let herself be drawn to him. It seemed to her just a natural way to react. A very pleasant sensation was rising within her. It began when she felt his arm touching her shoulders. It increased as he whispered close to her ear. After a moment she turned her head slightly to look at him and found his face right where she thought it would be—extremely close to her own.

"This is interesting, Maria," he said. "They are sitting in the Committee of the Whole. It is a parliamentary mechanism to avoid some of the strict rules of the House. It may sound like splitting hairs but there is a good reason for it. Generally speaking, the Committee of the Whole is used to conduct debate on issues of major importance. You can tell the difference by looking on the wall. If the mace is there, the House is in session and if it's not there, the Committee of the Whole is sitting. Another way to tell is how they address the main man up there. He's either Mr. Speaker or Mr. Chairman. Sometimes the Members get confused. A lot of times the rest of the world gets confused."

When she turned toward him to acknowledge what he had said, their faces—their lips—were very close together. Her closeness broke his concentration. He froze in place. After a moment he felt a distinct, reluctant need to clear his throat. It was the only way to get his voice going again.

"Ahem. The man speaking in the well is Congressman Stephen Solarz from New York. He's Jewish and even though he's a Democrat he's been aggressively working to get this resolution passed."

For the time being, Maria was not concentrating too clearly on the debates either. Neither was she thinking of Kassim or the assignment he had given her.

"Who is it?" she asked as though she had not heard—not caring a bit what he might answer.

"Solarz—Congressman Solarz—a Democrat from New York. He's very liberal and generally votes against the President. But in this case, because he is such a staunch supporter and promoter of Israel's interests, he's working hard to get this resolution passed for the President."

"Oh," she said, the message still not generating enough stimulus to interfere with what she preferred thinking about.

With great reluctance Nephi moved his arm from her shoulder and straightened himself in his chair. Relying on extreme peripheral vision, he noticed that she had lingered in the same position, even looking toward him rather than at the action on the floor. Then she moved in her seat too, straightening slightly but still leaning against him as much as the chair would permit.

In a moment what the gentleman from New York was saying began to penetrate the pleasant, emotional veneer that she had allowed to rise around her and protect her even from her own thoughts. What had he said? They had to make it safe for all nations in the Middle East? His words, his line of reasoning made the muscles in her back stiffen and her hands tighten into fists. The best thing about this man was the annoying tone of his voice. Solarz's voice wasn't all that bad. She just thought it was because what he was saying had crashed so recklessly into her consciousness.

She did not hate Jews. Never had. But for the past two years most of the people with whom she had been associating did hate Jews. They wouldn't admit it openly, but Maria knew they did. Of course, those same people had a great hatred for many things. She hadn't really hated those other things either. But given time and given opportunity, many of their beliefs had managed to intrude deeply into her psyche. In order to maintain the level of antagonism she wanted to apply against her parents, she had outwardly championed their causes, had walked in their demonstrations and had lived their lifestyle. Without sensing a change in herself, she had become one of them.

Now this traitorous Solarz was saying things that attacked the very heart of one of her causes—Palestinian relief. Of course, she hated war. But war was secondary. Had the war held hope for the Palestinians, she knew her mentors would have spoken for it. The twists and inconsistencies of her actions for the past two years rebelled. She erected another barrier around her against the words that man was using to attack her. She felt the assault crowding her. She couldn't listen to him any longer. She wanted to shout him down.

But she could not. Out of respect for Nephi, she had to honor his request and her promise.

"I need to get out of here," she finally whispered.

Nephi nodded and they filed out of their seats, moving to the aisle and up the stairs to the door.

Outside she admitted, "I'm sorry. I just didn't want to hear any more."

"It's all right."

She headed for the corridor through which they had come. It was the only familiar place where there would be a measure of privacy. And she needed a place where she could be away from the crowd.

"What's the matter?" Nephi asked.

"It's this war. It's all wrong. Why can't they see that, Nephi? We're going to get ourselves drawn into something we can't get out of. Another Vietnam. You know? This country is heading for Armageddon. You wait and see."

Nephi stepped to her side. He already knew she felt strongly about this, but it surprised him to see her so intensely emotional about it.

"Come on, Maria. There may not be any war at all. And if there is, President Bush has promised there would not be another long, protracted conflict."

"And you trust him?"

"Sure."

"Then you're more naive than I thought you were," she chided.

"Well, okay," he said without guile.

His innocent acceptance of her attack stopped her from saying anything more. Actually, it put an end to her intense rebellion against what she just had seen and heard.

What was she doing? Why was she reacting this way? she asked herself quickly. She liked this man, really liked him. He had been a gentleman and had gone out of his way to be nice to her. He had done nothing to her—except make her feel something kind of wonderful, something she had not felt before with any man.

What was she really doing? To him? To this beautiful building? To her own country? She had come with him only so she could turn him—compromise him. Kassim had ordered it. She was doing it. They had come there to make a statement about the war. Whatever it was had to be something awful. She hadn't asked what was in those bottles. She didn't want to know. But she knew it would not be pleasant. She had talked herself into believing it was just some kind of stink bomb. But deep inside her she knew Kassim was not the kind of man who would settle for making a stink. He destroyed things. He killed people. She knew that, even though she had never heard him say so. She just had not wanted to admit it before.

What she had done in coming here was wrong. What Kassim wanted her to do with this man was wrong.

The only thing that was right about this whole deal was him, this man with the funny name. She liked being with him. She could not betray him. For she held in her heart another deep-seated fear. Whatever Kassim wanted to do with him, after she had managed to turn him, would not be pleasant. It was most likely to be serious. It was quite likely this man with the funny name could get killed.

"I'm sorry," she said simply.

And there he was doing it again. He smiled at her. He had no idea what was happening to him. And there was that smile again—that innocent, wonderful, gentle smile.

"There's nothing to be sorry for," he said calmly.

"Yes, there is," she said. "You don't understand."

"Sure I do. This is a very emotional issue with you. I can see that. But there's nothing here we can't work out."

She looked at his face. So innocent. She didn't think there were any men left in the world who could look like that. Trouble was, he showed all the classic signs of being hooked. There was no question in her mind that she could go back to Kassim's apartment right now having accomplished her mission. She was convinced that this man, this wonderful man with the funny name, was in such a state of emotion that he surely would do whatever she asked him to do.

"You really don't understand, do you?" she said again in that urgent tone.

"Why do I have to understand anything?"

"What do you mean? You think I should—that we should forget about what's going on here?"

He shrugged his shoulders and forced a question on his face.

"Why not?"

She looked at him again and couldn't believe how relaxed he was. Of course, he had no idea what Kassim had planned for him. Maybe he wouldn't be so much at ease if he really knew what kind of a trap Kassim had ready to spring on him. She thought about warning him, telling him everything. She even started to speak— to reveal what she and Kassim were doing. But as quickly as she started, she cut off the thought. At the moment she was not in the best position to say anything about it. She could see exactly what would happen if she did. She would be arrested. It would be the greatest offense against her parents she had ever accomplished. While that might have been acceptable, the worst part of that scenario was not. She probably would lose Nephi. She had a strong feeling she would regret doing that.

"Come on, Maria. Lighten up. There's not a thing you or I can do about what's going on in there today. But we can do something for ourselves, can't we?"

She had to nod in agreement. But she included a shrug of her shoulders along with it. And a reluctant smile.

"We've got a couple of hours to spend together here. Why don't we make the most of them?"

Nephi quickly estimated the time they would be debating in there. Two hours maybe. It could go longer. It could go shorter. He wouldn't have to worry about meeting his boss until they completed action in the Committee of the Whole. Then they still would have to go through the motions in regular session and take the vote.

His biggest problem right now was to hold on tightly to this woman. If only he could do that then he would be satisfied. Also, he tried telling himself, there would still be a way for him to fulfill his responsibilities to his boss.

"Could I interest you in some lunch?" he asked.

She suddenly realized how nice it would be to have lunch with this man. She nodded and they headed for the Members' Dining Room on the first floor. He took her hand and guided her back to the hall outside the House gallery. He led her to the east staircase and showed her the painting of the signing of the Constitution.

"They didn't have it so easy back then, either," he said to her. "I'll bet there were a lot of concerned men and women standing around outside, wringing their hands, while those men were doing their best to give birth to a nation."

That was an interesting thing for him to say, she thought. And she purposely walked as close to him as she could, taking hold of his arm and drawing it to her. Since his shoulder was so handy, she even leaned her head on it for a moment.

Then it occurred to her that she had not done such a thing since she was in high school. She had not wanted to since then. People would have considered such a thing to be childish. But she didn't care what anyone might think. She was enjoying this means of expressing herself. She only hoped Nephi would enjoy it too. Whatever anyone else thought was their problem.

As for what Nephi was thinking at the moment when he felt her near him and knew she had put her head on his shoulder: This was a whole lot better than just dreaming about her.

CHAPTER 5

THEY FOLLOWED THE WAITER TO A TABLE IN THE CORNER OF
the room. That suited them fine. The dining room was crowded
and they both wanted to be as alone as possible. Each hoped for
the chance to say things and didn't want to worry about others
overhearing.

The Members' Dining Room is reserved for members of
Congress, staff members and their guests. A special area located
in an adjoining room is set aside for members of the press. It's
located on the first floor—the same floor as the Hall of Columns.
The main dining hall is larger and more ornate than the two
other rooms. With a high ceiling, this full service restaurant
maintains the integrity of the Capitol's decor. When Congressmen want privacy, they slip into the private dining room reserved
strictly for their needs.

Maria and Nephi both ordered soup and salad, and when the
waiter left, Maria felt it was time for her to mend a fence or two.

"I'm so sorry, Nephi." She forced a nervous smile. "You probably think I'm strange, don't you?"

"No. As a matter of fact, I think you're pretty terrific."

"You're kidding!" His choice of words caught her off guard.

"Well, if it makes you uncomfortable—maybe just a little
terrific," he said, a faint smile on his face.

"It's all right, you know. You really don't have to go back on
your word." She liked the way he put things—just a bit differently
than other people. What a refreshing personality.

"Actually, I wasn't kidding at all. And I consider myself a pretty good judge of character. Look, Maria. I know you're concerned about the war. We all are. But for some reason, what you're feeling seems to run a bit deeper than what the rest of us do."

She shook her head. "This whole thing has really gotten complicated." If he only knew the half of it, Maria thought to herself as she finished her comment. She had not figured on discovering such a fascinating person in this man with a funny name—her assignment from Kassim. In the short time they had spent together he had impressed her with his sincerity. The contrast between him and Kassim had opened her mind to a whole new set of choices— choices she had never before considered possible. At the moment these new leanings had created the complications in her mind.

If she only knew the half of it, Nephi thought to himself while nodding in agreement. The war had managed to bring the two of them from their divergent lives to this moment where they could share lunch and a few hours together. To him, the whole of it represented a prelude to their future together. For they would have a future and they would be together. Of that he was more certain at this moment than he had ever been—since he was twelve.

They looked at each other and smiled. Then they laughed— but for different reasons.

"See," Nephi said, leaning back so the waiter could serve his salad. "That wasn't so complicated."

"Couldn't we just ignore the whole thing?" she suggested, thinking how good it would be just to forget about Kassim and what he planned to do.

"Sure, why not," Nephi agreed. "Let's just enjoy ourselves and put everything else on hold."

If we could only be that lucky, Maria thought to herself as she jabbed at her salad with her fork. Kassim would demand his moment of reckoning. That would not be pleasant. But what could he do to her? Nothing. So, why not just enjoy this moment with Nephi?

Wouldn't that be something? Nephi thought, hoping the Lord might just help him get through to her—help him convince her that a whole new, exciting life awaited them if they could find it together. After a bite of salad he began the conversation again.

"So, talk to me. Tell me about yourself."

"Why?" she asked, surprised at his request.

He shrugged. "I guess I'm the curious type. I like to know things about my friends. I'd like to know all about you."

"Why?" she repeated, the question surprising her even more.

"I like you."

"I know," she admitted. And for the first time in years, she wondered if what she felt that very moment was showing up as some kind of a blush on her face. But that possibility meant nothing to her. For she plunged into another modest confession. "I like you, too."

I wonder if she has the slightest idea how deeply I really care for her? he thought, looking past the flowers, into her eyes. I wonder if she even suspects how happy the two of us could be—will be?

It's so strange to feel this way, she thought looking up at him in a sheepish way and discovering him looking at her. After everything I've done, after all the jerks I've been with, after all the demonstrations I've been in to protest and complain about this country, I really believe I'm falling for this conservative reactionary. I wonder if he could ever go for a girl like me? He's so straight. I know he likes me. He said so a minute ago and now his eyes are telling me the same thing. But will he like me after he finds out about me—*all* about me?

Through the rest of the meal they talked about their childhoods. She found it difficult to speak about her childhood at first, but soon it became fun. And she found herself wanting to tell him more and more.

He just kept asking her questions about where she had been in the world. It was all she needed to review so many pleasant times with her parents. It was hard for her to get him to tell as much about himself. All he would say was that he had grown up in a little town in Utah and had not been anywhere until he went on his mission. He told her a little about missionary life and then a little about what he did for the Congressman, but that was about all. She vowed to make him tell her more—and if he refused, she would find out for herself one day.

Each time she told him a story about where she had lived, she could not avoid relating those times with her parents. And for the first time in years she actually remembered them as people who loved her, who had shared their lives with her. For the first time in a long while she didn't think of them as tyrants, trying to force her to believe as they believed, or live as they lived, or do what they did. Sitting there with Nephi she remembered how they always seemed to know stories to tell her about the places they went. When he mentioned how much research her parents must have done to keep up her interest, Maria had to agree. Maria had never quite thought of it that way.

Funny. By the end of lunch she caught herself wanting to call her mother when she got home and just talk with her. Her mother really would like this man. So would her dad. For some reason, that made Maria feel good.

Nephi paid the check and settled with a generous tip. If the rest of the tour turned out like their lunch, he thought he might even tip the Capitol policemen stationed at the door on their way out.

First thing he wanted to do was take her upstairs to the Hall of Statues. That was up one flight, around the hall to the right and through the hyphen. Just before entering the Hall of Statues, Nephi stopped.

"You recognize this guy?" he asked, jerking a thumb at a statue in the corner.

"Will Rogers," she read off the name tag. "Oh, yeah."

"Oklahoma's favorite son. He's the one who coined the phrase, 'All I know is what I read in the newspapers.'" Nephi paused for a minute and then continued. "He'd probably have something colorful to say about the way the press mangles news these days. He had a great wit. He would take every opportunity to pick on Congress, you know. Those were hard times, back then, and he gave everyone a chance to laugh for a minute at a common foe. Once he said something like he never wanted to turn his back on Congress. So, when they were deciding on a spot for his statue, they lovingly situated him so he would never have his back turned to Congress. See? He's facing that door over there. That's one of the entrances to the House Chambers."

"You're kidding."

"Nope. So now you can sleep better at night knowing Will Rogers still keeps his eye on the government."

She responded with a smile, a shake of her head and a gentle punch to his shoulder.

"And this beautiful room is what used to be the House Chambers." Nephi gestured by moving his arm in a sweeping arc above his head. The domed ceiling varied slightly from the perfect dome they would see in the Rotunda. Even so, it curved pleasingly but was interrupted slightly on one side to accommodate two fireplaces.

"They gussied it up for the Bicentennial and it's been in this state ever since. Come here, I want to show you a couple of interesting things."

Immediately to the left they looked at a display of old furniture and decorations, original to the House. Back to the right of the hyphen stood the statue of Hawaii's King Kamahamaha. The magnificent statue done in ebony and gold had been adorned by visitors who had draped orchid leis over his outstretched arm.

"That's nice," Maria observed. "They have a great reverence for King Kamahamaha in the islands. Now it reaches all the way to Washington."

"I don't know why they have hidden him back here. It's a replica of the one they have of him in front of their own Capitol. I think it's the most impressive statue of the bunch. And even though he's hidden away back here, all the Hawaiians seem to find him," Nephi added. "I've seen his whole arm just covered with flowers."

Around a row of statues that seemed to hide Kamahamaha, Nephi pointed out the statue of Brigham Young. They had placed him in the corner by the fireplace.

"Would you like to find the statues from the state where you were born?" he asked Maria.

"You don't have any. I was born in Germany. Remember? Mom wanted to wait for the last minute before flying home. But I fooled her. She didn't get back. I was born in a genuine, bona fide United States Air Force Base hospital."

"Well, just so you got here eventually. This country would have been a lonely place without you."

She smiled at him. It was fun to have someone say things like that.

"Now. Stand over here. And wait," he ordered.

He left her standing on a spot about 30 feet into the middle of the room. Then he walked away from her. He turned so she could not see his face.

"Can you hear me, Maria?" he said softly.

"Yes," she answered, surprised to have heard him.

"It's the dome," he pointed to the ceiling arching above them. And he walked back to her. "Over where I was standing is a plate to show where John Quincy Adams died. They found him slumped over at his desk. At first they didn't think anything of it. The story is that he was the first to discover the strange acoustical qualities of the room. He would slump over and listen to what the opposition was planning. They had no idea how he seemed to know what their plans were. They thought him to be some kind of genius. He would block every move they made."

"That was cheating," her sense of fair play caused her to say.

"Of course it was cheating. But what goes around, comes around. When they found out what was happening, they began feeding him false information."

She could laugh at that. And he led her into the Rotunda. The room was filled with tourists. They had been herded into manageable areas cordoned off by brass, self-standing posts and braided ropes. From place to place there were men and women in red blazers shouting to their groups. When they moved around they held an umbrella or hat to identify them to the members of their group.

"I don't have a funny hat or an umbrella, but will you follow me around?" he asked.

"Sure," she responded without hesitation. "Anywhere."

For a moment they lingered to satisfy themselves with the full implications of that little exchange. And a much more confident young man with a funny name took Maria by the elbow and continued conducting his tour.

"You can see statues of our big-time heroes at the four entrances to the Rotunda: George Washington, Thomas Jefferson, Abraham Lincoln and the others. Over there is the second statue from Utah—Philo Farnsworth. That's a cathode ray tube—television tube—he's holding."

"He's from Utah?"

"Yes. Born in the thriving metropolis of Beaver, Utah. He worked all over the place, but Utah has a solid claim on him. The important thing is that he is a figure of national importance. He has had a significant impact on all our lives."

"For good or bad?" she asked.

"Both," Nephi replied. And he went right on explaining what had been included in the most central room of the Capitol.

"Around us are paintings that portray various stages in the history of our nation, from exploration to the surrender of Cornwallis to Washington and, later, Washington's resignation from the army. He made it before Congress when Congress was working out of Annapolis. These were done by various painters of the day. There's one of Pocahontas, only she's getting baptized, not saving John Smith. And there's DeSoto trying to find the fountain of youth."

He led her to a spot near the center of the room and positioned her so she was just in front of him.

"Now, look up," he told her.

"I have been. You can't help it."

"Yeh, I know. But look up from here."

She tilted her head back. He was standing so close to her that her hair brushed softly against his cheek again. He placed his hand on her shoulder—to steady her, of course. And he pointed upward with his right hand.

"Constantino Brumudi, a naturalized American citizen, painted all those figures way up there. They are heroic figures one-and-a-half-life size. They had to be that big so they would look normal size from way down here. Notice Washington surrounded by all those women."

"His harem?"

"Not quite," he responded. "He's sitting between Miss Liberty and Miss Victory. The other thirteen women represent the thirteen original states. And below that are groupings of figures representing what made the country great."

"What's that?"

"Notice the lady with the sword—right under Washington. She's Freedom."

"She's got a sword."

"Of course. We won our freedom with the sword, so to speak. Back then swords were a big deal."

"And what are the other things?" Her question clearly indicated a desire to ignore his previous answer.

"They represent arts and sciences, the sea, commerce, mechanics and agriculture."

My gosh, it's great standing here with her almost in my arms, Nephi thought. Her perfume is fantastic! Let's see, what else can I point out to her so we can stay like this a little longer? Oh, yeh. The frescos.

This is nice just standing here with his hand on my shoulder and his arm holding me up, Maria thought. I wonder what else I can ask him so we can stay like this a little longer?

"Maria," he began. "See that ring of frescos about halfway up the dome?"

"Yes."

"The figures look like sculptures, but it's a flat painting. Brumudi did the first part. He started it when he was seventy-two, twelve years after he finished the dome. He finished six panels and was beginning the seventh when he fell from the scaffold."

"Oh, no!"

"Oh, yes. It was tragic. But he didn't hit the floor. Apparently he held on. He just hung there until rescuers could get him down. But the experience was a little much for the old man. He never recovered.

"Then they hired a painter by the name of Filippo Costaggini, I think was his name. They didn't like him much. Can you see up there how his figures are so stiff?"

"Oh, yeah. A big difference."

"Well, they fired him on the spot when they found he had painted his own portrait into the picture."

"No kidding? Where?"

"See that tree trunk right there? See what looks like a gnarled part of the trunk? That's his face."

"Oh, yeah. That wasn't so smart."

"No. But it did solve a chronic problem they had with his style. The only thing is they just left it the way it was the day they fired him. They didn't do anything with it until quite recently. It remained unfinished from 1888 to 1953 when a painter named Allyn Cox was hired to complete it. He did much better than Costaggini. Looks a lot like Brumudi's work, not so stiff."

Having said that he reluctantly removed his hand from her shoulder and took half a step away from her. To his pleasure, he found himself looking into a beautiful face that smiled at him so charmingly that he nearly forgot where he was.

"Thank you," she said in a soft voice, hardly audible over the echoing noises of the crowd.

"You're welcome," he answered in a voice just as soft.

"I guess I should be going," she said without meaning it.

It's really dumb to be like this, she scolded herself. You're acting like a 14-year-old kid. And you have no right to expect anything but heartache if you keep on like this. What's this nice guy going to do when he finds out you came here because Kassim wanted you to turn him? That's going to make him furious. And if he doesn't find out—if he turns because of you—Kassim will use him like he uses everything else around him. Including you.

"It's up to you," Nephi said with reluctance. "I don't have anything to do until they take the vote. Then it will be a furious race with deadlines. After that I'll be free."

"How long will that be?"

"I have no idea. Sometime tonight. Maybe this afternoon. Late."

Stay with me, Maria, were the words Nephi wanted to say. But they wouldn't come out. He feared she would take it the wrong way. This was difficult territory. He sensed, just sensed, something might be wrong. He had no idea of the danger lurking near them both. From the moment he saw her in the entrance to the Longworth Building, he had felt an incredible force within his breast. At different times he had supposed that force to be his emotions, his nerves, and perhaps even the Holy Spirit. But there had been little effort to classify its true source. He knew it could have been fabricated by his carnal interests in this girl. It might even have been from an evil source. His state of mind and emotions had rendered ineffective his ability to recognize it to be a prompting of the Spirit. It had been given to him to confirm the validity of all those dreams. It had surged within him as she spoke of her experiences and as he had silently matched them with his sketches.

In the same way he misunderstood new promptings that were given to him as they spoke of parting

It was clear to him that in spite of the short time they had actually known each other, they were building what looked to be a solid relationship. That provided the foundation for his thought to let her go—for now. He loved this girl. He had waited so long to find her. This afternoon had been great—far better than he had any right to expect. He knew very well that she liked him. That was easy enought to tell. But he wanted her to like him more than anything—more than anyone. Unconsciously that fixation overwhelmed his thoughts, his judgement, and his ability to reason. A strong negative feeling—actually a warning—bounced off his obsession and went unheeded. Had he recognized the warning and inquired about it he might have prevented grief from entering their lives.

But instead of inquiring he merely concluded that she just had not told him everything. He assumed the negative feeling had come because she called him "naive" and said he "didn't understand." He presumed she had probably said those things because of her past—her indescretions. He was willing to allow her her secrets no matter how badly he felt about her past.

He couldn't help but wonder how much of a past she had. Odds weighed heavily against the possibility of her reaching this point in her life as a virgin. The way things were in the world today few girls with beauty like hers could have survived adolescence a virgin. Over the years he had dealt with this scenario many times. And he had concluded that once they had found each other they would start anew. For him it would be required to forgive anything that had gone on before. He willingly had done so in his heart. It would remain for her to repent of whatever she might have done before they met. That would leave everything up to the Lord. He had no doubt the Lord would forgive her. That made it easy for him. He had been in love with her since he was twelve.

His carnal interpretation had been partially correct. Most certainly she felt concerned with what he would think when he discovered her past. But her most pressing concern involved her entanglement with Kassim. At this point, Nephi had no idea of this element of her thoughts and her increased concern with how it threatened his safety.

"Well, I wouldn't want to keep you from anything," he added without really wanting to.

"I've had a wonderful time," she said, hoping he would find some way to stop her from leaving.

"So have I. I'm sorry I don't have my car here. I'd be happy to drop you wherever you needed to go."

"Thanks. I'll just take the Metro."

"Where are you going now?"

She shrugged. There was absolutely nothing she really wanted to do except spend more time with this man. And she didn't care how funny his name was. In fact, she was beginning to like it. Nephi.

"I have to run some errands," she lied. "I'll have to pick up my car first. It's not far."

"I see." He knew nothing more he could say except, perhaps—yes, he would say this. He had to say this. "Could I see you again?"

"Oh, yes," she answered instantly.

"When?"

"Anytime."

"Really?"

"Sure," she said, satisfied to have this much of a commitment. She started to step away from him.

"Just a second."

"Yes?" she said, happy for the delay.

"Ah, I don't know how to reach you."

She laughed and walked back to his side, giggling as she fumbled with her purse.

"You'll never find me in the book," she said. "I have my own apartment. But I sometimes can be reached at my parent's place. They have an apartment in Ballston. Actually, I'm staying there while they're out of town. I think Dad's over in England or some place. I don't know. But I'm watching their apartment for them."

She handed him a piece of paper with her phone numbers on it—and her addresses.

She gave a wave of her hand again and walked away from him—again.

As she disappeared into the crowd, Nephi felt that a hole opened up in his soul. Their time together had been short, but they had managed to create a bond between them.

He meandered back through the Hall of Statues, past Will Rogers and into the hall that surrounded the House Chambers. He walked down the stairs to the first floor and made his way to the little known stairway leading to the basement. It seemed like a better idea for him to walk through the tunnel than to fight with the demonstrators outside.

The tunnel connecting the Capitol with the House Office Buildings curved slightly so it would emerge mainly under the Cannon Building. Few people ever took the sidewalk. Most people who used the tunnel walked in a broad area slightly below the raised sidewalk. Across from the sidewalk, on the other side of the tunnel, were massive pipes covered with many layers of cracked and peeling paint. On the opposite wall were pictures drawn by high school students. They brightened a dreary path for those working on the Hill.

But the lines and colors and shapes of the works blended into a blur before Nephi. His mind was focused on his Elena—his Maria.

In his office Nephi leaned back in his chair. No one was there. If Roy Ivars had come in, he had left again. Nephi didn't care. The only reason he noticed the television monitor was to make sure he would be on time following the vote on this resolution. But his mind was far away from politics. He was thinking of Maria—again matching everything Maria had told him about her life with the sketches he had done. He thought also of his circumstances when he had made those sketches. Every day of the two years he spent proselyting for the Mormon Church he fully expected to see her face on the other side of each new door he knocked on.

Then, after he had completed his mission and had enrolled at

Brigham Young University, his natural tendency was to search for her there. After all, BYU had more than a casual reputation as a marriage factory. Surely he would find her on campus somewhere. Surely she would be there waiting for him, looking for him—around the next shelf of books in the library or in the next class.

How he had managed to do so well in either of those experiences had been a miracle in its own right. Thoughts of her had crowded into his time significantly. But it was a new ballgame now. All the thinking, planning, and dreaming was over. Reality had given a new dimension to his life. Fulfillment was at hand.

After Congress completed its historic vote to give President Bush authority to use force against Iraq, Nephi hustled over to the Capitol. He found his boss and shuttled him to meetings with reporters representing the two major newspapers and the television and radio stations back in the district. From these interviews Nephi got the direction and language for his own press release.

He returned to the office to write something for the weekly papers. As soon as his pants hit his swivel chair he began to click off the words as if he had been writing for 30 years. He not only wrote the piece quickly, he wrote it well. Hersch didn't have to correct a single word.

He was out of there in record time. And even though he had to ride the Metro system home, he didn't mind. It gave him a chance to get back to thinking about something important—Maria. In fact, he could think about her for the rest of the weekend and nobody would be able to interfere.

* * * *

Kassim hung up the phone. The expression on his face had changed little during the conversation. He had been trained too well to allow such things to bother him. He had received such orders before.

There had been no mistake. There would be no excuses. President Saddam Hussein himself had issued the order. Kassim was to have everything in place so that the instant word was received that the United States had begun the unprovoked attack on Iraq or any of its provinces—including Kuwait—he was to complete the assignment.

That meant he would have to plant the bombs in the Capitol as soon as possible. Also, he would have to rig the bombs so they would explode by a radio device.

He could see two problems: first, he would have to get those bottles inside the Capitol; and second, he would have to make sure the radio frequency he used was not one the police or anyone else might be using.

His greatest problem was that he would have to have Nicholes help him. He had found that only staff members were able to carry odd items into the Capitol without being questioned. Nicholes was his best chance. If Nicholes would not do it, then he would use that girl—Sariah. Yes. He would use her. But he would rather use Nicholes.

Maria had not returned to his apartment before he had to leave and make his regular contact with his control in Paris. Surely she would be waiting there for him by now. He fully expected her to report positively on her assignment. If Nicholes had not turned, surely he would turn during the weekend. Maria would provide him with proper incentive. Too bad she had not become a true believer. Time grew short for her to accept the true path. He could not trust her completely until she did. He would press for that the next time he saw her.

He circled his apartment building as he was accustomed to do each time he returned to his residential base. After the short walk from the elevator, he unlocked the door and discovered Maria sitting on his couch waiting for him.

"What is this?" he asked her warmly. "You come into my house to wait for me and you sit there with your coat on? I will not have it. Has Fatima been rude to you?"

"No," Maria spoke quickly, lest she lose her nerve. She stood up and faced him before she continued. "Fatima has not been rude to me."

Kassim smiled and took off his coat.

"Then why are you waiting like that? We have business to attend to. You have a report to give me. And I have a new assignment for you. Then there will be time for us to share each other when we are finished."

"That is why I came. I wondered if I should come at all."

"What?" he said, showing some surprise.

"I will not help you turn that man," she announced.

"The boy?" Kassim questioned. "The boy from Congressman Hersch's office?"

"That's right—him. I will not help you use him. In fact, I am finished helping you anymore."

Kassim was more annoyed than surprised. An infidel could never be trusted. And as hard as he had tried to protect her and to teach her, it had come to this. He would still find a use for her though, he thought. And he approached her with a smile on his face.

"It is all right," he said. "But perhaps we should talk about it for just a minute."

He didn't wait for an answer. He had managed to narrow the range between them sufficiently.

His first blow was to her face—a simple, but powerful, smash to her cheek. It sent her tumbling backwards. She flipped over the couch and crumpled on the floor.

The blow came so fast she did not realize what had happened. It had been delivered with such power that she lost consciousness. When she opened her eyes, his face was all she could see. She felt him straddling her, his weight on her body, his knees pressing her arms against the floor. In his fingers he held the thin cigar he had been smoking.

CHAPTER 6

News Briefs
Sunday, January 13, 1991

WASHINGTON, D.C.—Congress on Saturday gave President Bush authority to wage war in the Persian Gulf and leading lawmakers urged national unity in the wake of the vote.

The Senate voted 52-47 to empower President Bush to "use United States armed forces" to expel Iraq from Kuwait. A short time later, the House followed with a 250-183 vote.

President Bush called it a clear signal that Iraq "cannot scorn the Jan. 15 deadline."

House Speaker Thomas Foley said, "This is the practical equivalent of a war resolution."

Sen. Edward Kennedy, D-Mass., said, "We have not gone the last mile for peace, and until we do the United States Senate should never, never, never vote for war."

But others held that Saddam Hussein's refusal to withdraw his troops from Kuwait left them with no choice.

"Sanctions without a credible military threat would never have any impact," Senate Republican Leader Bob Dole stressed.

BAGHDAD, IRAQ— U.N. Secretary-General Javier Perez de Cuellar is expected to meet with Iraqi President Saddam Hussein today in an effort to head off hostilities.

"I come here as a messenger of peace," the U.N. Chief said. "I am not bringing any specific proposal . . . I bring only my good will to find a peaceful solution . . . I bring the wish of the international community for a peaceful solution.

ALEXANDRIA, VA —

IN THE EARLY HOURS OF THE SABBATH MORNING NEPHI dreamed of her again. Never before had the dream come on successive nights. And never before had he felt such intense responsibilities toward her. As far as he was concerned she was his. And although she didn't exactly understand things yet, he was hers. She would come to realize that in time. If they had any time.

The picture he sketched placed her at the brink of a cliff—a cliff he knew to be high and dangerous.

Walking into his apartment the night before he had been filled with emotions stemming from many different sources. Like many others, he brought with him a consciousness of the impending conflict with Iraq. His particular apartment complex provided billeting quarters for regular and reserve military personnel enrolled in numerous courses offered at the Pentagon and any one of several military bases in the vicinity. It might have been his imagination, but he thought he could see his temporary neighbors walking with greater purpose than they had done before. Salutes between enlisted men and women and officers snapped with greater energy.

Watching them, living among them, Nephi felt they had accepted increased responsibilities even though their courses had not changed nor had their orders. One neighbor served in a reserve unit in Texas. He had come to participate in the Inspector General Course. The course prepared him to inspect other reserve units. He would be assigned to visit a given unit with the commanding general. While the general would deal with the officers, his job would be to find out what was really going on. For he would sniff out specifics by working with the enlisted men—especially with the non-commissioned officers.

There was no doubt in Nephi's mind that this particular man walked straighter and more deliberately. They met on the elevator. The man's uniform had the tightest creases the fabric could carry.

"How's school?" Nephi asked.

"Tense," came the sergeant's reply.

Aside from the threat of war and his own small role in having set the stage for it, the rest of Nephi's emotional state that night had centered around Maria having entered his life. Lingering thoughts of her revolved in his soul—how gracefully she had moved, how soft and mellow had been the tone of her voice, how sensitive her feelings, how responsive to his touch and his words—how real she was. Mingled with his memories of his day with her, his thoughts reached into their histories—what she had told him, what he had felt when he had sketched her experiences. He even allowed himself to consider their future—how and where he would ask her to marry him, where they would marry, which temple it would be in.

By the time he retired that night, euphoria had wrapped around him more completely than his sheet and blanket.

Sleep had never been an automatic event in Nephi's life. His mind hated the oblivion his body required. Something during his days always seemed to claim analysis or evaluation. This night his day's experiences were legion. The war and everything everyone had said about it all day filled one large compartment. Maria filled all the rest. They persisted until Nephi felt a need to apply a structured technique to liberate his mind and relax it. He chose to envision himself at the bottom of a deep, dark box. He shaped every thought into a firefly. Systematically he gently nudged each light up and over the edge of the box.

The technique worked. When he lifted the final idea up and over the edge, sleep filled the void.

But almost immediately something else hit him.

It came as an enormous wave, washing around him, pounding him with an oppressive darkness. He first thought it had been the power of the adversary, and he consciously rebuked Lucifer and his followers by the power of the priesthood and in the name of Jesus Christ.

But the suffocating force refused to budge.

That meant either he had slipped and no longer qualified to exercise his priesthood in such a way, or else he had misjudged the source of the feeling. The instant the second possibility entered his mind the power that had overcome him surged in confirmation.

What he felt had come from the Lord.

Setting aside all else, he humbled himself, asked for forgiveness and listened.

As he did this the ominous quality of the feeling subsided but its serious nature remained. Also in that moment his memory quickened, forcing him to recall exactly how the Lord had tried to communicate with him several times during the day. He could not hide from this disclosure.

To be shown so vividly how he had failed sent Nephi into a state of semi-shock. He loved the Lord and anxiously sought to serve Him in every possible way. He had spent much time and energy preparing himself to qualify for the gifts of the Spirit. And after having learned so much about receiving answers from the other side of the veil, it devastated him to realize how badly he had failed to recognize obvious promptings of the Spirit at one of the most critical times of his life.

At the very least he had allowed distractions to prevent him from honoring the prompting of the Spirit. Clearly he had offended the Lord because he had ignored what the Lord had extended as a gift—a gift that could have blessed both him and Maria. And that made it worse. For in failing his responsibilities to Maria, he knew it was possible he could lose her—forever.

Powerful feelings surged in him now from within his heart and mind. Never had he believed himself capable of failing the Lord in such a way, of failing himself and now of failing his "Elena." To lose her seemed to him like losing his quest for immortality and eternal life.

The emotions crowding his soul massed into a panic. But through these feelings he could still sense that there was a way to correct his error. He had no idea what it might be. He just knew the Lord had prepared a way. He had to find it.

At an appropriate moment he asked if it was expedient to inquire about solving this problem. On receiving permission to proceed, he asked specifically if there was a way to correct matters. There was. By carefully asking a series of questions and listening intently, he learned what he could do. Complete details were not given. First, he learned Maria was not at her home. It was imperative he find her as soon as possible. But he would have to depend on someone who would be sent to help him. On finding her, they were both to flee into hiding.

The whole experience repeated itself two more times. Each time he learned more completely how he had failed. Each time his concern for Maria's safety increased. But if she was in danger, he could not understand why he had to wait for someone to help him. A sense of urgency built within him. But so did his determination not to fail again. Someone would come. That had been promised. He would have to wait. That was all there was to it.

Fatigue finally overcame his anguish and concern. But shortly after he fell asleep, there came the dream of Maria on the edge of the cliff. It did not bring peace and consolation to his soul.

After he finished his sketch, he searched for a way to reclaim the strength he needed to continue. He dragged himself into the shower. Soon it would be dawn. He figured he would have to follow his normal routine for the Sabbath. But by the time he turned off the water, he knew this would not be a normal Sunday for him.

A strong impression matured within him. He was to prepare for the day and leave his apartment.

Morning had barely encroached on the neighborhood when Nephi left his apartment to look for Maria. Even so, they had been waiting for him. Both men stepped from the grey sedan and approached his car before Nephi could get his key into the ignition.

"Excuse me, sir," one of them said. He held his ID so that Nephi could see it clearly.

It consisted of a mug shot, a small badge and some printing with three prominent letters: FBI.

"My name is Agent Dalton, Howard Dalton. Is your name Nicholes? Nephi Nicholes?" He mispronounced it Neh-fee, with the accent on the first syllable.

"Yes. Only you pronounce it Knee as in your leg and Phi as in Beta Kappa."

"Nephi," the agent corrected himself and continued, "Nicholes? Nephi Nicholes, press secretary to Congressman Hersch?"

"Yes."

"Well, Mr. Nicholes, I wonder if you would mind coming with us. This is not an arrest. We would just like to ask you some questions and discuss a few things down at headquarters."

"What is this all about?"

"I really can't tell you, Mr. Nicholes. My instructions are to ask for your cooperation in a matter of imminent national security."

Nephi looked at them. They had to be great poker players. Had they been sent to help him find Maria? A faint approval rose within Nephi's chest. "Okay," he said, reluctantly accepting their invitation. They wanted him to ride with them. But he negotiated, asking them to allow him to drive his own car. They agreed he could do that so long as the extra man would ride with Nephi. They implied it would be the best way to get Nephi into their parking garage.

Fair enough, Nephi thought, and moved some files from the passenger seat. In tandem Nephi followed the FBI car directly to the headquarters building on Pennsylvania Avenue.

After they had arranged parking, the two agents escorted Nephi through the parking facility to a bank of elevators and up to the fourth floor. Down the hall to the right they entered through a door marked, "Washington, D.C., Metropolitan Field Office." It was a large room crammed with desks opening into several small rooms at both ends. The two agents directed him to turn left and they headed down an informal aisle between the desks toward a circular table with three men already seated around it. No one else had come into work this weekend.

The man seated in the center stood and extended his hand. "Thank you for coming down here, Mr. Nicholes. My name is Levant, Robert Levant. I'm a Squad Supervisor and these men are all members of a special team. We are responsible for a number of assignments, Mr. Nicholes. But at this time we are deeply concerned about terrorism."

"Terrorism?" Nephi repeated with astonishment. What in the world would they want to talk with him about that for?

"Yes. And we brought you down here to show you a few things. Would you please step in here?"

The room had no windows—it was obviously a projection room. Loose chairs in scattered array awaited them. When they all were seated, the lights went down and an image came up on the screen. It was a picture of a shop front somewhere. It had been heavily damaged.

"This is a popular shop on Kaiserstrasse in Dusseldorf, Germany. The owners catered to tourists, mostly American tourists," Levant's voice said calmly. "And this is a picture of the American Express office in Copenhagen, Denmark."

Debris filled the street and people bent over bodies on the ground.

The next picture was more familiar—the American Embassy in Lebanon. And then they showed him a series of pictures of the disastrous bombing of the U.S. Marine compound in Lebanon.

"We could show you dozens more, Mr. Nicholes. But we don't want to belabor the point. Terrorism around the world is increasing. That it hasn't happened extensively here in the United States has been a miracle of sorts. We like to think we are part of that miracle because we work very hard to prevent such things happening on our streets.

"But we face a serious problem here. With war imminent against Saddam Hussein, we know he has a network of terrorists working on a global basis. The full extent of it is not completely known. We firmly believe we have a line on all the known terrorists he may have planted in this country."

"That's great," Nephi said.

"At the moment we're working on a case that has been a bit testy. We brought you here this morning to ask you to help us."

"What can I possibly do?" Nephi asked, sobered by the things he had seen and fearful of what he might learn.

When the next slide came up, fears pierced his composure.

It was a picture of Elena—that is, Maria.

"Do you know this woman?" Levant asked.

"Yes."

"Do you know who she is?"

"Yes. Her name is Maria Moore. I believe she is the daughter of General Arnold G. Moore of the United States Air Force." He said the latter part in hopes it would quash anything further they might say about her.

"That is correct," Inspector Levant said in a voice completely void of emotion. "Now, do you know this man?"

It was a picture of the sleazebucket, al-Jarwi.

"Yes. I met him yesterday in my office when I met Miss Moore. I believe he is a cultural attaché with the Embassy of Yemen."

"That's what he claims. We have not yet filed a challenge to his credentials. But it is possible we will in the near future."

They showed pictures of several other people. Four of them Nephi recognized from the Ellipse. He told Levant he did not know their names.

"Mr. Nicholes . . ." the Inspector's voice began.

Nephi interrupted. "You can call me Nephi. I'm too young to be called Mister."

"Okay, Nephi," Levant responded. "We know you work for Congressman Hersch. Do you consider yourself loyal to him?"

"Of course."

"How do you feel about your country?"

It was a stupid question. Nephi didn't feel he had to explain how he felt about his country. But he did.

"I love it."

"Yes. That's what we expected you to say."

Why should they doubt my loyalty? Nephi asked himself. The prospects here were not too encouraging. Maria's involvement here concerned him too. They had not explained how she was connected with al-Jarwi and why they were in the process of challenging his credentials. His lack of knowledge extended his fear. He felt uncomfortable enough to shift around in his chair and to clear his throat. He doubted these people had been sent by the Lord to help him find her. But he felt impressed to be patient.

"Now, please don't get upset," Levant explained. "We didn't bring you here to upset you. I hope you can appreciate that these are dangerous times. And we have a difficult task here. Believe me. I hope you understand that you wouldn't be here today, and we never would have told you as much as we have told you already, if we had the least suspicion that you were anything but loyal to your country. I only asked you that because I needed to hear for myself what your response would be."

Nephi shifted in his seat. They didn't make it easy for him to exercise patience.

"Go on," he invited.

"Thank you," Levant responded. "Just how well do you know Miss Moore?"

What should he say? What could he say? He couldn't very well tell the FBI that he knew her almost as well as her parents knew her—that he had been dreaming of her since he was twelve, or that he had been drawing pictures of her all that time or that he loved her and intended to marry her. He had to back way off from anything he knew or felt about her, especially what he had experienced in the past twenty-four hours.

"I really just met her. I took her on a tour of the Capitol. We had lunch together. She seems like a very nice girl."

"I want you to keep an open mind here, Nephi. Sometimes people are not what they seem to be. For your own information, I would like to give you a little background on Miss Moore."

A series of pictures came up on the screen. The first was of a group of people on a very European-looking campus. Levant said it was in Frankfurt. The second was the same place only showing a closeup of one man singled out with a circle.

"This is Kurt Grundermann. He is a political activist working out of Frankfurt, Germany. He is known to have connections with several subversive organizations in Europe and is definitely tied in with the Abu Nidal faction of the PLO."

When another picture came up, it was of a group having dinner and drinks at a Hofbrau. Nephi noticed Maria sitting at the table, just two places down the line from Grundermann. She was leaning forward, looking at him as he was speaking and gesturing to the crowd.

"Miss Moore has lived in Germany for the past two years. She lived off and on with her parents. Her father was stationed at the Ramstein Air Force Base near Kaiserslautern—which is near Frankfurt." Levant's voice changed from its clinical mode to a more conversational mode. "I don't want to belabor this, Nephi, but I wanted you to see the kind of company Miss Moore was willing to keep when she was in Germany—at the very same time her father held an extremely sensitive position. We have no evidence that she did anything illegal, but she was seen frequently in Grundermann's company. Furthermore, during that time she was seen in most of the demonstrations we know Grundermann organized. You can see her in this frame—right there, right in front."

Levant ordered the projectionist to begin the next series of slides. First picture up was of Kassim.

"As you know, this man's name is Kassim al-Jarwi. You mentioned he uses the cover in Washington that he is one of the cultural attachés for Yemen."

Then they began showing a series of pictures of him. One of him as a soldier. Another of him with his head wrapped in a head cloth like Yasser Arafat. There was a picture of a soldier running a desert obstacle course—they said it was al-Jarwi training in a PLO camp near Tripoli. Another picture showed him throwing a hand grenade.

Levant began reading his dossier. "Trained by the Abu Nidal branch of the PLO. Further training in East Germany. Experience as a chemical engineer and fully capable of creating a bomb out of chemicals commonly found in the average American household. Generally prefers letting others make his bombs. Quite capable of modifying ordnance to suit his needs.

"Listen carefully to this part, Nephi," Levant emphasized as a new series of pictures played on the screen.

They were of Kassim putting the make on beautiful women. They even had a picture of him and Maria.

"Al-Jarwi is a sadistic killer who gathers around him young, impressionable people to help him in his plots. He is especially successful in charming women who seem to develop a strong loyalty to him in a relatively short time.

"He is known to use torture techniques on those who turn against him. He is rapidly climbing in the Abu Nidal organization and is believed to be on loan to the Iraqi government's network of international terrorists. The specific reason for his being in the United States is not known. The chances of his being here to coordinate or to personally create terrorism because of the threat of war with Iraq is highly likely.

"Al-Jarwi survives by creating plots that place his recruits in jeopardy while he remains in the background with a number of avenues for escape. He has been known to try out his weapons on his less enthusiastic recruits. He has been trained to sacrifice any or all of his recruits or even his full-time associates to accomplish his mission. He has no real friends. His political position is maintained through fear and mutual aspirations. He is deeply involved with secret projects within the PLO even though the PLO and the Nidal group are enemies.

"Now, Mr. Nicholes," Levant repeated. "Think about how well you know Miss Moore—how well you want to know her."

At the same time he said that, they repeated the series of slides on al-Jarwi's romantic activities in the same basic sequence. The sequence with the first girl showed her having a great time with al-Jarwi. It seemed as romantic as any story Nephi could have imagined. They sat at a table in an open air cafe. They walked along a river. They held hands and kissed under large trees in a park. But before the series with a second girl began, they showed a new slide of the first girl. It was of her body as it lay in the morgue—vicious lacerations and what they said were cigarette burns covered her face. The second girl's body also had marks on it—large dots—on her arms, breasts and abdomen.

Each victim brought increased apprehension to Nephi's heart and mind. He suppressed a natural reaction to throw up when he saw the brutal way those women had been treated.

They began the series on Maria. Each picture caused Nephi's stomach to tighten. He would not be able to handle seeing Maria like the others. They came to the final picture—of her getting into the limousine just yesterday. Nephi realized that if the camera man had centered a little to the left he would have been in this picture too. He wondered if they might have caught him in one of their other pictures by chance. That they hadn't shown him in any of their shots hadn't brought him relief. But he did exhale deeply when they did not show a picture of Maria in the same final pose as those other women.

Now he knew the nature of the cliff she was on. Now he knew the urgency of finding her.

"How well do you know Miss Moore?" Levant asked, again showing no emotion.

Nephi struggled. He wanted to blurt out that he loved her.

But he stopped short of that. But he did speak in a very firm voice.

"Well enough to know that I would be very upset if she was ever treated so badly."

"That's what we thought," Levant said, for the first time betraying a little emotion.

The lights went up and Nephi found himself looking at Levant who was leaning toward him.

"Nephi, this little group you see around you here is part of a SWAT team working out of the Washington Metropolitan Field Office. We're all volunteers here. Everyone on this squad has received special training. We all carry our normal case loads. All this is extra.

"We're responsible for anti-terrorist activities in this area. Frankly, Nephi, this business with Saddam Hussein has me worried stiff. Right now we have a line on three possible terrorist attacks. Two of them we pretty well have under control. But this guy, al-Jarwi, has us buffaloed. So far, we don't have enough on him here in the United States to make a case against him. Everything he has done has been outside this country.

"Believe me. We are very close to nailing that guy. With the war powers act in force now, our powers are much broader than they were before. We don't have to catch him in the act or anything like that. We can just nail him on suspicion. But the diplomatic situation is a bit tricky here. He's actually documented by Yemen. Yemen has sided with Iraq. But Yemen technically is considered neutral. And the State Department is not interested in offending the Yemeni delegation here. As a matter of fact, there is a strong possibility they have no idea what al-Jarwi is doing here. In any case, it won't take much to declare him persona non grata. We just need a bit more evidence than we have."

"But I don't know him. And I don't know if I want to get to know him. He just showed up at our office."

"You know Miss Moore, don't you?"

Nephi looked at him. Suddenly he got the idea this Levant guy had been watching them through the tour. He hadn't noticed anyone watching them. But he had no reason to notice anyone. He was too busy noticing Maria. Everyone else had faded into the background.

"You know I do."

"That I do," Levant said with a knowing smile. "And here's your assignment. All we're asking is that you get to know Miss Moore a little better and get her to talk about al-Jarwi. If anything comes up in the conversation, just let us know. Okay?" Nephi looked at him. What he asked seemed harmless on the surface. But when it came to what he wanted to do with Maria, he didn't want spying going on in their relationship. How could he be honest with her if he was pumping her for information? That's not the best way to generate a sense of trust and confidence in a budding romance.

"Look, Mr. Levant. I kind of like that girl. I'd really like to get to know her better. And, who knows, I just might get serious about her."

"That's just fine. It would probably be doing her a great service, you know? If she could break away from al-Jarwi it could save her from ending up like one of his other girlfriends. We have no quarrel with what you do. All we want is to get a line on al-Jarwi that will allow us to simply send him out of the country as fast as we can get him out of here."

Nephi looked at Levant and then at the other agents. They all showed no emotion except for Dalton. And all he displayed were some extra worry lines on his brow. But he too looked at Nephi intently.

That was all the pressure they applied.

But it was enough.

With some reservations, Nephi simply said, "Okay."

And the worry lines disappeared from the brow of Howard Dalton. Robert Levant let go with a heavy sigh and leaned back in his chair.

A knock came on the door and it opened without the chance for anyone to answer.

"Someone to see you, Bob," the agent spoke in a businesslike way.

"I'll be right there," Levant responded. Then he turned back to Nephi. "Now, we don't want any heroics here. We don't need them. All we need is a little more information. We'll take it from there. Just let us know. And it's highly likely that Miss Moore will never know whether you said anything or not. We keep everything quite confidential."

Nephi nodded. He took hold of Levant's hand to seal their agreement. This man carried an impressive handshake. He only hoped this commitment wouldn't damage his relationship with Maria. It couldn't.

Outside, Nephi looked over the room to reorient himself. It startled him somewhat to notice that seated near the door through which he had first come sat a familiar figure. Yussef Makal, his receptionist's fiancé.

"Yussef," Nephi called to him when he got closer. "What are you doing here? You in some sort of trouble?"

"Nephi!" Yussef looked up for the first time. "No. No trouble. I . . . I'm . . ." he let his voice trail off.

"Yussef has come to talk with me," Levant said. "That's all. Nothing more than that. Good-bye, Mr. Nicholes. Thank you for your help. It's been a pleasure to meet you."

Nephi took hold of Levant's hand again. Levant was pretending the parting was permanent. So Nephi followed suit.

"Thank you for your time."

Nephi made his exit. Agent Dalton came right after him.

"You know that man?" Dalton asked.

"Yes."

"How?"

"He's engaged to the receptionist working in our office. They make a terrific couple. What's he doing here?"

"I shouldn't tell you this. But it will be much better if you know. Yussef is one of our sources. He has been a great help to us. He seems to know a great deal about al-Jarwi. The only thing is, he's a little gung ho, if you know what I mean."

"Yes. He's greatly concerned about his country. I know he feels frustrated because he has a great desire to help his country, but doesn't know how to go about it."

Dalton looked at Nephi and smiled. The agent knew very well what Yussef was doing. It wasn't healthy. He was taking more risks these days than many of his countrymen. Dalton worried that Yussef might jeopardize the whole case they had against al-Jarwi without knowing it.

And that's exactly what Levant was telling Yussef as they talked in one of the private rooms.

"You have got to stop this, Yussef. I don't want you hurt."

"I will not get hurt," Yussef said boldly. "But I will hurt my enemies."

"You could screw up our case. And get yourself killed. Look at this. You've brought us some great information here: three places you saw al-Jarwi go into. And a fourth you were not sure of. How could you get this information?"

"I followed him."

"You followed him?" Levant almost shouted. "Now that's exactly what I mean. Did he see you?"

"Of course not. I would not be here if he had seen me. He would have killed me."

"He still could. And he still might. You know you can't keep this up. He's bound to spot you sometime. Then all this information will be useless. He will not go back to a place that has been compromised."

"I am very careful. He has not seen me. I just lost him somewhere in McLean. No matter. I will find that place, too."

"No, you will not!" Levant said. "You let my men follow him. You've given us exactly what we need." Then he calmed himself. The man had done an incredible job. Perhaps the key to this whole case was right here. "When did he visit this place in Rockville?"

"Thursday night. Actually Friday morning. About 3 a.m."

"You followed him at that time of night?" Levant exploded.

"Yes," Yussef answered calmly.

"He could have seen you. Killed you."

"But he did not. And now you have this information. And I must go."

"What are you going to do now?"

"Right now?"

"Yes.

"I am going to bed. I am tired."

"What then?"

"I will not say. You will try to stop me."

"I most certainly will. I don't want you to be killed, Yussef."

"But you will not stop me."

"I will if I have to. I can put you under protective custody.

Heaven only knows you need protection—from yourself."

"Good. Do it. Then deport me. I will be in my own country. And I will fight my country's enemies face to face. I do not consider what I do as legitimate fighting. It is the only way I have. So I do it."

Levant looked at the man. He was left with one reaction. He simply shook his head. Here was a man who first brought him information about al-Jarwi two months ago. It had triggered the whole investigation. They would not have requested information from Interpol had it not been for this Kuwaiti patriot. And he had been insulted when Levant had offered him money. But the more Yussef did, the more liable he was to be discovered by the terrorist. He was jeopardizing not merely his own life, but the case against al-Jarwi as well.

"Yussef. What can I say?"

"Thank you," Yussef answered him with a huge smile. "You can just say thank you."

Nephi said he knew his way to the parking lot and Dalton just left him at the elevators. But Nephi didn't take the next elevator down. He felt impressed to hang back a little to see if Yussef came out.

He did and they rode down together. When Yussef punched the main floor button Nephi guessed that he had come on the Metro.

"Could I give you a ride?"

"Thank you," Yussef answered. "It will give us a chance to talk."

In the car Yussef apologized and asked Nephi to forgive him for inquiring. "But may I ask what you were doing there?"

Dalton's warning echoed in his ear. He thought for a moment about not saying anything. But the idea came to him to tell him that he had been asked to watch Maria. And that he intended to do absolutely nothing more. In that way he would be able to help them and allow them to conduct the investigation in a legal way.

So that is what he said in answer to Yussef's question.

"This Maria you speak of—she is a woman just slightly taller than Sariah?"

"Yes."

"Skin just slightly fairer than Sariah's skin?"

"Yes."

"And she is beautiful?"

"Very."

"Ah—and you love her?"

"Yes."

Yussef shook his head slowly.

"Then I must exercise my right as a friend to you. Even though it may destroy that friendship, I must tell you."

"What? What could possibly destroy our friendship?"

"This news I have. It is possible that your lady is not your lady."

"What are you talking about?"

"I am talking about your lady. It is possible she is the one Levant and his men call Maria when I have heard them talk about this case. She is the daughter of an Air Force General?"

"Yes. She is a General's daughter."

"Then I have bad news for you, my friend. You must drop her at once."

"Yussef," Nephi pronounced the name deliberately. "Will you please tell me what you're going to tell me?"

"I can tell you only what I saw. Your woman entered the apartment of al-Jarwi last night. And she has not come out of it at all. At least not before I left my post."

"What?" Nephi exclaimed, causing him to lose control of the car for a moment, turning dangerously into the lane of on-coming traffic.

"Your lady, the one known as Maria. I saw her enter al-Jarwi's apartment. And she spent the night with him."

Nephi could not believe what he heard. At least he could not believe the conclusions of what he had heard.

Thoughts from his carnal mind flooded into his consciousness. Accusations encroached from a more sinister source. This was the girl who nestled against you in the Rotunda? This was the girl whose perfume drugged your senses until you had been entrapped by your own thoughts? This was the girl who spoke in such an inviting way? A Jezebel?

With that word he realized the emotional trend and stopped himself. He silently rebuked the carnal and evil thoughts that had invaded his soul, and a more calm assessment came to his mind.

She had not betrayed him. She had remained true to their brief friendship. And she now stood at the edge of that cliff.

"Yussef. You have got to take me to al-Jarwi's apartment."

"Are you sure?"

"Yes. I am dead sure. Maria is in trouble—serious trouble."

And there came upon him a confirmation with such intensity that it was impossible to ignore.

On the way to al-Jarwi's apartment Nephi's mind replayed those pictures of the brutalized women who had trusted the terrorist. Those poor women had turned from him. If Maria had gone up there on one of those errands she said she had to run—and it had been soon after they had been together in the Capitol, then she just might have revealed her true feelings to the terrorist. If she had done such a thing she was in danger of becoming another picture in Levant's file.

And it would have been his fault. He would have been the cause of any changes al-Jarwi might have detected. What condemned him even more had to do with not having acknowledged the prompting of the Spirit in a critical moment. He would never do that again if he could possibly help it.

Plainly he had loosened the soil around her feet at the edge of the cliff. But the greater condemnation bothered him more. He knew he had denied her a chance to have avoided the cliff and its dangers altogether.

The thought made him shudder.

"You feel strongly for this woman," Yussef stated more than asked.

"Yes," Nephi admitted. "Very."

"As strongly as I feel for Sariah?"

"I am sure of that. And I strongly believe she is in danger. I don't think she would spend the night there of her own accord."

Nephi told his Kuwaiti friend what he had seen at FBI headquarters. Yussef began pounding his leg with his fist.

"It is time we do something about this prince of Satan."

Dalton's warning rose again in Nephi's mind. Was Yussef out

of control? Or did Dalton just want to be more in control? Such was the nature of the games people played in Washington. Were the agents concerned about people? Or was their concern about the case?

Of course, Nephi recalled they had expressed concern about both. But there was no way they could help in this situation. What was he to tell them? That he had a dream and that he suspected Maria was inside al-Jarwi's apartment undergoing torture?

They would laugh at him. There was nothing official agencies could do.

But he was not a part of any official agency. Except for one. And when he remembered that, the plan came into focus in his mind.

The apartment Yussef identified as al-Jarwi's apartment building was just outside Bethesda, Maryland. It was a new building with a security system and all the amenities desired by the wealthy.

Yussef pointed to a bright red sports car and told Nephi that he saw the woman, Maria, get out of it and walk into the building.

"About half-an-hour later, Kassim pulled into his garage. Then nothing else happened until this morning. Kassim left. But I saw nothing of the woman."

"She's still in there, Yussef. I know it."

The Kuwaiti was thoughtful as he analyzed what he knew about the situation.

"Yes," he concluded. "It is highly possible that your woman is still inside. And you may very well be right. If she had simply spent the night with al-Jarwi, she would have left before he left— or with him. He would not have left her in his apartment alone."

"I'm going in," Nephi said.

"You can't."

"Then you go in."

"I can't. I mean, we shouldn't."

"We have to. It's the only way. By the time the agency gets all the legal work out of the way, she'll be dead."

"All right," Yussef spoke with firmness. "Then we'll both go in."

Nephi reached in the back and retrieved his briefcase.

"You have a plan?" Yussef asked.

"What is his apartment number?"

"Seven fourteen."

Nephi repeated it and took from his briefcase a manila envelope. It had his boss's name on it. Nephi wrote al-Jarwi's name on it along with the address.

"We need to deliver this to Kassim al-Jarwi," he told his friend. He said the same thing to the security guard at the desk.

"I'll take it," the security guard said in a firm, bureaucratic way.

Nephi pulled the envelope back.

"Not unless you have House and Pentagon security clearance."

The guard shook his head. "Nope. But there are no deliveries except those I know about. And I don't know about you. Sorry."

"So am I. These are urgent documents. I must deliver them personally. Mr. al-Jarwi has to sign for these himself."

"Mr. al-Jarwi is out," the guard said smugly.

"That's all right. In an emergency I am authorized to place them in the care of a trusted member of his household. No one else. I could not possibly leave it down here. I have to go upstairs and leave it with someone there. National security. You understand?"

"I think so," the guard said with a nod.

"Is there anyone in his household at home?"

"Yes. There is a woman, I believe."

Great, Nephi thought. It had to be Maria. She had to be the one the guard was talking about.

"Is she still there?" Nephi chastised himself for hurrying and for saying "still." But the guard didn't catch it.

"I think so."

"Then I'll just go up and see how long it will be before Mr. al-Jarwi returns," Nephi said, making an effort to collect his ID as if he was going to leave.

"I'll just hold onto this until you get back," the guard held up the ID with a grin on his face.

Nephi shot out his hand to snatch his ID away from the guard. Then he took out a business card and handed it to the guard.

"Here. You take that. I'll keep my ID. The woman up there won't believe me without it."

For some reason the guard thought that reasonable. He watched the two of them move toward the elevator and smiled.

"You wait here," he pointed at Yussef.

And Yussef shrugged his shoulders at Nephi. "If you're not down in ten minutes, I'll be up there in one," he said quietly, so that the guard wouldn't hear.

Nephi stood before the gray metal door with the raised number 714 on it. He had no legal right to do what he was doing. But he knew this obstacle separated him from Maria. Was he justified in doing this? He had felt strongly that the Spirit had justified his coming this far. He paused to inquire if he should go on.

What he felt was an intense burning within his bosom. His whole body felt as if it had been wrapped tightly—as if something was squeezing every square inch of it. Then he listened. There were words rising within him, quietly, calmly.

"Press on."

Nephi touched the doorbell. He could not hear anything. But in less than a minute the door opened slightly. The face of a woman appeared in the crack, the distance carefully held steady by a thick chain.

"Yes?" she said with an accent.

"My name is Nephi Nicholes. I'm with Congressman Hersch's office. I have some important papers here for Kassim al-Jarwi. Is he in?"

"No."

"This is very urgent. Here is my identification. Would it be possible for me to come in and wait for him?"

She took the identification, looked at it and handed it back through the crack in the door. She said nothing. She remembered Kassim had said something about a man from one of the Congressional offices. She couldn't recall what it was all about. Kassim talked in too many riddles for her. She wished he would let her know more about his business so she could know better how to stay out of his way. She hated it when Kassim was angry at her. She hated it when he beat her. One day he would deal with her as he had done those others. It was just a matter of time. The thought of it sometimes made her cry.

Nephi just watched the door close. Then it opened again, this time widely. He saw a beautiful woman gesturing for him to enter.

He had seen this woman before. Yes. She had been at the demonstration. She had been standing next to Maria. They appeared to be friends.

"Thank you," he said, stepping inside. "Will Mr. al-Jarwi be long?"

"I do not know. He did not tell me. Please be seated."

"Well, if you don't mind," he said to her, turning so he was facing her. "I really don't have that much time. What I really need to do is to pick up Maria and leave."

"What?" the woman said in disbelief. This filthy American dog had tricked her. She began to run for the bedroom. She knew where Kassim kept his extra weapons.

But Nephi caught her and took hold of her arms. He held her away from him, far enough so she could not kick him. He forced her toward the hallway.

"Where is Maria?"

"She is not here. She left."

He laughed at her. And he just kept pushing her to the first door in the hallway.

"Why don't I believe you?"

He opened the door. It was a spacious bedroom. There were two doors inside the bedroom. Probably a closet and a bath, he thought. He decided to check the other rooms first. Then if she wasn't in any of them he would come back.

His intuitive decision served him well. The second door was a bathroom. But the third door had a sliding bolt to keep it closed—locked to anyone inside.

He opened the door and found it dark. He found the light switch on the outside and turned it on. All he saw at first was a room with foam rubber for wall paper. As he pushed the door more, he found it to be a very small room. It had no windows. But it did have a single bed—a folding bed—jammed inside. There was not much room around it.

Nephi forced the woman inside and then cautiously entered himself.

"Get out of here!" he heard a woman scream.

"Maria! It's me!" Nephi exclaimed.

After a second in shock Maria allowed her mind to accept him.

"Nephi? Nephi! It is you!" and she jumped at him from where she was crouched in the corner.

The weight of her crashing into him forced him back a step or two and they blocked the doorway so that the other woman couldn't escape.

"I thought I'd never see you again," Maria said sobbing into his shirt.

It felt so good to hold her, to comfort her—but he couldn't ignore for very long the danger they still faced. If al-Jarwi found them in his apartment, he would kill them both.

He guided Maria through the door and then, turning to the other woman said, "We're leaving. I'm going to lock you in here. Al-Jarwi will let you out when he comes home."

"No!" the woman cried.

"I won't hurt you. He'll let you out."

"You don't understand. He will hurt me. When he finds out I let you in and you took Maria, he will make me take her place. You can't leave me here."

Nephi looked at Maria. There was a huge, swollen bruise on her face.

"What did he do to you?"

"Not as much as he was going to do," she said.

"Please, take me with you," the woman pleaded over and over again, her tears flowing freely down her face. "Don't leave me here! He'll kill me!"

Vivid recollection of the pictures of al-Jarwi's victims played in his mind and Nephi could not deny her.

"You must follow my orders," he said firmly.

"Yes. Yes," she accepted with emotion. "You will not be sorry. I can tell you much about what he does. And yes," she seemed excited. "I will give you something."

She pressed through the door past Nephi and Maria. She hurried to his bedroom.

Nephi suddenly thought she might be going for a weapon. If she was able to get a gun, they would be through. He ran after her. By the time he reached the door, she already was on her way out. She held in her hand a simple, plastic grocery bag—with three two-liter bottles of soda pop.

"I give you these to show how grateful I am and how true I will be to you for saving me," she said, having fallen to her knees before him.

"It is all right. There's no need for all of this. Let's just get out of here."

The funny looking procession walked from the elevator into the lobby. Al-Jarwi's woman led the way. She looked about as casual as anyone could look. The shopping bag gave her the appearance of domesticity even though she was dressed in very expensive clothes. Behind her were Nephi and Maria. They walked in a clumsy way. Maria simply would not let go of him. She had been clinging to him since she had pounced on him in al-Jarwi's special room. Nephi didn't mind it at all. But it did look a little abnormal. Especially with Maria's swollen, discolored face and torn blouse.

Yussef joined them as they walked past the front desk, the guard didn't even look up until they were upon him. He was responsible more for people going in than coming out. Nephi paused long enough to reach over and snatch up his card.

"He wasn't there. You won't be needing this."

"Hey! Wait a minute. I'm calling the police."

"That's okay. That's right where we're going—to the police."

It was a little lie. But Nephi couldn't help himself.

They hurried to Nephi's car and held a brief, impromptu meeting.

"You take my car and the woman, Yussef. We'll take Maria's car and we'll follow you to whatever safe place you pick—a market, a park—anywhere away from here. Okay?"

Yussef nodded and took the bag with the soda pop from the woman. Then he waited, impatiently watching through his rear view mirror while Maria groped for a key box under her car's bumper. Nephi unlocked the door and held it for her. Why was he taking all this precious time playing the gentleman? Yussef was exasperated at his friend's priorities.

"He actually went around and opened the door for her," he said aloud.

The woman looked at the two and smiled. "That is nice," she said. "He loves her." Yussef shrugged his shoulders and grunted.

Yussef made many turns before he stopped in the parking lot of a secluded neighborhood playground. For the first time, he looked seriously at the woman. He knew her. She was the one known as Fatima. They had no family name for her. She had been seen with al-Jarwi in several countries. Kassim had never married. Officials had assumed Fatima was a convenience for him.

Yussef let her leave the car when Maria arrived. But he watched both women carefully as he walked toward Nephi.

"Her name is Fatima. She is al-Jarwi's woman. They are not married. They are just together and have been for some time."

"I think she just divorced him," Nephi said. And he explained all that went on inside al-Jarwi's apartment.

"Then Maria is not badly hurt?"

"Bruises. She complains of a sharp pain in her side. He probably broke a rib or two. But the excitement hasn't worn off yet. She probably hasn't felt the full extent of the pain."

Yussef nodded. "When she does, she is likely to be very sore."

"I know. But I will take care of her."

"What do you mean by that, my friend?"

"I mean that I am going to take that beautiful woman and disappear for awhile."

Yussef shook his head. "That is not wise, my friend. It would be much better for you to let the Bureau protect you."

"I'm sure it would, Yussef. But I have this very strong feeling that I need to spend some time alone with her." That made Yussef smile as he had done many times with other bachelor friends.

"Separate rooms all the way," Nephi reacted to the look his friend was giving him.

And that made Yussef laugh out loud, as he also had done many times with other bachelor friends.

"I repent having told you anything of my plans," Nephi said, a little irritation creeping into his voice.

"I am sorry," Yussef tried to stop the enjoyment he was having at the expense of his serious-minded friend. How could he tell him that he would have trusted him with his own sister, or even with Sariah, on such an occasion? He could not. On the other hand, why should he tell him? It was great fun watching him squirm. "It's just that I remembered another friend of mine who did the same thing. Two separate rooms—one slightly used."

At this point Nephi understood that Yussef was joking with him. At least he hoped Yussef was joking with him. Unfortunately, he needed Yussef to be serious for a minute. He had to tell someone. He did not want to run off alone without telling someone he trusted. And Yussef was one of two people in this part of the world that he could trust. The other was Roy Ivars.

A few paces away from the men, Maria began talking with Fatima.

"Thank you," she told the woman. "I know you stopped Kassim from hurting me any more than he did last night. I don't know what you did but I'm glad you did it."

"It was nothing," Fatima replied. "Nothing I have not done before. He loves to hurt people. He only needed to be reminded that it would be better to take his time with you. It was the blessing of Allah that your man came to save you."

"To save both of us," Maria added.

"Yes."

"What will you do now?"

"I do not know. Perhaps your friend's friend will help me. He seems to be someone important." She walked to Nephi's car and took from it the plastic bag.

"This is for saving my life," she said, holding the bag for either of the men to take.

"Thank you," Nephi responded, a little unsure why he was thanking her for three bottles of soda pop.

Maria recognized the bag and its contents.

"That's what Kassim wanted us to carry into the Capitol."

"That's right," Nephi acknowledge. "I thought I had seen it before."

"You will want these. They are very important to Kassim. He told me these would help to bring the Great Satan down to its knees."

Yussef took the bag from Nephi's hands. He placed it on the ground.

"This is very important. These bottles could be bombs of some sort." Yussef looked at Nephi. "I must borrow your car. I must take these to the lab."

"No," Nephi responded. "Take Maria's car. I will need mine."

"Fair enough."

"Just let me get something out of the trunk," Maria asked. She took from it an overnight case. She smiled at Nephi.

Yussef smiled too.

The woman, Fatima, smiled. But hers was softer, filled with more understanding. The same idea that filled Yussef's mind also filled hers. But her expression had been tempered by a different perspective. She could not help wondering if she ever would find a man who would consider her of value enough to risk his life to save her—or someone who would open the door of a car for her.

She took hold of the door handle and stepped into the red car. She had no idea what would happen to her. The man Yussef would take her to the authorities. They would question her. If she cooperated, she would be protected. This, after all, was the United States of America. It was a place she had read about. It had been such a remote possibility she never could have dreamed she would have this chance. But now, her separation from Kassim had been accomplished. He would never expect her to have fled on her own. He would not be coming after her.

She was free.

CHAPTER 7

WHEN YUSSEF DROVE AWAY IN MARIA'S CAR, SHE STEPPED closer to Nephi and took hold of his arm. She didn't care about her car. She needed the security she felt in Nephi's nearness. She had just experienced the most horrifying hours of her life. And he had plucked her from enduring the excruciating pain that surely awaited her.

Kassim had smashed her in the face and had threatened her by holding his cigar so close to her cheek that she cried in fear. Just remembering the intense spot of heat tightened the muscles in her face, and she closed her eyes and drew up the corner of her lips into a pained expression. She could remember Fatima's voice, calling to him, saying something in Arabic. Then he had stopped. But he taunted Maria with an interpretation saying that Fatima had suggested he would enjoy it more if he took his time. He had agreed and had said something about a safe house where no one could hear or interfere. Then he laughed and dragged her down the hall locking her in that horrible, dark room to await his pleasure.

She knew that nothing she could have done would have prevented Kassim from killing her. And she knew the end would not have come until after he had satisfied his appetites for dispensing pain. She had tried to comfort and prepare herself for the coming end by remembering all the good things she had done in her life, with her parents, with her friends—not the pseudo friends of these past two years, but rather her real friends, like Eleanor—and her newest friend, Nephi. Actually he had dominated her thoughts during those dark hours.

When the door had opened she cringed into the farthest corner she could find. She had decided to fight Kassim in hopes she could find an early death. But it was Nephi's wonderful face that she had seen coming through that door, not Kassim's. The instant she saw it her fear fled and was replaced by exhilaration. She still could feel that exhilaration although much of it had subsided. In its place had grown an attachment to this man with the marvelous name. As long as he remained within her reach, she felt safe. Her nightmare was over.

Over—except for the memories of threats, the memories of pain that almost was and could still be.

She tightened her grip on Nephi's arm desperately hoping he could protect her from the mental anguish she feared.

"Thank you," she said softly.

He turned to look at her.

"You're welcome."

Oh, how she loved his smile. It came from deep inside him. And it made her feel as if he meant it for her alone.

She watched him for only a moment then slipped into his arms. It seemed such a natural place for her to be. She did not want to let go of him.

Nephi returned her embrace and held her for a few moments. It was the first time they had been so close—unless all that business at the apartment could be counted. No. That came with her rescue. This was the first genuine, bona fide expression of love and trust between them. She resisted only when he tightened his grip and her bruised ribs complained. It was only a flinch, but it was enough to remind him to hold her more tenderly. Then in the tenderness of his touch, he kissed her.

A group of teenage boys taking their spring training began to whistle and holler from the playground's baseball diamond. Nephi waved at them and held up his hands as if in victory. The kids gave another cheer. Maria held onto Nephi with one hand, but turned so she could wave at them, too. The group hollered even more.

"Let's get out of here," he said while his arms were in the air. "I'd kind of like to talk with you where it's a bit more private."

"Yes, I'd like that," she said while Nephi opened the door.

Then he noticed the dishevelled quality of her blouse.

"Well . . . first of all," he said, "it might be well for us to find some place where you'll be safe . . . and . . . where you can take a stitch or two in your shirt."

Suddenly aware of her attire, she wrapped her arms across the front of her. Nothing serious had been exposed, but the fabric had been torn. She pulled at the cloth to make it cover as best she could and willingly hid herself in the front seat of the car.

"Those boys will think you've been mean to me," she teased.

"But now they know we made up. Would you rather stay here?"

"No. But you might have said something about my blouse sooner."

"Actually, I just noticed myself."

"Sure," she said, "And Kassim is out buying me flowers."

Nephi laughed, enjoying her sense of humor. "You want to go back and get them?"

"No thanks. They'll probably be plastic."

He started the motor and drove from the lot. It took thirty minutes to get to Ballston. He parked near the back entrance of the tall apartment building, and they entered through a seldom used door. Nephi was thinking they might be successful in making it to the apartment without anyone seeing them. But then they found themselves sharing the elevator with a middle-aged woman. She stared at Nephi in a very disapproving way. He fully expected her to say "Shame on you," or something worse. But she didn't. He thought of telling the woman that he had beaten her when she refused to have their twelfth child. But he decided not to. Even so, the non-exchange brought a smile to his face.

"What are you smiling about?" Maria asked when they got out of the elevator.

"Nothing. That woman, I guess. She really thought I was a scoundrel."

Maria was certain it was not that simple. She almost accused him of harboring some ulterior motives in coming up here. But she lost her opportunity. Nephi already had his finger on the bell.

"Nephi!" Roy Ivars exclaimed when he opened the door. "What are you doing here? Come in."

"Am I glad you're home! We need your help."

"Sure," Roy agreed. "Tina, we have company," he called.

"Who is it?" came a voice from down the hall. A very pretty woman entered the room and hurried toward them. "Nephi," she called out. "It's good to see you. And you brought a friend."

"This is Maria—Maria Moore."

"I don't believe it," Tina said with a big smile on her face. "Little Maria? Yes, that is you. For goodness sakes, you've grown up. Last time we saw you was in Japan. How are your folks?"

"My folks?" Maria said, surprised by this stranger who had recognized her. But this stranger did look familiar—a face from long ago. The question traced through her memory linking past with present inviting thoughts again of her parents. She had thought a great deal of her mother and father while she was locked in that room—her parents and Nephi. She had calculated exactly how long it had been since she had talked to them—even longer since she had talked *with* them.

"I'm sure they're all right. I haven't talked with Mom since just before they left. They went to England, but I think Dad's in the Persian Gulf now. I don't know for sure."

Tina looked at her. It required a bit of effort to keep up a positive front. But she managed. Tina had been gifted with a natural desire to make people around her feel comfortable—to help them if she could.

She had heard that Rita had been having trouble with one of her daughters. Maybe this was the one. This one certainly looked like she needed help. Actually, she looked as if she had been in a fight.

"Shame on you, Nephi," Tina Ivars scolded. "What have you been doing to this lovely girl?"

Nephi shrugged his shoulders to plead innocence and was about to speak, but Tina had grabbed hold of Maria's hand and was already leading her away.

"Come with me, Maria. Let's get you cleaned up."

"It wasn't him, Mrs. Ivars. It was somebody else," Maria said as she allowed herself to be led away.

Roy invited his friend and fellow staff member to sit down.

"Did you come here just to get her fixed up? Or did you want to tell me about it?"

"A little of one, a lot of the other, if you don't mind," Nephi sat back, relieved with the chance to confide in someone.

Roy gestured with his hands. "Lay it on me, man. What else are friends and attorneys for?"

Nephi told his story from the point of meeting al-Jarwi and Maria in the office.

"I got your notes and saw your tracks," Roy interrupted. "Incidentally, that was a good story you wrote. Best so far. She must have a good influence on you."

Nephi nodded and plunged back into the story. A compliment always helps, but at this time in his life he didn't really care if his story had been nominated for the Pulitzer Prize. He told of his meeting with Levant at FBI headquarters, the slides he had seen and the report he had heard. Then he mentioned having connected with Yussef.

"Our Yussef? Sariah's Yussef?"

"The very one," Nephi said. Then he began telling how the Kuwaiti helped him locate Maria and free her from the terrorist's apartment.

"That's pretty bizarre for a Congressional press secretary from Utah County," Roy said. "Is that where she got that bruise on her face and the torn blouse?"

Nephi nodded.

Roy shook his head. "Have they caught the guy yet?"

"I don't know. I doubt it. But Yussef says they probably have enough on him now to take him into custody."

"He'll come after you, you know. You won't be safe until he's out of the way."

Nephi kept thinking of the cliff.

"Yes. That's why we're here—we need a favor."

"Sure. Whatever you need. You want to stay here? You're welcome to. But this might not be the best place for you to hide. It would be too easy for him to trace you to this apartment. Maybe you need to get out of town for awhile. Yeah. Take off. Take an assignment to conduct an unofficial Congressional survey somewhere, research, anything."

"Funny you should say that," Nephi smiled.

"Yeah. Just get away from here. And keep moving. Call me every day. But keep moving. He won't be able to track you down that way. Call, then move."

"Would you do me a favor and call Levant for me? He's going to be bent out of shape when he finds out I went in there and got Maria out of al-Jarwi's apartment. I don't want him getting mad at me. I know it was pretty stupid, but I just had to. You know."

"Sure, Nephi. And don't worry about him. I kind of think he'll be glad you've left town. Probably give you brownie points for it."

Nephi nodded. For the first time since the middle of last night, he felt like giving himself brownie points. He felt good about the way things were working out. He was just about to haul Maria safely off that cliff.

In the bathroom, Tina Ivars gently cleaned Maria's cheek. Her eyes narrowed in empathy when what she thought was just dirt turned out to be deep bruises.

"How did you get this?" she asked. "Somebody hit you. Who was it, Maria? You need to report whoever it was. That's a terrible abrasion. The blow that caused it could have killed you. Who was it? We need to put him away."

"It was a man named Kassim, Kassim al-Jarwi."

"He's dirt. Any man who hits a woman is just plain dirt. Don't worry, dear, I'll be careful. I'm a trained nurse. This will be tender here for a few days. But there'll be some discoloration for a lot longer than that. You're going to have to use a lot of makeup."

"I know. And thanks. You're really kind. I appreciate it very much." Maria said. "I'm beginning to feel better already."

"You know, you sound just like your Mama," Tina said with a smile.

"You know her very well?"

"Oh, yes," Tina said with enthusiasm. "We were best of friends. Back then we used to go to church together."

"You're Catholic?" Maria asked.

"Used to be. When I first married Roy I was Catholic. But as I learned more about his religion, it made so much sense. Then I made the mistake of asking questions and soon it was plain to me that being baptized into The Church of Jesus Christ of Latter-day Saints, the Mormon Church, was the right thing to do. Now I'm a Mormon."

"I've known some Mormons. They lived a pretty strict life. It must be difficut."

"Goodness, no. There are so many things to do. You're busy all the time. It's fun. Especially if you have children. When you have children it's a lot more fun. At first I think I did it because of Roy, you know? But somewhere along the way I got a testimony that it was the true church."

"Testimony?"

"Yes. It's something you feel—something you get from the Lord." She laughed. "It's kind of hard to explain. But when it happens to you, you'll know what I mean."

Maria looked up at her. She wished all things were that simple. But she couldn't believe the Lord would give her anything. She had done too many rotten things in her life. How could she straighten everything out? It seemed impossible she could ever be as happy as this woman—or her mother.

Tina noticed how sad Maria looked—slumped down and frowning.

"Now, what's this? How come you're so down? You should be happy. You've got a lot of friends looking out for you. And you've got a man out there who loves you. I know he loves you—I saw the way he was looking at you. He loves you a lot—or my name isn't Agustina Maria Consuela Menendez Ivars." She laughed. "Now you know why they call me Tina."

Maria laughed with her. Then she looked in the mirror at the woman. As nice as this woman had been to her, something within made her wish it had been her own mother tending to her needs—sharing this moment. And her laughter turned to a flood of tears. For the first time since she had been locked in that room she allowed herself to cry.

"There, there," Tina leaned over and held her as she had done so many times with her own children. "It's all right. Everything's going to be all right."

"No, it's not," Maria argued with a tear-stained voice. "I've been so rotten all my life—to Mother and Dad and to everyone around me. All I do is run around with people who really don't care about me . . . they just want to use me . . . and dumb old Maria just goes right along with them and thumbs her nose at her parents and everyone who . . . really loves her. And by the time I meet this terrific guy I'm so beat up and scuzzy I don't deserve to be in the same room with him."

"Scuzzy?" Tina asked in a light-hearted way, ignoring the details of what she had just heard. "Where did you get such a marvelous word like that? Scuzzy?"

Maria looked up at the woman. Through her tears she couldn't tell what kind of expression she had. It seemed inconceivable that anyone had not heard the word.

"Scuzzy? I don't know. Everyone knows what scuzzy is."

"Why don't you tell me what you think it is."

"It's rotten, filthy, dirty—all those kind of things."

"Oh," Tina said as if she had learned the world's greatest secret. "You mean the same thing as that rotten, filthy, dirty vermin who hit you?"

"No, not like that."

"Not like that?" Tina clearly was working the girl. Only the girl hadn't caught on yet. "So, is scuzzy worse or better than the man who hit you?"

Maria thought for a moment and the tears and the emotions seemed to evaporate. She *wasn't* like Kassim. She wasn't like Kurt. She wasn't really like so many of the people she had known and had associated with for the past two years.

She was like her Mom, and like her Dad. She was more like this woman than all those others.

"Better than him," she admitted timidly.

"Ah," Tina exclaimed with clearly an exaggerated expression. She kneeled in front of the girl and took hold of her hands. "Now you listen to me, Maria. You are a child of our Father in Heaven. And He loves you. Or He wouldn't have given you such great parents who love you very much. I know because your Mama told me many times how much she loves you. And now you have made some mistakes, right?"

Maria found herself nodding her head slowly—as she had done with her own mother a long time ago.

"But didn't you know? That's why we came here to earth—to experience good and evil. The smart thing to do is choose to do good things. But it's hard to always do good when there is so much that's really scuzzy all around us. The trouble with all that scuzzy stuff—it all looks like so much fun. Doesn't it? But when you find out how bad it is for you, you know, you can still choose what to do. You can turn around. It's not too late, believe me. You can find your way back to the right path."

Maria looked into the eyes of this marvelous woman and saw something as deep and as good as she had seen in Nephi's eyes. But it had been different with him. He was a man, an attractive man. And she felt so different around men. It was hard for her to speak of her past with men. But here in this lovely bathroom, this stranger was telling her everything she so desperately needed— wanted—someone to tell her. She didn't like the life she was living. At first it had been new and dangerous and exciting. It had definitely separated her from her parents as well as her virtue.

But the newness had worn off in a matter of weeks. She tried to get out. But she wasn't strong enough to break away. They kept dragging her deeper and deeper into their lives. Shortly before her parents forced her to leave Germany with them, she had almost generated strength enough to break with her "friends." But Kurt kept telling her it was too late, that she had gone too far and that she had no place in the world except her place with them.

He was wrong. She had been wrong to let them lead her around for so long.

"It's such a sordid story, a stupid, sordid story," Maria admitted. "I'm not so sure I will ever be able to get rid of my past. I mean, what's Nephi going to say when he finds out?"

Tina looked at her. Well! That's interesting. She loves him, too. That's nice. If they can get over their hangups they'll make a cute couple, she thought.

"I'll tell you, Maria. If you pick the right moment and tell him in the right way—dump everything on him about your past—if you do that and he turns his back on you, then he doesn't deserve you."

"You think?" Maria's voice regained hope.

"I know."

Maria began to brush her own hair. But she had more questions she wanted Tina to answer.

"You think he would ever convert to Catholic?"

"Never in a million years."

"Then I'll have to convert to Mormon."

Tina smiled. "It isn't that easy, Maria. On the other hand, it isn't that hard. You just have to know what you're doing. But I guarantee, it's well worth it."

*　　*　　*　　*

Yussef drove directly to FBI headquarters from the playground parking lot. He assured Fatima that she was doing the right thing in telling her story to the men he knew.

"They will be pleased with you," he told her in Arabic. "You will have given them the evidence they need to get al-Jarwi out of the country. Also, they are in a position to offer you sanctuary."

She nodded her head and agreed to speak with them. She did not tell him that she already had decided to cooperate and that she was ready to make some serious changes in her life. It was just as well that she let him believe he had convinced her.

Yussef's story caught Robert Levant's attention immediately. He handled Fatima's testimony with precision, driving down the excitement he felt. When the woman finished, he thanked her. Actually, he could have taken hold of her and danced around the room. His case against the terrorist was more than complete. Had al-Jarwi been the ambassador himself, the case would have held up.

She had been his mistress for five years. She had never been accepted by him either as a wife or as an official concubine. He had just used her and had expected her to follow him blindly.

The size and weight of al-Jarwi's file nearly doubled. The number of names she revealed provided excellent cross references for the master file. Levant even had enough evidence to deport three other people, all members of the Iraqi delegation.

The bombs, of course, were taken directly to the lab.

Levant issued orders to arrest the chemist.

After Fatima's statement was typed up and signed, Levant ordered the paperwork completed to arrest Kassim al-Jarwi. He was to be taken into protective custody. At the same time, another set of papers were hand delivered to a special office in the State Department to declare him persona non grata. As soon as they caught him, they would have him out of the country within 24 hours.

Kassim returned to his apartment shortly after Nephi had left with Maria and Fatima. He quickly ascertained that he had been discovered and was in danger of being caught. Why no one was there waiting for him, he could not figure out. They had made a big mistake. Also, they had made a mistake in taking the bombs. Now he knew they were onto him and he would simply change his plan. He gathered a few items he felt might be useful, and he left—just minutes before a team of FBI agents arrived to watch the apartment. Al-Jarwi sat in his car watching them charge into his building. He smiled at his good fortune. They had not interfered at all with his work. In fact, it was likely to be better for him to work from one of the safe houses he had established in the past three months. Perhaps he would move from one to the other. Yes, that would be best.

His base would be the house in McLean. The others might be located more conveniently, but the house in McLean was situated on a larger, more secluded lot. More security equipment had been installed there. Also, he had converted a room in the basement where he could work with any reluctant or rebellious informant. The other locations could be used as alternates. Each contained ample stores of weapons and ammunition.

First thing in the morning he would contact that press secretary. At the same time he would reach Sariah. While he had decided to change his plan, he still would use them—if not directly, then indirectly.

Too bad he did not live in the days of the Prophet Mohammed and Ali, he thought. Issues had been more clearly defined in those days. Then there were believers and there were infidels. Believers merely struck down enemies with the sword in open conflict between men. It was strength against strength. And the strength of Allah filled the arms of true believers with the strength of ten men. On the other hand, certain pleasures made this new kind of warfare palatable—the stealth and cunning—the opportunities to convince people to follow the true cause. But the old kind of war still fascinated Kassim. He had studied it through his life and had worked hard to become a master swordsman. Had this been such a war—a war of strength and swords—that press secretary and the traitorous woman, Maria, would already be lying in their own blood.

*　*　*　*

News Briefs
Monday, January 14, 1991

OTTAWA, CANADA—Secretary of State James A. Baker III said today that the opportunity to avert war in the Persian Gulf is up to Iraq. He made the statement following a tour of nations allied against Iraq's five-month occupation of Kuwait.

Baker said he was disappointed that the U.N. peace mission to Baghdad had apparently failed.

BAGHDAD, IRAQ—Members of Iraq's National Assembly, meeting in an emergency session today, voted to give Saddam full authority over the gulf crisis and shouted they were willing to back Saddam with their blood and souls.

A spokesman for Saddam Hussein said that he remained firm and will not withdraw from Kuwait.

"The time for surrender has gone forever," the Iraqi President was quoted as having said. "Any last-minute chance for peace must come from them [the U.S.], not us."

WASHINGTON, D.C.—President Bush on Sunday called Iraq's intention to keep troops in Kuwait beyond the Tuesday midnight EST withdrawal deadline "a tremendous mistake."

NEW YORK CITY—U.N. Secretary-General Javier Perez de Cuellar returned today from peace talks with Saddam Hussein in Baghdad and reported he was unsuccessful in negotiating a settlement to Iraq's occupation of Kuwait.

"God only knows if there will be war," he said.

BALLSTON, VA —

At breakfast, Nephi asked Roy if he could swap cars for a few days.

"Sure," Roy said without hesitation. "I've always thought that somehow you got the best parking place of all the office staff. Take the clunker. I'll take your car—and your parking place."

Roy's idea of a clunker was his older Mercedes—with 165,000 miles on it. But it still ran like a precision watch. Roy had serviced it much more frequently than the manufacturer had recommended. Twice as often, he had told Nephi once. Obviously, it paid off.

"You can have my spot until I get back. Deal?" Nephi said with a smile.

"Deal. But I think I'll just take yours in and park it," Roy said. "It will be safe down there. Tina and I can get along with one car for a while."

"If they have enough on al-Jarwi to put him away, I would imagine they'll just pick him up. Then we will be able to get back to a normal life."

"Don't worry about things at the office. Ron isn't in and won't be until next week. We really won't need you until he comes back."

*   *   *   *

"Where to now?" Maria asked as they drove out of the apartment garage.

"I'd like to pick up a couple of things at my place. It'll only take a minute."

"Fine thing," she complained. "You get to go to your place. But I don't get to go to mine."

"Didn't you get enough stuff from Tina?"

"Well, if you like living in borrowed clothes. Of course, we could always go shopping." She smiled at him and watched for a reaction. Funny thing. She just caught herself saying the same thing she had heard her mother say to her father many times. And he had responded just as her father had.

He laughed.

He had sisters. He knew. These were the games girls played. And while the laugh was supposed to be his part in the game, he knew that sooner or later they would end up somewhere looking at things for her to wear—maybe even for both of them to wear.

His main concern now was to slip into his own apartment, get a few things and get out of there without being seen—especially by al-Jarwi. He drove completely around the apartment complex to make sure the terrorist's car wasn't around. Maria said she knew what all his cars looked like. At different times, she said, he had driven three cars—all of them fast, all of them silver-gray, and all of them German. He parked in the visitor spaces on the west side. He didn't want to chance being seen—even though he was driving a strange car. They walked to his building and entered it from the rear.

He let her into his apartment on the third floor and felt grateful for having left the place tidy. She turned to step into the kitchen, then strolled back around the counter into the living room. "This is nice," she mused.

"Thanks," he yelled back at her. "But the furniture is rented. A package deal. Only the books and a couple of prints are mine."

That's all right, she thought to herself. It's just right for two. And it wouldn't take much to fix up a place like this.

He crammed a few items into the large gym bag that was handy. On their way out, an impulse caused him to grab the old case with the sketches in it.

With enough turns and back-tracking to assure them that they were not being followed, Nephi made his way to the Beltway. He had driven randomly and had ended up in Springfield. It was one of the few places he knew. Now he could head for the Shirley Highway.

"I've always wanted to see Williamsburg. You game?" he asked.

"That's the old colonial town they restored?"

"That's it. Be there in a couple of hours or so. That okay?"

She smiled. It was nice to have a man ask her for a change. "That's fine," she said, settling down for a short nap. She had slept well enough at the Ivars after they had finally gone to bed.

Tina slipped her a sleeping pill. Maria didn't argue with her. She knew it would keep her from dreaming of her experience. But she had slept so hard that she woke up groggy and still felt a bit sluggish. Steady parkway travelling had not helped to arouse her and the second she closed her eyes she began thinking of al-Jarwi and what he had done to her. Quickly she opened them again and looked at Nephi. Yes. He was still there for her.

Driving south on I-95, Nephi felt alternate emotions of comfort and agitation. Maria rested in the bucket seat beside him. She seemed relaxed enough. Certainly she remained beautiful enough. A measure of puffiness lingered on her face, but what discoloration might have existed had been almost covered by makeup. She had on a smart looking skirt and sweater outfit Tina had loaned her. Tina had packed other clothes in a medium-sized suitcase they carried now in the trunk. The clothes belonged to Tina's daughter who visited regularly from her home in New Jersey.

Having Maria safely in his care relieved much of Nephi's concerns. He still experienced a wash of emotions when he relived seeing her cringing in that room. How close he had come to losing her! Too close. But how marvelous had been the blessing granted him by the Lord. How stupid had been his own contribution in placing her in that precarious position in the first place.

Nothing beats obedience, he repeated to himself. And the reminder caused him to once again search his impressions for any possible information he might have missed in planning this trip.

He had been told the Lord would send someone to help him find her and that he should take her and flee. At first he had thought the FBI agents had been the ones who had been sent. But it turned out to have been Yussef. How interesting that his friend had been involved in this by the Lord.

But not much else had come to Nephi about the fleeing part of his instruction. He felt comfortable staying with the Ivars last night. And he had spent considerable time trying to get a fix on which direction he should go. When the idea of heading down to Williamsburg came to mind—it had been a place he simply wanted to see sometime before he went back to Utah—he received a very moderate approval through the Spirit. He wondered about going in a different direction. Apparently that direction would have been all right as well. For something as serious as this, it seemed strange to Nephi that he would be left on his own in this decision. But as long as he had been given this much information, he would continue with what he had received and simply enjoy.

That brought him to the next disquieting part of this journey. Ahead, somewhere at the end of this tree-lined parkway, he would need to find accommodations for them—the two of them. Nothing had been given him on how to handle this situation. And the closer he got to it, the more nervous he became.

Looking at Maria set off tingling sensations within his body—a body already filled with serious desires to possess her. Touching her—and being together made it impossible to refrain from touching her—only intensified those desires. For a moment he considered following his carnal inclinations. After all, hadn't all this been arranged by the Lord, Himself? Hadn't they been thrown together—told to flee? Together?

Whoa!

There were booby traps in such reasoning. That much he knew. Since nothing had been given about how to deal with these compromising circumstances it was time to remain on guard.

Society in general no longer frowned on unmarried couples traveling without a chaperone, but Nephi had accepted the responsibility of living within the bounds the Lord had set for sexual relationships between men and women—those bounds were marriage. He knew that stepping outside the commitment he had made to the Lord could seriously jeopardize any fullness of joy they could have together.

In order to receive this joy he would need to deny himself immediate pleasures. But this knowledge only intensified within him his natural drive to experience those pleasures. It seemed ironic to Nephi that having the woman of his dreams sitting beside him in the flesh had the potential of becoming a horrible nightmare.

Nephi found what he hoped would be an ideal situation for them. One of the motels not far from Williamsburg offered rooms with kitchens. It was an older place, square and boxy with ivy crawling all over the walls and overhangs. The dark, heavy wooden beams reminded Nephi of the older motels in Utah. Only someone had kept this one well painted and properly repaired. Several of the units with kitchens connected with units that did not have a kitchen.

"The clerk said they get a lot of large families and these rooms work well for them," Nephi explained. He cleared his throat. "We're not a large family, but it's perfect for us," he continued, hoping she would understand. "We can each have some privacy and still be together. Okay?"

She stood in the open doorway that joined the two units. She leaned on the door jam and looked at him. Then she looked back and forth into the two rooms. Beyond that reaction, she simply shrugged.

She had wondered how this man would deal with this situation. Somehow it seemed natural he would arrange for separate rooms. She loved him a lot. He had saved her life. Other men might have thought that was reason enough to expect certain rewards. But not Nephi. He seemed to *really* care about her. These separate rooms proved it. She needed space—for the moment—and he was sensitive to that. She wasn't certain she would need so much space later on. But for now, of course, it was the perfect thing for him to have done.

"It's fine," she added and smiled.

"Now all I need to know is, can you cook?" he asked.

"No," she admitted. "Not really. Well, a few things. Not like my mom, though."

"Fine. Then I'll take the room with the kitchen. You can have the other one."

"Okay. But I'll expect room service," she teased, half seriously.

He looked at her and felt tempted to agree. But he wasn't going to allow all this planning to be shot down the tubes with one casual remark.

"Oh, no," he responded. "You're not getting off that easy. If you don't cook, I'll teach you. And the first two rules are, first, we take all our meals in here. That means we sit up to the table like a regular family."

"Okay," she smiled, amused at how he pretended to be in charge. "And what's the second?"

"The second is, that whoever cooks doesn't have to do the dishes."

"Figures!" she said, before plying him with a better idea. "Let's eat out."

They spent the rest of the day wandering around Williamsburg. The restored 18th century community extends east from the William and Mary College campus about 50 miles east and south of Richmond. The project began back in 1926 with the blessing and support of John D. Rockefeller. By the time Nephi and Maria discovered the village it had become a well-trampled community situated on about 127 acres. Duke of Gloucester Street begins at the college campus on the west and runs east to where the Capitol Building had been rebuilt. Shops and inns line this main street, their colonial sameness individualized by signs and colors.

On the east side of the restored Capitol building, they saw where the firebrand Patrick Henry had delivered his "Give me liberty or give me death" speech before the House of Burgesses.

"He was my kind of man," Maria teased, as they stood in the crowd listening to the tour guide describe what the Burgesses did during colonial times.

"I thought you didn't like war," Nephi said, trying to dull her remark.

"I don't. I hate violence of all kinds. But I admire someone with the strength of character to stand up and take a stand."

Nephi ran his fingers through his hair as he followed her and the rest of the tour group out the door. Maria's opinions confused him a little.

Extending north from the corner where the Burton Parish Church stood were the Palace Green and the Governor's Palace—both beautifully restored. Massive oaks and other species of trees, still dormant from winter, promised ample shade along both sides of the Green and throughout the community.

Mingling with tourists were the Colonial Williamsburg employees. They were the ones dressed in various types of colonial garb. Many had been assigned as guides and explained what went on in the various shops that lined the street. There was the printing and bookbinder shop, the silversmith's shop, the black-smith shop, and others. In the old courthouse, Nephi and Maria watched carpenters working to restore its eighteenth century character. Holes and impressions in the walls betrayed where partitions had been placed over the years when the building had been used for other purposes. All this interested Maria, but only because the craftsmen used the same kind of tools available to carpenters when the building was built. When she was ready to leave, Nephi lagged back.

"I love working with wood," he confessed.

"Will you make me something?"

"Sure. What would you like?"

"I don't know. Surprise me."

"How about a house?" he suggested.

Instantly her eyes looked at him. She couldn't tell for sure if he was kidding or not.

"A house? A whole house? Can you do that?"

"My Uncle Fred is a contractor. I used to help him all the time. Actually, I put myself through school building houses."

She was impressed. But still she didn't let him stay in the courthouse more than a few minutes longer. Then she dragged him across the street to a place where a few women were sewing clothes. The guide explained that everything they wore in colonial times had to be sewn by hand. She mentioned the name of Thomas Saint, an Englishman who invented a crude sewing machine in 1790, and then rattled off a number of other names and dates. She finished by noting how an American named Isaac Singer invented a machine that incorporated a foot treadle and a yielding presser foot. Until then, all clothes had been sewn by hand. Fine stitching occupied much of the time of women, the interpreter said.

"You like to sew?" he asked.

"No," she said emphatically. "Not like that, anyway. But I do appreciate something sewn well."

"Fine thing. Can't cook. Can't sew. What are you good at, Maria."

"I know how to hold up signs in a crowd."

"That all?"

"A few other things."

"The women in my family all know how to sew," Nephi said with exaggerated pride.

"Well, I guess I'd better learn, then, hadn't I?"

"It would be a good thing. Sure does help when you're raising a family."

"I think I'd like to learn how to do that, too," she said. For a moment they looked very seriously at each other. But nothing further was said right then. Instead, to put off the subject, they went shopping.

They were reluctant to end their day together, but both being tired they crashed on the beds in Nephi's half of their motel "suite." Maria let herself fall on top of the nearest of the two queen-sized beds. He chose to crash on the second bed. After a moment, she looked over at him and wondered when he would make his move. They had shared a day filled with such warm expressions of love and concern for each other, mingled with flurries of unspoken expectations. The closest thing to a disagreement that had risen between them had come when they went through the Governor's Palace.

The woman, wearing a colonial dress of blue flowered fabric trimmed at the neck and wrists with filmy lace, had led them down the front walk into the large, three-story brick structure. The entry hall had been decorated with weaponry—muscats, swords and pistols—hung in circular designs on the darkly stained wood panels and beams.

"Why do they always have to make so much out of war and killing?" she had asked.

"Didn't you hear the guide? That was the way things were back then. The governor showed off a lot of weapons because weapons were a sign of power."

"Well, we don't have to make such a big thing of it now, do we?" she asked. "I mean in Eastern Europe and now in the Persian Gulf?"

Nephi stood up a little straighter. Because of the nature of his job he felt he had a clearer point of view on the subject. "Don't you think someone might just take advantage of us if we decided to weaken our military posture unilaterally?"

"I don't think they'd be talking about war with Saddam Hussein if they hadn't spent so much money on weaponry—it's all so sophisticated that it probably won't work. It's not to defend ourselves, you know. Saddam Hussein is no real threat to us. They have picked this fight just so they can use up all the weapons they can't use on the Russians. That's all—and oil."

"But if we hadn't been strong, Maria, all those great things in Eastern Europe never would have happened. Now the cold war is over."

"See, I was right. The minute the cold war is over and they couldn't use all that junk on Communists, they had to get rid of it somewhere. All of a sudden they absolutely have to go to war with Iraq." Her face grew flushed. "It doesn't make sense—No! It makes a lot of sense—but only when you realize people just want to go to war all the time and kill each other."

"Maria, with all due respect," Nephi said, in a gentler voice, "I didn't pick this fight with Kassim al-Jarwi. But it kind of looks like I'm into one now, doesn't it? And what's my motivation? Survival. Along with the survival of someone I love."

The fight ended there. It had been a short one, but not a sweet one. She still felt strongly about war being stupid and unnecessary. But she had no way to argue against Nephi's last remark.

They both would have preferred letting the subject go, but it was not to be. At the motel, after they had rested for a few minutes, Maria got up and stretched. Nephi, still lying on the bed, reached over and turned on the television. The news was on and covered nothing but the war. There were reports on negotiations, troop movements and departing warships. There were touching shots of weeping families watching their men and women shipping out. Maria wanted to comment on the sadness and unfairness of it all. But wisely she said nothing. She felt a great relief when they found something else they could watch.

Actually, she would have preferred not watching anything. She wanted to get on with more important matters. So much had been exchanged between them through the day. She knew exactly what he had in mind—at least she thought she did. But since they had returned to the motel, he had avoided any of those provocative remarks that had been flying around all day. They left briefly to pick up a pizza and she teased him, asking if this was the way he was going to teach her how to cook. His reply hadn't been much more than a smile. They talked a little while they ate, but Maria noticed he had changed noticeably from earlier in the day. It almost appeared as if he had turned himself off to her—that he was trying to avoid her.

None of this made any sense to her. No one she had ever been with before had ever acted this way. Was he shy and waiting until the clock showed a proper bed time? Some men were like that. She had no idea what would cause him to act as he was acting. He liked her. She knew that. And she had been sending signals to him all day. Surely he hadn't missed any of those invitations. Well, she decided, if he was waiting for an official bed time, this was as good a time as any to test that theory.

"I guess I'm more tired than I thought I was," she began.

All he did was nod his head up and down. He didn't even look away from some stupid commercial.

"Good night," she said, the invitation strong in her voice.

"Good night," he responded as flatly.

She lightened her tone. "Sleep tight."

That evoked a more encouraging response from him. But not the one she had hoped for. He smiled. They had learned about sleeping tight back at Williamsburg. People in colonial times slept on beds with rope webbings. Whenever the bed sagged, they would just tighten the ropes. Thus, "sleep tight."

The last half of the saying had to do with bed bugs—in the ticks, or mattresses.

"Don't let the bed bugs bite," he said.

She waited for him to get up. She even tried closing her eyes tightly and willing him to get up. But it didn't work. Nothing worked. By this time, if it had been Kassim, the jerk would have been tearing at her buttons. If she had been back in Germany, hot old Kurt would have been finished by now. Neither of them would have needed any encouragement at all.

This guy hadn't budged. She couldn't accuse him of being dead. Just now he had spoken to her. All afternoon he had been sending messages that he wanted to play house together. But he certainly wasn't playing his part tonight.

"Good night," she said one last time before disappearing through the connecting door.

One of Nephi's rules had been to close the door so each of them would have privacy in getting dressed. The last one to retire would be responsible for opening it in case something happened. But she was the first to retire and she left it open—one final invitation to him, if he changed his mind.

The second she disappeared from the room, Nephi let out the breath he had been holding. It was over. No. Wait. She hadn't closed the door. It wasn't over yet. Oh, man. She was in there making all those sounds—and then not making sounds. Whatever she was doing, it was driving his imagination wild.

She had no idea what she was doing to him. All he would have to do was walk in there. Nature would take its course. And he would enjoy every minute of it—every second—every millisecond.

But he was determined to stay the course. And he pretended he was weighted down by cement.

He wanted that woman. There was no question about that.

He wanted her more than anything else in this world.

But he didn't want her just for the night.

He wanted her forever.

It was another restless night for Nephi. His carnal mind played havoc with his psyche. She was there—right there in the next room. She was so desirable. There was little doubt in his mind they would be getting married anyway. It probably would not be the first time for her. So, why not?

It just wasn't right.

It would lead to serious complications.

He couldn't—well, he could, but he couldn't.

He wouldn't.

He didn't.

Then, when he finally did fall asleep he felt no relief.

He dreamed of her again.

She was there, on the cliff. Only this time there was a new ingredient added to the scene.

He was standing there with her—holding her. But they were perilously close to slipping over the edge.

CHAPTER 8

News Brief
Tuesday, January 15, 1991

NEW YORK CITY—A flurry of last-minute proposals that could head off an imminent conflict in the Persian Gulf were not given much chance of succeeding today.

U.N. Secretary-General Javier Perez de Cuellar said that Saddam Hussein left him without any reason to have real hope of averting war.

In the meantime, France has proposed that the Security Council agree to Saddam's demand for an international conference on the Palestinian question if Hussein ends the occupation of Kuwait.

However, Thomas R. Pickering, U.S. Ambassador to the U.N., told reporters that it was not the appropriate time nor the appropriate circumstances to present such a proposal, with linkage of the Palestinian question to the crisis in the Persian Gulf.

BAGHDAD, IRAQ—Hundreds of thousands of Iraqis staged government-organized demonstrations today in support of Saddam Hussein and in defiance of the fast-approaching U.N. deadline, which calls for an Iraqi withdrawal from Kuwait.

TUNIS, TUNISIA—Two top aides to PLO leader Yasser Arafat were assassinated Monday, apparently by a renegade bodyguard linked to terrorist Abu Nidal.

The gunman used an AK-47 assault rifle to kill Salah Khalaf, Arafat's second in command, and Hayel Abdel-Hamid, the PLO's security chief. Also killed was Abu Mohammed al-Omari, Khalaf's chief bodyguard.

Several Palestinians were arrested. The main suspect, Hamza Abu Zeid, was taken into custody. However, it was not clear who the suspect may have been working for.

WASHINGTON, D.C. —

Y USSEF CALLED THE FBI'S WASHINGTON METROPOLITAN Field Office. The panic in his voice increased when the operator wouldn't put him through to Levant.

"He's not answering his phone," the operator said in a cool professional voice. She put him on hold and Yussef's frustrations increased. "Would you speak with Agent Dalton instead?" she asked when she came back on. Yes. He would even speak with Agent Dalton. He hated talking with Dalton. Dalton had offended Yussef many times and Yussef had classified the highly skilled FBI agent as a bureaucratic clerk, incapable of thinking for himself.

This conversation merely strengthened that opinion.

"Look, Dalton, Sariah is missing. No one has seen her. She left her office shortly after six o'clock last night. We had a date. She did not meet me. She did not go home. Unless she meets me, she always goes home—the same way—the same time. If she ever varies from that, she calls someone. She called no one. She is gone. Isn't it obvious that something has happened to her? Can't you see that this son-of-a-devil's boil, Kassim al-Jarwi, has taken her."

"Wait a minute, Yussef. Back up. Who is this Sariah?"

"She is my beloved—my betrothed."

"Oh yeah," Dalton said recalling what Nephi had told him.

"Yes. And she is missing, I tell you. It cannot be anything other than that. She would never do such a thing. I'm telling you, al-Jarwi has done this. That filthy scum has taken her. He has her just as he had Maria Moore."

"Calm down, Yussef. There could be any number of reasons why she is missing. She may not be missing at all. And if she is, what makes you think it has to be al-Jarwi?"

"My Sariah works with Nephi Nicholes in Congressman Hersch's office."

Dalton took a few seconds to put together a plan.

"Get in here right now, Yussef. I will start a search for her immediately."

* * * *

Kassim al-Jarwi stood at the stove in the barren, suburban kitchen and cursed under his breath. He hated to cook. Nothing turned out right when he cooked for himself—not even on a fancy range like this decadent contraption before him. In the desert he would do anything to avoid cooking—even if it meant fasting for days. Only when forced to do so would he cook for himself. He cursed those who had reduced him to this position. If only Fatima were here. She would be doing this. Where was she? Why had they taken her? She knew nothing. She was merely a convenience to him.

Strange, Kassim thought. What he missed was not so much her presence in bed. It was her hand at cooking. She would have loved this kitchen. All the appliances had been specially constructed and built into this house—double ovens as well as a microwave and an extra-wide refrigerator requiring two doors. Somehow Fatima would have seen to it that meals from this kitchen became special delights. She had a way to turn the most simple foods into delicacies. Ah, yes. And then she would tell him stories—stories of old, stories of defenders of the true faith. How wondrous were those stories—brave men—riding swift horses—swords flashing—the blood of infidels spilled upon the ground. Glorious!

No. Never. She would not have left on her own. There had been signs of a struggle. They must have drugged her. The poor defenseless woman. Surely she struggled as best she could before the drugs took effect. No. She would not have let them take her without a struggle. Not Fatima. She had been with him for too many years. She could not have walked out. They had to have taken her. Yes, he kept telling himself. They stole her away as they had stolen everything else.

He scraped the tilted pan, forcing the scrambled eggs to slide onto the plate next to the dark, nearly burnt toast.

But what they had taken from him did not concern him at this moment. What he had taken from them did. After he ate the tasteless eggs he would go downstairs and talk once more with the woman.

It had been so easy to take Sariah. He thought it would have been hard to find her. But he was blessed with the brilliant idea to simply wait for her and follow her. He had only to be patient and to wait for the right moment. Such a gullible woman. But, then, most women were so gullible, weren't they? All he had to do was promise her information about her family. The letters were in his car. She had come willingly. He did not need to use force until they reached the car's door. And he had used precisely the right amount of chemical—just a touch of it with the syringe in her arm. She had slept the whole drive. She did not waken until he had her in place at the safe house.

Such a beautiful body. He hated to think that she might continue to resist. He would have to deal with her more carefully, he cautioned himself. He could not damage her too much or she would not be able to perform her task. On the other hand, he smiled, there could be other benefits if she refused altogether.

His control in Paris had applied great pressure on him to move quickly. His most recent instructions from Baghdad were to be ready to strike as soon as the deadline was past. They did not expect the United States to attack until much later. But he needed to have everything in place by tonight. If the Americans struck in a sneak attack, then he was free to act at the earliest possible time. That meant he was ordered to attack immediately after.

He wished again that Fatima was with him. She would have been helpful with this woman. Oh, well. He would have to use his own techniques.

In the motel near Williamsburg, it was barely getting light when Nephi finished his drawing. He had debated considerably whether he should do the drawing or not. He kept telling himself that he was not into self-portraits. But habit did him in. Now that it was finished he felt somewhat vindicated. It was not exactly him. But it could not have been anyone else.

"What are you doing?" her drowsy voice drifted into the room from the connecting doorway.

He tried to slip the sketch pad into its case before she could see it. She was too fast for him.

"Drawing? You're sitting here drawing in the middle of the night?" She stepped over to the couch and casually picked up one of the books.

Her interest left Nephi with nothing he could say. He had never been able to tell anyone about what he had been doing. He had less of an idea how he could tell Maria about these sketches and his dreams—especially this early in their relationship. He even had considered destroying the drawings—now that he had found her.

It was too late now for any such option. He had been discovered. It felt a lot like he had been caught with the crown jewels.

"These are nice," she said, turning the pages of the first book he had used. "You did these yourself?"

He still couldn't speak.

She finished the first book and set it back in the case. At the same time she picked up the second one.

This one would probably give him away. A chill rippled across the stiffened muscles of his back. He still didn't know what he would tell her. There was no way she was ready for a gospel discussion—of the Holy Spirit and the plan of salvation—at least that's what he thought. Ready or not, though, something like that was on its way.

"These are all of girls. Couldn't you draw anything else?" she teased.

She turned another page. It was the same girl as on the page before. She turned back and studied the two pictures. Yes. They were of the same girl. Definitely the same girl.

Was she *his* girl? Could he be in love with someone else? That would explain why he didn't try anything last night. But, no. Even though she had not asked about another girl, that didn't seem possible. She just knew she was not invading someone else's territory—his actions over the past couple of days said just the opposite. She had been expecting to hear a proposal of marriage at any time.

Maybe he was already married, she thought. After all, he is a Mormon. Did they still marry more than one woman? No. She remembered there was a story on television once where a bunch of polygamists claimed they were Mormons. The church in Salt Lake City—the one Nephi belonged to—denied their claim. Besides, his shirts had not been laundered by a wife who loved him.

On the other hand, there was no doubt these were sketches of the same girl.

She turned the page—and it was like looking into a mirror.

For the first time the girl could be seen in a closeup, her features larger, more distinct. It was a picture of her.

"When did you do this?" she asked.

He looked at the drawing. There was a date written in tiny numbers at the edge of the drawing. It was hardly noticeable.

"Three years ago." He pointed to the numbers.

"You're kidding," she said. And she flipped back to see if the others were dated. They were. Then she flipped back to the portrait.

It was really good. And she remembered she had worn her hair that way back then.

"How did you know? How did you do this?"

He didn't have the foggiest idea what to say. So he just looked at her. The smile he tried to craft on his face came out completely wrong. There was no confidence in it, no strength. The shrug that went with it didn't help a bit.

She turned in her place on the couch, putting a little distance between them—as well as her knee.

She went back to the page where she was standing beside a Shinto shrine in Japan. And she looked at him. He hadn't changed his expression. He just sat there looking like a lovable puppy who had been caught chewing up a slipper.

But this was no slipper. And there she was in that garden with all the statues of Buddha. It was uncanny. How did he know she had stopped there with her parents? Her dad's back was turned. But it was him for sure.

She moved ahead to the page where she was in the base hospital with appendicitis.

"I had a severe pain in my side for three days after I drew that," he managed to say. But it came out so sheepishly, he wished he hadn't said it at all.

She smiled cautiously, shook her head and continued.

There she was in Australia. And there she was in those gardens in Thailand.

When she got to the picture of her with her friends in the Hofbrau in Frankfurt, she closed the book. She feared what she might find next.

"All right," she said sitting up straight. "What's going on here? I want an answer and I want it now."

Nephi still was having trouble. In such times it was his practice to think twice before he spoke. And then to speak only when he was certain that what he was about to say was justified by the Spirit.

But as he sat there watching her look at these precious pictures he had drawn of her, there had been a void of thought in his mind. He pressed himself to ask silently, but urgently, for help. Until it came he would have to stall. And to stall, all he could think to do was to shrug his shoulders and gesture with his hand.

The Spirit eased into his mind and heart.

"You don't like them?" he asked. That bought him a little more time. And during that brief period he felt the confidence rising within him as the Spirit filled his soul.

"I love them, Nephi. That's not the point. How did all those pictures of me get into your mind and onto this paper? I mean there is something really strange going on here."

"You really want to know? Couldn't you just ignore how they were drawn and enjoy them for what they are?"

"No," she said.

He shrugged and took a deep breath. When he let it out, he began.

"Okay, I'll tell you and I promise you it will be the truth. But there's a good chance you're going to find it hard to believe."

She framed as much of a skeptic's look on her face as she could create.

When he began, his voice was as calm as she had ever heard it. Gone were the nervous gestures, the hesitation, the stalling, and the weakness in his voice. Back was the strong, confident man to whom she had been attracted.

Aside from his expressions and demeanor, something else was going on—inside her. It began so gradually she wasn't aware it was there. When she did realize something new had been added to her life, she had no idea what it might be. But she knew something was far from normal. Her mind was so much more alert. She felt a warmth in and around her heart. Every word he spoke seemed to come alive in her mind.

"I had the dream first when I was twelve years old. I had no idea what was going on. I was embarrassed to tell anyone, even my mom. But I was into cartooning at the time and I just pulled out that first pad and drew what I could remember of the dream. You had to have been in some kind of school back then."

"Dream?" Maria asked softly but in disbelief. She tried to remember back that far. It was easier than she thought. It was a school on a base in Germany. She could still remember painting at those easels.

"When the dream came back a few months later," he continued, "it was even harder for me to tell anyone about it. But it was so real. Both of them had been so very real. The first one came when I was just beginning to learn about the Church. I had just been ordained a deacon. That's the first office in the Aaronic Priesthood. We spend a lot of time in our Church training young men to assume leadership positions. It all begins when you're twelve and are ordained a deacon.

"Well, on top of what I was learning about the priesthood, I began reading the scriptures. And the dreams just started. I didn't understand much about what was going on, but I did know enough to realize that what had happened had come from the Spirit. All I could figure was that it was a blessing of some sort. At the time I couldn't figure out why the Lord was sending me dreams of a girl—a pretty girl at that—when I was much more interested in receiving dreams of my future as a fantastic sports figure or something.

"In the next couple of years I received a number of dreams. They were of you in all sorts of places. By then I was noticing girls more. And since I had no choice in the matter, I just figured I'd sit back and enjoy dreaming about this cute girl traipsing all over the world. I'd try to draw them as best I could.

"Well, the dreams became more and more frequent. I came to really enjoy them. There you were—whoever you were—visiting all these exotic places, Maria. And in a sense, I was there with you. I got the feeling that when you moved or took some kind of trip I would have a dream about your new place.

"Then when I came to Washington I started having them more frequently than ever. I had one of you last Saturday. That was when I first saw you—on the subway—going to the demonstration."

"You saw me there?"

"Yes."

"Before we met at your office?"

"Yes."

"And you saw me get into the limousine with Kassim?"

"Yes."

She turned her head. She remembered exactly what she had done when she first saw Kassim.

"I'm sorry. I didn't know you were there."

"It's all right. I understand. You had no way of knowing that I was there at all—or why I would be there."

"I hope you understand that I didn't know what a jerk Kassim was when I did that."

"It's all right, Maria" he said again, in an effort to reassure her that he meant it. He was relieved to hear her respond like that. It wasn't what she said. Rather, it was the tone of her voice. It was the first evidence he had that she just might believe him.

"But it's still hard for me to understand exactly how you could know so much about me—and the places I went. These are very accurate drawings. It's scary."

"Well, the dreams came in scenes, you know? Kind of like snapshots. I didn't see a whole lot of movement. But the last scene I would see would be extremely vivid. The very first time I remember that it remained in my mind so long and so sharp, I tested it by opening my eyes. The reality of the world around me didn't interfere in the least. It was like my mind had a separate eye, so to speak. And those images would just linger there whether I had my physical eyes opened or closed. And the visualization always lingered long enough for me to finish the drawing. Can you understand what I'm saying?"

"Not really. But I promise you, I'm trying."

"I told you when I started that it was going to be hard for you to understand. It's hard enough for me to explain it to you, and I understand exactly what's going on. You know, you really should know a lot more about the gospel before I go into it."

"The gospel? What has the gospel got to do with all this?"

He had reached the very place he had hoped this conversation would take them. Again, it wasn't the question itself so much as it was the tone she used to ask it. It sounded like she wanted to know—like she truly wanted to know. It wasn't the skeptic's tone or any sort of attempt to ridicule him and what he was trying to explain. She was seriously trying to understand.

"What I have been given, Maria—really, what *we* have been given—has been a gift from the Lord. You don't have to believe it. But it's true."

Then he began to tell her that they were children of our Father in Heaven. He explained how they had grown up in the spirit world before the earth was created. He told her that while he was on his mission he had been given information about his dreams—that he and Maria had fallen in love before they came to earth and had wanted to be together forever. He told her the Lord had given them a promise that they could be together. They also had been told that the way for them would not be easy.

The explanation was lengthy. But words poured into his mind as he spoke. He looked directly into her eyes and somehow he knew she was accepting what he said, absorbing his thoughts and words as they were delivered to her.

What he assumed was happening to her actually *was* happening within her. There was no way she could prove what he said. But she knew it was true. Somehow she knew it. She remembered what Tina had told her about, what was it? A testimony? Yes. But Tina was talking about learning about their religion. This was different. This was personal. Did their church—did their God provide such individual attention so that things like this could happen?

It must be, because it most certainly was happening. She could tell by just looking in his eyes. It was as if he was speaking to her with his eyes, through his eyes—his mouth was giving her a message, and his eyes were saying the same thing only more. And the same message was also coming from another source. She had never felt such a thing. It was a wonderful feeling. It was so wonderful she wanted to tell everyone about it. But in thinking of it, she knew there was no way she could explain it.

A number of points of evidence were coming to her mind—points she could not ignore. For instance, the attraction to him had been so quick, so intense. How else could that have happened except that they had known each other before?—before either of them were born on this earth? What had Tina said? It just made good sense? Well, this strange thing somehow was beginning to make sense to her. But she still had no idea how she would tell her mother or anyone else.

"Why us? I mean, why me? Nephi, I can understand you going through all this, but why me?" The unspoken part of her question had to do with the things she had done that did not seem to merit the kind of reward this represented. But that thought was overwhelmed by a feeling—a greater sense of peace than she had ever felt in her life. It was more than just peace. It was as if she felt fulfillment for the first time. And yet, that didn't even describe it completely.

Nephi searched for an answer to her question. An easy one was given him.

"Why not you? Why not me? If the Lord wants to give us a great opportunity like this, why not take it and be grateful?"

She asked more questions. And he provided answers as he felt impressed to give them. They talked about Mormon temples. They talked about what it took to become a member of the Church.

As he spoke, the words drilled into the inner depths of her heart and mind. As intense as the feeling had been before, she found her whole body encased by some kind of pressure. By all rights, she should have been feeling pain. Instead, it was a pleasant feeling. And there was no question in her mind. What he was saying was true.

"I didn't plan to tell you in this way, Maria. When you walked through that door I knew I would have to tell you. I wasn't sure how you would react. I was so frightened that you would just laugh. That would have been extremely difficult for me. I've lived with this whole thing for so long. In a sense, I've lived with you all that time. And I knew I would love you the minute I saw you.

"Maria, I do love you and I want you to marry me. Will you?"

"Yes," she said without hesitation. "I probably would have said 'yes' yesterday. I was kind of hoping you would ask. Once or twice I got a little scared that you wouldn't. But yes. Today I say yes. After hearing about all this, I say yes."

"That's great," was his response. Kind of dumb. Certainly not profound. But those were the words that came from his mouth at the same time he released a heavy sigh. The burden no longer was a burden. All was well. And he felt all washed out.

He leaned toward her. She leaned to meet him and they kissed.

Then she sat back suddenly.

"You know it's all wrong," she announced.

"What's wrong?"

"These pictures," she began turning the pages of the second book. "At least this one."

"What's wrong with this one?"

It was the picture where he had written the name "Elena" on the drawing."

"That's not Elena."

"I know. It should be Maria."

"No. There should be a Spanish tilde over the n. You know the little squiggle? My folks named me Maria Eleña. Without the tilde it's pronounced differently."

"You're kidding?" Nephi said as if he disbelieved her. Actually he was filled with wonder. The voice had been right all along—and he had been right to expect something more. Maria—and that little squiggle. That was all. What an incredible thing.

"No. I don't kid about things like my name. When I was a little girl the kids in my class used to tease me so much about it—it was a popular song a long time ago, you know—Maria Eleña. Well, I just hated it. I didn't want that name. So I simply ignored it. I haven't used it in years. In fact no one in Washington knows about it except for my mother and father."

"And now me."
"And now you."
"Maria Eleña Moore."
"Maria Eleña Moore Nicholes," she added.

They finished breakfast at a nearby pancake house and Nephi stopped at the entrance to call Washington. He had promised Roy he would keep in touch while they were moving around.

"Sariah is missing," Roy reported. "Yussef is very upset. I had to tell him I knew all about what you did and what he was doing. When I told him that, he dumped everything on me. The guy's in a panic. I had a call from the FBI. They're upset because Yussef is running around doing stupid things. He's out of control. You may be the only one he trusts. How soon can you get up here?"

"We'll leave right away. I'll be there as soon as I can drive from Williamsburg."

"Williamsburg? Why did you go all the way down there? Couldn't you find some place a little closer?"

"You're lucky we didn't go to Utah."

"I guess I am at that. See you soon."

Back at the motel Nephi called Maria from her room where she was packing. He wondered if he should tell her what Roy had said. He didn't much like the idea of breaking the news and telling her of his plans. But she had to know.

"Sit down, sweetheart," he said softly. "We need to talk this over for a minute."

She held herself rigid fearing greatly what he was about to tell her. She had felt so safe here—with him—so far away from Washington, D.C., where a horrible man was still on the loose.

She watched him take out the third sketch book and open it. But he held the book close to his chest so she could not see which drawing it was. She felt the blood drain from her face. Was this when he would make her confess all the things she had done? She wasn't ready to do anything like that. And she would resent the obligation of having to do so.

"I told you that the dreams came more frequently when I got out here to Washington. Well, this one was one of those dreams."

He turned the book so she could see the picture. It brought to her mind recollections of the meeting Kassim had taken her to. There were people there she didn't like. But they all seemed dedicated to stopping the war. She told Nephi exactly what had happened.

She was relieved that he did not condemn her, neither by expression—which would have been enough to devastate her—nor by word.

"This is the one I did Saturday," he said. "Where is this place?"

"I have no idea," she said, taking the book and holding it so she could study it. "No. I've never been in this place. I wouldn't mind. It looks elegant, with the fountain and all." She handed the book back to him.

"Now look, Maria. I won't put your life in the balance again. I won't force you to do something you don't want to do. But Yussef needs my help. He thinks al-Jarwi has kidnapped Sariah."

"The woman who works for you?"

"Yes. They are betrothed. It's a little like us. It's more than a normal engagement."

She smiled at that.

"I need to go back and help," he told her.

"Why?"

"Because he's a friend. Without him I never would have found where al-Jarwi lived—never would have found you."

She shuddered and withdrew from him, slumping slightly into the couch. She knew Yussef had played some kind of role in her rescue. She remembered him being there in the lobby. But she hated thinking of going back there. It would bother her just to be in town. She would be looking at every man who had the slightest resemblance of Kassim—and there were probably hundreds. She would be looking for him and for the places he might hide.

Still, there was a thought in her mind that she owed this Yussef something. Her father had taught her to keep her promises and to be loyal to her friends. Why had she remembered that now? Why couldn't she just stay here? Why couldn't Nephi just stay here with her?

Because, was the only answer she found.

"I'm going, too."

"No, you're not," Nephi said.

"You can't stop me."

"But you can't go. There's too much danger for you."

He turned the page to the dream of her on the cliff.

"This is what I dreamed of you Sunday morning. I didn't like it then, I don't like it now."

She took it and looked at it and began to tremble.

"What were you drawing this morning?" she asked.

"It doesn't matter," he said quickly, reaching for the book.

She held it away from his reach and turned the page.

She looked at him for a moment and then at the latest sketch.

"You're on that cliff, too. You're in as much danger as I am."

"No, I'm not. I'm there to protect you."

"Good. Then stay here with me."

"I can't. I have to help Yussef. I can't abandon him."

"Then neither can I. He helped me too, you know. And if you're going somewhere, that's where I'm going. You can't do anything about that."

"What if I tie you up?"

"Don't be stupid," she said. "You wouldn't know how. And besides, I would be up there the minute I could get a plane or bus or train. I'd even hitchhike. And what if Kassim stopped to pick me up. Then where would you be?" She was upset and her words came out angrily.

They packed quickly and took their things to the car. But Maria wouldn't leave until she had taken a picture of the very place where they had talked that morning and another of the rooms and another of the motel itself.

She smiled and thanked him for waiting patiently in the car for her. As he drove from the motel she told him she wanted the pictures to show their grandchildren.

"You don't want to show them to our children?"

"Maybe, if they behave. But considering all the trouble I gave my parents, couldn't we skip over the children part of it and get right into the grandchildren? I understand they're a lot easier to handle."

He laughed. "You weren't that bad of a child."

"I was too. I was rotten," she said with emphasis.

"No, you weren't. You were a cute little thing. I know you had a great time with your parents. It wasn't until you got older that you turned rotten."

She winced at his words. But then she realized the tone of voice he used was not at all hateful or accusatory.

"How much do you know?" she asked, dreading the answer.

"Enough," he said nonchalantly.

"And you still love me?"

"Of course."

"You want to know all the details?"

"Only if you want to tell me. Do you want to tell me?"

"No," she said. Then she thought about the danger of loose ends. "Would you still love me if it was really horrible?"

"Look, Maria," he said.

"Eleña," she corrected him. "To you I will always be Eleña."

He looked away from the road for a moment and smiled at her.

"Look, Eleña. What you did before we met was an entirely different lifetime than the one we've begun. Isn't it?"

"Yes."

"Do you want all those things to interfere with our future?"

"No."

"Then all you have to do is turn away from them. It's what's known as repentance."

"Do I have to confess?"

"Well, to a certain extent. I wouldn't worry so much about that as much as I would worry about approaching the Savior in a humble way and asking Him to forgive you. All the rest is mechanical. And when you know He's forgiven you, it will be over."

"Will you forgive me?" she asked a few miles down the parkway.

"You haven't offended me. You have brought me nothing but happiness. I have nothing to forgive."

"Sure you do. I mean all this affects your life too, you know."

"Well, I guess in a way it does."

"Well, will you?"

"Will I what?"

"Forgive me?"

"Certainly. I love you. So does the Savior. You don't think you would have felt what you felt back there if He didn't love you, do you?"

"No. I guess not."

"Then if He can love you and forgive you, why shouldn't I?"

She settled back with a smile of content on her face.

"Nephi?"

"Yes."

"How do you know how I felt back there?"

"Because I felt it, too. It was something special we were given to share—just the three of us."

"Three of us?"

"You, me and the Lord."

That sounded strange, but it certainly had to be something like that.

"I love you, Nephi."

"I know."

And the car pressed on toward an unknown future, edging them closer and closer to the brink of the cliff.

CHAPTER 9

NORTHERN VIRGINIA —

ELEÑA WANTED TO ENJOY THE LUSH GREEN COUNTRYSIDE found on both sides of I-64 as they traveled northward, but ugly images from her past kept demanding her attention. She found it impossible to prevent the dreadful scenes from flashing through her consciousness. When she could, she forced more pleasant memories before her. What made it all worse was the knowlege that with each turn of the wheels she and Nephi were getting nearer and nearer to where Kassim al-Jarwi waited. He no longer meant anything to her; now all he represented was a vicious obstacle to the most promising expectations of her life.

The previous night had been a restless one. Every sound in or around her motel room had awakened her. Each time she had hoped it would be Nephi. But he had not come to her.

She wakened one last time and noticed morning's first light showing through the drawn drapes. She relaxed then, knowing that if he hadn't tried to be with her last night, he wouldn't try in the morning. It surprised her not to feel disappointed or insulted. She knew he loved her. He had shown it in too many ways. But his not coming to her seemed so unnatural.

On the other hand, it made a lot of sense. Her mother had talked with her about men. She hadn't paid much attention to her mother then, but parts of what she had said drifted upward from some recessed corner in her memory. Men showed respect by showing restraint, her mother had said. But Maria Eleña Moore had never met a man who had shown any restraint at all—until she met Nephi. Then, while laying there as morning encroached on her room, there came a smile upon her that radiated from deep inside her soul. It carried warmth and assurance that she had been considered by at least one man as something more than an object to possess or exploit.

When she discovered him sitting in his room drawing, she had no idea what she would learn from him. Looking back on that conversation, it all seemed a kind of blur in her mind. Dreams over the years—a premortal life where they had a personal contact with each other and with their Father in Heaven—God. It was an incredible story—an unbelievable story. But to her the most incredible part of it remained the intense feeling that had taken hold of her as he spoke of these things. Its power and beauty had literally overwhelmed her. The feeling, more than anything, had convinced her that what he was saying was true. Much of that feeling lingered with her in a kind of afterglow counteracting her fear of returning to where Kassim waited.

"Why can't everybody just be nice to each other? Be happy?" she asked.

"Not everybody's in love like you are."

"Too bad. They don't know what they're missing."

Nephi smiled. "You've got that right."

"Nephi," she said, after another mile had passed. "How come people always have to make war?"

"So long as there are conflicts of wills, there will be war."

"Then why can't we just set our conflicts in neutral?"

"Wouldn't that be great? But I'm afraid it's too much to hope for right now. Probably won't happen for awhile."

"What do you mean, awhile?"

"Ever hear of the second coming of Christ?"

"Yes. Of course."

"When He comes, the Millennium begins. That's when there will be peace. Until then there will be opposition in all things. Good—evil. Happiness—misery. Peace—war. Unfortunately, it's something you can count on."

"I don't want to. And the Millennium is too far away."

"It might come sooner than you think."

"You think so? That would be interesting. But couldn't we just get started with a little Millennium right now?"

"Sure. We could. But we won't. The odds are against anything like that succeeding. The United Nations isn't doing too well, is it?"

"Well, it could if we'd give it a chance."

"Oh, they'll keep trying. But they won't be able to stop men fighting with each other."

"I don't see why."

"Well, Elefia, conflicts among God's children date back to before the world was created—back in our premortal life."

"Back then? Like what you were talking about this morning?"

"Yes, but there's even more than what we talked about this morning. There was a massive rebellion against Father's plan. Lucifer started it. At one time he held a respected position as the Son of the Morning. But he rebelled against Father and became the adversary. He talked a third of Father's children into following him. It turned into open rebellion—or in other words, war. Lucifer and his followers were overwhelmed and cast out of heaven. They were the ones who introduced war and conflicts here on earth shortly after Adam and Eve began raising their family. That's when all this business about war began. It's been going on ever since. And there won't be any peace on earth until the Savior comes again and Lucifer and his followers are cast out a second time."

She had heard some of this before. It had never been explained quite that way.

"Why would God let that kind of thing go on? I think that's terrible."

"In a way, I agree that sometimes it's tragic. Only there's a very good reason for allowing these things to continue."

"What could that possibly be? I mean, there's so much pain and suffering involved in war."

"Pretty sad when you look up close. But from the Lord's perspective there's a greater purpose. See, we're looking at life from a very constricted point of view—like having blinders on—

looking only between birth and death. But He sees things from an eternal perspective. He knows what each of us was before coming here and He knows who among us has the capacity to rise above these problems of mortality."

"Well, if He knows, why doesn't He relieve some of the pain?"

"That's a good question. But you see, even if He knows, we don't know. And, in a way, each of us is proving all this to himself or herself. So, the bottom line is that the Lord uses these conflicts to prove his children. Actually, it's the best way for us to prove to ourselves that we're worthy. And when we learn to resist all the conflicts that would destroy us, then we end up understanding how they have strengthened us. Along the way we learn to choose good rather than evil, right rather than wrong, truth rather than counterfeits, peace rather than war."

"I still don't see why they won't leave us alone—those of us who choose to live in peace."

"People like Hitler and Stalin and Saddam Hussein see peace-loving people as an opportunity for conquest."

"But we don't have to go to war, do we?"

"Let me explain it this way, Eleña. The biggest battles any of us face are fought every day within ourselves. War is just an extension of those same conflicts. But sometimes it's easier to go to war than to conquer one's self. If we can't even win those inner struggles, how can we win the ones with our neighbors?"

"What if we just don't fight our neighbors?"

"That would be fine. But I don't remember picking a fight with Kassim al-Jarwi. And still we're in a heck of a war with him, aren't we?"

"But he's trying to kill us, not just fight with us. Didn't God command us, 'Thou shalt not kill?'"

"Oh, yes. But did you know that at other times he commanded, 'Thou shalt utterly destroy.' Sometimes there is a good reason to go to war."

"Oh, yeah? What reason could be that good?"

"Well, for instance, when people become so corrupt they don't deserve to live on the earth. It's time to send them on their way so the rest of us can go on about our business in relative peace. And then, of course, we all have the right to protect ourselves, our families, homes and freedoms. Really, beyond self-protection, it should be the Lord who determines when war should take place."

"So who's going to decide that? And how can the rest of us tell when war is right?"

"That's why we need prophets who can keep us in line with what the Lord wants. And that's why the Lord has given us so many gifts of the Spirit—so we can receive confirmation of what the Lord has given His prophets. Not just with the decision to go to war or to make peace with a neighbor, but with the battles that go on within the heart and mind of each individual. That's the real battle ground. And the Lord's willing to keep his promises. All we have to do is listen. To ask and listen and obey."

"Oh, is that all?" she scoffed. "That seems so hard, so remote."

"In one sense it is hard. You have to pay the price the Lord asks. You have to qualify for answers from Him. But it's not nearly so remote as you think. Didn't you receive a confirmation about what we talked about this morning?"

"Yes. As a matter of fact, I did," she looked at him and smiled. It had been a wonderful feeling. "But I can't say I qualified for it. I mean, I didn't do anything special for it."

"Sure you did. You just don't know when."

"Oh," she responded. There wasn't much she could say to that.

"And look at it this way, Elefia. Wasn't that a lot easier than being left on your own to believe what I told you? I mean, would you have believed me if you had heard me say those things without some kind of backup?"

"I'm sure I would not have. It's bothering me to think of having to tell someone else about what you said."

"Oh, I don't think other people need to know about it. Can't we just keep that to ourselves?"

"Okay," she looked at him and caught him glancing at her, smiling at her. That would really be better, she thought. She would just tell her mother she fell in love with this neat guy. Her mother would understand "neat."

"But with the Spirit you knew I was telling you the truth, didn't you?"

"Yes."

"And it makes a lot of sense to rely on the Spirit in other matters as well. It simply helps us avoid mistakes and problems we might encounter along the way."

"You mean like going to war?" she asked.

"Like going to war," he answered. "You know, sometimes it's better—easier—to go to war than to avoid it. But it should be the Lord who makes the decisions."

"Well, I'd feel better about going to war if the Lord decided it was best. At least that would be better than Congress making the decision, or some president. But I'm still going to have to think about it a little. I just don't feel right about the whole thing."

"It must be your loving nature," he said.

She smiled at him. She felt comfortable believing he meant that as a compliment. But she could not feel comfortable believing there could ever be any reason or justification for one person to shed the blood of another person. Surely there had to be a better way.

MCLEAN, VA —

Kassim al-Jarwi felt secure in the safe house he had established in this secluded McLean neighborhood. He had looked there because of its proximity to the operational base of the American Central Intelligence Agency. His only concern had been the lack of alternate escape routes. Only one road led into the residential neighborhood. But the back fence did border a ravine which had been converted into a sylvan park. Should he have to flee he could walk through the complex system of underbrush, or he could ride a trail bike or even a motorcycle through the pathways lacing the public park. In some ways that was more acceptable than fleeing in a licensed vehicle. Anyone chasing him in a car would have to drive over a mile around the ravine to cut him off.

The house was well suited for his purposes. He had a large master bedroom on the main floor and there were six other bedrooms: one on the main floor with his own, three on the second floor and two in the basement. There was a large family room in the basement. The builders had conveniently added extra insulation to reduce the excessive noise children might make there.

While noise from children did not concern the terrorist, noise from his prisoners did. He had planned to bring the Moore girl here. But it had not been convenient that night. Fatima had suggested he might want to take his time interrogating the girl. She was right. But he couldn't make the transfer immediately. There had been some difficulties contacting his control in Paris. By the time he had returned from a different safe house, they had ransacked his apartment and had stolen both Maria and Fatima from him. His opportunity to bring the traitor to these more suitable environs was gone.

He had not made such a mistake with Sariah. He had brought her directly to this place. With the extra precautions he had taken to add more insulation to her room, he was certain no one had heard her screams. After all, the nearest neighbor was no closer than 250 feet away. With the dense growth of shrubs and trees in between, and with the bucket he had put over Sariah's head, the chance that anyone outside the room had heard anything at all was extremely slim.

Of course, there was nothing she knew that could help him. Her value to him had always been to carry the bottles of chemicals into the Capitol. It still was—if he could get her to turn. She had been a stubborn one. But still he had hopes that something he might do would cause her to change her mind. Of course, if he did much more to her, she might not be able to handle even the simplest of tasks—to carry the lightest of containers.

It was not his fault. That filthy Maria was to blame. If she had only followed instructions and turned the other contact they had—what was his name?—Nicholes, yes, Nephi Nicholes—nothing would have happened to Sariah. There would have been no need for her to be here.

He suspected from the beginning that Maria was not fully committed. Kurt Grundermann had recommended her. He said she would do anything for the man who was "nice" to her. But

Kassim knew now that Grundermann had been wrong. The signs had been obvious. He should have dropped her long ago. Anyone as reluctant as she had been to become a true believer could not be trusted. And he had seen other signs as well.

But he had not expected her to be turned so quickly by the very mark she had been sent to recruit. Recruiting him should not have been so hard. There was not even a need to tell the boy what he was doing. In fact, it would have been better to tell him nothing. They could have gotten him to carry the bottles inside as if it had been some kind of gift or for some reception. Before Nicholes would have known what he had done, the mission would have been accomplished.

Kassim's mind returned to the girl in the basement. What a pity. He never truly enjoyed torturing women—except, of course, those who betrayed him. To those who deserved such treatment, Kassim considered the experience to be something of a religious rite. As for this Sariah woman, she was beautiful. There had been moments when he had been tempted to let her escape to his bedroom—for an hour or so. Perhaps he still would. He had been careful not to damage anything that could be seen or that which might be useful to his own passions. That had proven to be the best policy in such cases.

What bothered him most was the time factor. Very little remained. In fact, there was little chance he could be in place with his bombs in the Capital—certainly not by the devilish U.N. deadline—and probably not by the time the United States committed its first act of aggression. Morning papers had reported preparations under way in Baghdad to protect citizens against air raids. Kassim knew President Hussein was waiting for a couple of days to show himself not a coward. Then there would be a true peace agenda.

He himself would need to follow Saddam's most honorable example of patience. He should not panic into a mistake—like rushing the bombing of the American Capitol building. Yes. It would be better to simply prepare a new plan. This time he would create a foolproof one he could execute without being forced to depend on others. Destroying the American Capitol certainly would have made a dramatic statement. It would have sent a message around the world that even the Great Satan, with all its defenses, and with all its money, could not prevent war from touching its people.

Had he succeeded with that plan, they would have been in a position to demand the withdrawal of foreign troops from the Middle East. Such a thing still could happen by hitting the most strategic objective at the right moment. He needed a target that would cause the whole world to fear the powerful forces of Islam. Islam with one leader—Saddam Hussein. Non-Arabian armies most certainly would be withdrawn from the Middle East. Attention could then be focused upon the Palestinian question in the most strategic way. A unified Islam would crush Israel and drive the intruders into the sea.

Truly, Saddam would become the great leader of all Islam—the Great Mahdi—the infallible, divinely guided one. Islam, under his leadership, would soon control most of the world's oil supply. Wealth and power would flow downward to the faithful. Kassim could, even now, visualize himself as one of the most faithful—one of the most favored—for greatness and respect.

Kassim knew there was to be a place for him inside the Palestine Liberation Organization. If only Hamza had finished his work. He had been planted inside the PLO as a bodyguard. But he had only managed to kill the traitorous Salah Khalaf and Hayel, the security chief. There were three others who had been targeted. With all of them gone, Yasser Arafat's organization would have been purged of traitors. And the chairman's dependence upon Saddam would have become complete.

Kassim knew a prime position in the newly structured organization awaited him. Because that incompetent fool, Hamza, had not been thorough, there still were several things that needed to be done in Tunisia—things which Baghdad would recognize to be of value. But he would need to finish his work here. That would place him in the perfect position to take care of matters in Tunisia.

Kassim pounded the table in front of him. He had had enough of depending on others and being let down by their weaknesses. There was no time for that now. He would undertake only those projects that he could control by himself. Little by little he would gain control over things elsewhere.

This was the first step. His former plan, to place a binary bomb in the Capitol, had depended too heavily on unreliable resources. He had hoped the operation would result in establishing a dependable, effective network of operatives within the decaying government of the United States.

Now he would work alone. There had always been an alternative. He had seen it when he had decided on using a gas device instead of an explosive device.

All he would have to do would be to target the largest possible gathering of people. They had to be influential in their own rights—political leaders, business and commercial leaders, social leaders. He had been inspired by Allah to collect a number of clippings from various papers. Each carried the report of a coming event where such leaders would be gathered. He shuffled through them one last time. One stood out from the rest. It would gather together the very people he wanted to be together for their final acts on earth.

It was to be a relief benefit for families of United States Air Force Reservists who had been called to active duty in the immoral war. Senators, congressmen, generals and many others would be attending. Even the vice president would attend.

Yes. He would strike when the vice president was in attendance. It was Friday night—well within Baghdad's projected timetable. And how ironic it would be for him to hit this particular target—a branch of the vaunted, but over-rated, American Air Force. As those poor, misguided airmen would be flying into the steel trap of the impenetrable air defenses in Iraq, these poor, misguided socialites would dance their way to oblivion at a gala.

The message would be heard around the world:

"The Great Satan is truly vulnerable to the cunning, brave, dedicated warriors of Islam!"

Yussef began searching for Sariah the moment she missed her date with him. His work with the FBI had taught him to doubt, distrust and question everything and everyone around him—even those for whom he worked. In less than an hour he had worked himself up to a state of frenzy. Sariah had been such a fresh element in his life. Now that they were betrothed, she had become his responsibility. She had become the first member of his own family. Honor bound him to protect her and provide for her as if she were already his wife. Beyond honor, his great love for her demanded that he find her. He would deal harshly with anyone who dared harm his beloved.

When evidence revealed that she had been abducted, he had allowed his emotions to make a fool of himself before his leader, Inspector Levant, as well as before his friends.

He would permit himself no more foolishness in this matter. He would find her. He would find Kassim. And if Kassim had touched his beloved, he would kill him.

He knew where three of al-Jarwi's safe houses were. And methodically he visited them, studied them and eventually determined the terrorist had not used them to hide Sariah. Discouragement increased with each disappointment—each failure to find his enemy and his beloved. There remained the one place for him to look. It was where he had lost track of al-Jarwi during those surveillances—that neighborhood in McLean. It seemed such an impossible task. But at least in knowing the general neighborhood he had something to work with. And he had to do something—anything.

He drove to the spot where he had lost al-Jarwi. The highway curved at this point causing him to lose sight of his enemy. When Yussef cleared the curve al-Jarwi's car could not be seen. Only one street led from the highway he had been traveling. Yussef had concluded al-Jarwi had turned off there. But this was not an ideal location for a safe house. Access was too limited. There simply were no escape routes. Al-Jarwi was not one to corner himself in such a way.

Yussef studied his map carefully. He drove down the sense of panic he felt rising within his heart. This was his only lead and it did not look all that promising. He decided to drive the neighborhood anyway—maps were known to be wrong. Maybe it was so this time. He would look for an escape route al-Jarwi might use. His first task was to skirt the area, turning every corner and probing into every cul-de-sac. Sadly he found the map had been correct. The only way in was the only way out. He would search it anyway. What else could he do?

Many impressive homes had been built there on large, well landscaped lots. He charted the area on a tablet of graph paper he had in his briefcase, marking the location of each house. In all, there were thirty-two homes.

Beginning at the entrance he parked to observe as many homes as possible. What he watched for was something that would give him a reason to strike a house from his chart. Anything that showed signs of normal life would not be a place where Kassim al-Jarwi would be found.

Tedium engendered frustration and it required every measure of discipline for Yussef to hold to his plan. Homes with children were marked off. Homes where he could see normal people were marked off. Those homes where he could see no activity were the ones he suspected. One by one he checked them and marked them off. By 3 a. m. only two possibilities remained.

He parked out of sight of the first and walked into the cul-de-sac. The yards were huge. A dog began to bark. He kept to the shrubs as best he could.

He studied the house and noted the garage and the back entrance. A light shone from the second floor. Probably a bathroom because it seemed so small. But the reflection of it could be seen shining down a stairwell. From what he could see, the house had been decorated by an artistic person for family living.

The last house showed no such evidence. The windows had been covered and taped. It was almost impossible to tell whether or not a light was on inside. He was startled when a motion detector switched on an exterior light. Yussef quickly ducked out of sight. Then he began to be fortunate. The light went on again when a neighborhood cat walked across the lawn. Yussef took this opportunity to dash to the corner of the attached garage. If Kassim had checked on why the light had gone on, he would have seen just a cat.

Within a few minutes, Yussef found and neutralized the sensor.

Yussef then looked for holes in the window coverings. He found one that let him peek into a room. Little furniture adorned the room, barely enough to accommodate the lone man seated at the small, desk-size table.

But the man turned out to be al-Jarwi. He was studying something. Plastic containers sat on the table and on the floor around him. He seemed to be testing the plastic. Yussef saw him pour a chemical onto a piece. A yellowish smoke rose from it and al-Jarwi waved his hand in front of him to clear the smell.

Shortly after that, al-Jarwi moved from view and the room's light went off.

But al-Jarwi did not leave the house.

Neither did Yussef. He figured al-Jarwi would be asleep in about an hour. There would still be time for Yussef to find a way inside to look around. That same hour could have been used by Yussef to call the FBI. They would arrest al-Jarwi and that would be that. It certainly was the safe thing to do.

But what if al-Jarwi decided to leave while Yussef was phoning? They would miss him and he would be lost to them. It would be harder—perhaps impossible—to find him. Then, if al-Jarwi tried to flee, they would try to capture him. If he managed to escape without being shot, he could ride away without punishment at all. These Americans placed more emphasis on the law than they did on justice. They might not try to stop him—or even try to shoot him. Yussef vowed he would never allow such an opportunity to be missed.

The most important thing Yussef considered was what if al-Jarwi had hidden Sariah somewhere else? What if he was killed. They never would be able to find her. She would surely die. He could not allow that.

It took the Kuwaiti nearly an hour to creep around the house and to try every door and every window. Nothing was open. But he had found a slim prospect. The molding appeared loose around one of the window panes in the basement door. He took out his Swiss military knife and dug at the molding. It came out rather easily. So also did the window. But he had lost precious time trying to avoid detection. He reached through the opening and felt for the lock system. There were three dead bolts in place.

In a few seconds he stepped inside and turned on his penlight. He had entered what had to have been a utility room.

Through the only other door he found a large room with a fireplace. It was bare except for a bicycle and a small motorcycle parked in the center of the room.

Of course, Yussef thought, al-Jarwi would use these for his escape—through the backyard into the park. He could steal a car on the other side of the ravine. Across the room there was a stairway to the first floor. Beside the stairs was a closed door that opened to a hallway. At the end of the hall he found a bedroom. The bath was between it and another room. There was a simple bolt on the door. He moved it as quietly as he could. The door pushed open without any squeaking.

Inside, his light first picked up the end of a bed. A naked woman rested upon it.

Sariah.

And she was still alive.

Instantly his relief gave way to rage. He said nothing, uttered no sound. He just took a deep breath and whirled around. He raced for the stairs, taking an automatic from his waistband. He would kill al-Jarwi for doing this to his beloved.

Yussef found what had to be the master bedroom. He leaned his shoulder against the door and burst inside. Immediately he heard a deafening explosion—and another. He felt something hit him in the shoulder. He felt the floor against his face before the third explosion came.

Then he felt nothing.

WASHINGTON, D.C. —

Yussef had not yet begun to search the neighborhood in McLean when Nephi and Elena drove across the 14th Street Bridge into the capitol city. Miraculously, Nephi found a place to park Roy's "clunker." With no Congressional parking sticker on it, he had to find parking on the street—a nearly impossible task at this time of day. After circling for half-an-hour, he felt fortunate they only had to walk three blocks to the Longworth Building.

Once inside, Nephi felt more secure. But in talking with Roy Ivars his feeling of security diminished. They had not heard from Yussef. The FBI had tracked down every lead. Kassim remained at large and Sariah probably was being held by him.

"You folks are in the very same position you were in yesterday," Roy observed. "It seems to me that you can do one of two things. Either you can go back into hiding so this guy al-Jarwi can't find you. That way you can keep on waiting for the law to catch up with him. Or you can do everything you can to track this bugger down and put him away."

"Kill him?" Maria asked.

"Not necessarily. There are many ways to put someone away. I would hope you could do everything within the law. I don't want to have to defend you on a murder rap."

"So you're saying we should help the FBI?" Nephi asked.

"That would be the best, most responsible thing you could do. But you probably know already that it could get dangerous. I know they do everything they can to keep citizens out of danger. But sometimes that's impossible. You should be aware of that."

Nephi sat back in one of the stuffed chairs in the Congressman's private office. They had come back here to help Yussef and Sariah. That's the decision they gave to Roy.

"Okay. Fair enough. I'll tell you what I'm willing to do," Roy said. "I'm going to hire Maria, put her on the staff. That way she will have some place to go during the day. And we can work out something to protect her at night."

"Can you do that? Hire her?" Nephi asked.

"Sure—with the Congressman's approval. Don't worry. He'll do it. We are a bit short-handed right now. Even if Sariah were here we would not be up to par. Maria's smart enough to answer the phones, write letters and all that fun stuff we do around here."

"I could do that," she agreed. Then she looked at Nephi. "It would be fun working in the same office with you."

Roy could see they had something brewing between them. He hadn't been asleep when he was a bishop. It was hard to tell if they had slipped over the edge or not. As a bishop he had been able to tell when teenagers in his ward had gone beyond the limit. A certain quality of innocence simply would be missing from their eyes and expression. But Maria actually looked more innocent today than she had when she left his apartment yesterday morning. This put him at ease.

One thing Roy did notice was the number of times Maria looked over at Nephi. It was clear she liked him. At other times he thought he could detect a look of panic in her eyes. Rightfully so. She had been through a lot. Apparently she had placed considerable trust in Nephi. But they both needed help. He felt strongly impressed to provide whatever support they might need.

"You look pretty good, Maria," Roy tried to change the subject. "You feeling all right? How's your cheek?"

"Thanks. I'm all right," she said. But underneath the pancake makeup, the bruised places on her face still throbbed a little with soreness.

"Good. Then you're ready to go to work?"

"Yes. Whenever you want."

CHAPTER 10

News Brief
Wednesday, January 16, 1991

BAGHDAD, IRAQ—Saddam Hussein defied the United Nations deadline for withdrawing Iraqi troops from Kuwait in a radio broadcast to his country.

"I will not bargain over Iraq's rights," he said while assuring his troops that the whole nation was ready to fight in this "jihad" or holy war against the infidel invaders.

Later, Baghdad radio issued air raid instructions to citizens.

WASHINGTON, D.C—With the U.N. deadline having passed at midnight, White House press secretary Marlin Fitzwater told reporters that the Bush administration remained hopeful, but added: "There is a growing sense that we have to carry out our plans for the use of force with some resignation."

Meanwhile, President Bush met with Secretary of State James A. Baker III and Defense Secretary Dick Cheney in the Oval Office.

A few protestors remained through the night, standing vigil outside the protective fence surrounding 1600 Pennsylvania Avenue, despite a cold, steady rain in Washington.

MOSCOW—President Mikhail S. Gorbachev today urged the legislature to take temporary control of the media and suspend the nation's press law.

Lawmakers objected and instead voted to create a committee that would look into ways of ensuring "media objectivity."

It is assumed the Gorbachev proposal was the result of a critical article about the weekend Soviet military crackdown in Lithuania.

BALLSTON, VA —

THEY SPENT A RESTFUL NIGHT AT ROY AND TINA IVARS PLACE. At least Nephi got a lot more sleep. The pressures and temptations of being alone with her, virtually in the same room with Eleña, had been too excruciating to ever want to endure again—until after they were married when everything would be different. With the Ivars around he could relax a bit. Now all he had to think about was keeping al-Jarwi from shoving them off that cliff.

The three of them drove into Washington together. The first call Nephi made from his work station in the office had to be to FBI headquarters.

"I'm glad you called," Levant said. "I believe we can use you. We've just located Yussef's car. It's out in McLean. Will you meet me there? If Yussef is anywhere near there I want you to talk some sense into him. He trusts you. And so do I."

MCLEAN, VA —

By the time Nephi could drive to the address Levant had given him, offical vehicles of all kinds crowded the area. Nephi noticed immediately the lights from two ambulances backed into the driveway.

He parked as best he could and talked his way into the area with his Congressional ID and his business card. What it really took was a gesture from Levant motioning Nephi through.

A paramedic reached Levant at the same time.

"Well, they're both alive. Barely. I have no idea how the man survived. He's lost more blood than he should have. There's no way of knowing how he'll come out. We started an I.V. and are filling him with plasma as fast as we can. When we get to the hospital we'll start him on whole blood. When he's stabilized they'll be able to operate.

"Good thing he fell on his wound. That may have put enough pressure on it to have slowed the flow of blood some. We'll see," he shrugged at the end of his brief report. Then he started up again.

"By the way. The girl's in bad shape. She had some pretty ugly things done to her body. If you shoot the guy that did this and you call me to haul him—remind me to drive slowly. Okay?"

Levant waved at him. He had no time for joking around. But then again, it wasn't a bad idea. A bit off the acceptable list of behavior for law enforcement officers but very tempting. A wounded terrorist like him—with diplomatic status —just might beat the rap. Levant decided he would hate to see such a thing happen.

"Thanks for coming. Looks like we don't need you at the moment," Levant told Nephi. "We found'em both."

"Yussef and Sariah? Are they all right?"

Levant shook his head. "Medics are in there with them right now. We won't know for awhile."

"They're really close friends. I've got to keep track of them."

"Sure," Levant responded.

"What happened?"

"Well, when I talked with you we still hadn't found them. I was hoping that when we did you could help us convince Yussef to break off his search. But al-Jarwi did more convincing than we needed. Yussef told us he tracked al-Jarwi to McLean but he wouldn't tell us where. We spent all night tightening the loop down to this neighborhood. Pure luck we found the house. After we found Yussef's car, the police finally told us about the domestic squabble."

"Domestic squabble?" Nephi asked.

"Yeh. The lady in that house over there thought she heard gun shots. She hates her new neighbor—thought he was weird the way he lived with all the windows sealed up and such."

"She had that right," Nephi agreed.

Levant smiled. "Anyway, she turned on all her exterior lights and in a few seconds she saw a car whip out of the garage."

"Al-Jarwi?"

"Most likely. The neighbor called 911. But that report got lost in the shuffle until after we found Yussef's car.

"We might have had him if they'd just given us that report earlier. At least we could have gotten the medics here quicker."

Nephi shook his head. "Will you keep us posted? I mean both Miss Moore and I are very nervous with al-Jarwi on the loose."

"Sure. We'll keep you informed. If we can't reach you, I guess we can call that man in your office."

"Roy Ivars."

"Yeah. He phoned and told me you were heading out of town. How come you came back?"

"We wanted to help find Sariah and Yussef."

"That was good of you. Thanks anyway."

Dalton approached Levant with a sheath of clear plastic envelopes. He greeted Nephi and began talking cautiously to his boss.

Levant stepped closer to Nephi and held out the mass of plastic pages.

"Dalton found these inside. You're on the Hill. What do you make of them?"

They were clippings of social events scheduled for the near future. He had seen most of them as they had been announced in the Washington papers—part of his daily routine was to look for articles which might be of interest to the Congressman or one of the issues with which he was involved.

"Well, I'm no professional. But as long as you asked, I'll tell you. I think he's looking for a target to bomb. It seems to me that the most important clipping you should be reading is probably not here. It's pretty clear by these clippings he's looking for some kind of major event like these as a likely place to set off his bomb."

"And you don't think the real target is in this stack?"

"No, sir. I don't. I think he probably left here in a big hurry. I don't think he'd leave any part of his plan behind."

"Okay. You got any idea how we could find out what his new target might be?"

"Well, if you could find the papers these came out of, you might be able to match these stories to the holes left in those pages. If you're left with any holes in the papers and you don't have a story to fit in them, then you just might have a prime lead."

Levant looked at the Congressional staff member.

"You ever consider a career in the FBI?"

"No, sir."

"There's no question he's been trying to bomb something. Those three bottles you sent in with Yussef and that woman, Fatima, were binary bombs. You know what a binary bomb is?" Levant asked Nephi.

"Sort of."

"They're chemical weapons. They are made up of two chemicals. Each chemical is harmless by itself. But when the two are mixed, they give off a lethal gas."

"Al-Jarwi wanted to carry them into the Capitol building, you know. I just thought they were soda pop."

"In the state they were when you saw them they were as harmless as soda pop. You had to twist the cap. That would have released a chemical to dissolve the plastic. The two chemicals would have mixed and then you would have had a problem."

"Good thing we weren't thirsty."

"You would have had less than ten minutes until you would never have been thirsty again."

Nephi shook his head.

"Now tell me all about when he wanted you to carry those bottles into the Capitol for him."

"Sure. It was Saturday. First he wanted to go on a tour of the Capitol. He wanted Sariah to take him on the tour. When she wasn't there, I volunteered."

"You volunteered?" Levant repeated trying to withhold a snicker.

"Yeah," Nephi said, raising his arms and shrugging his shoulders. "I didn't know. But I did think it was funny that he suddenly decided he had things to do when I told him they wouldn't let him carry those bottles into the building."

"You told him that?"

"Oh, yes. They don't let people carry bags into the Capitol. They're very strict about that."

"But you could."

Nephi shrugged. He had to agree. The Capitol police could not possibly search all the Congressional staff members as they moved around attending to business. "I told him either he could leave the bag there in the office or leave it with the officer at the door."

"Hah! And that was when he did the Blue Ridge Mountain Quickstep. Right?"

"Right. But now that I look back on it, you know, it was Maria who carried them in. I guess it was supposed to look proper, the woman carrying in the groceries. It should have been a tip off when they got out of that big limo with such a common thing as two liters of soda pop."

"Little out of character?"

"A lot out of character. But at least he didn't make her carry the bag when he left."

"He took it?"

"Yeah. He talked Maria into staying. She didn't seem to want to stay—at first. We didn't hit it off until after he left."

"So it was al-Jarwi's idea for her to stay. Right?"

"Yes."

"And then he left—with the bag?"

"Yes."

"And the next time you saw that same bag with those bottles was when Fatima carried it out of al-Jarwi's apartment. Right?"

"That's right."

Levant strolled around for a few minutes. He spoke briefly to someone on his radio. He walked around some more. When he made his way back to where Nephi was standing he seemed less worried than he was before he took the walk.

"I thought you just might like to know. They found a stash of old newspapers in a corner of the garage."

"You knew all along, didn't you? How come you asked me?"

"Thought you might have a different angle. As it was, I think we might have a very strong lead here."

"You ever consider a career in the FBI?" Nephi asked with a smile on his face.

"Once or twice," Levant said.

*   *   *   *

The first bulletins began moving through the television and radio stations in the Washington area around 2 p.m. They reported briefly that United Nations forces had launched air attacks against selected, strategic targets in Iraq and Kuwait shortly after dark.

The war had begun.

*   *   *   *

Kassim al-Jarwi first heard the bulletin while registering at a hotel in Crystal City, right across the Potomac from D.C. He had spent most of the day bouncing from safe house to safe house discovering only one to be safe. He barely left that third one when he noticed a string of cars and vans drive up. The antennas clustered on top gave them away. He looked back and watched a crowd of armed officers running around the house. Some wore body armor with huge letters "FBI" on them. Others wore caps with the same message.

"Fools," he had mumbled. "They are a step behind and they will be two steps behind before I am through."

Also he had spent some time driving to the chemist's facility in Rockville. But he had been fortunate enough to spot two cars there staking out the facility.

On his way back he had stopped to purchase supplies. He would modify the bombs himself.

He had decided on a hotel room in Crystal City because of its proximity to Washington. They would not think he would dare register in such a nice place, so close. He would not have thought to register in anything less expensive. He thought it good strategy to remain under their noses.

Now at the desk he was forced to listen to the Imperialists broadcasting lies about the war. Every word of it filled him with ire. It took extreme concentration to maintain his poise. He could not afford to break his cover. It was not until he reached his room and had dismissed the bellhop that he allowed himself to vent his feelings.

"Cowardly infidels! These Americans have no honor."

He paced the room several times. Then he sat and stared at the television for a time. It was unbelievable. The numbers they reported could not possibly be true.

A thousand sorties. Impossible.

Wait.

An accounting of losses had not been given. Of course. This would give a much more objective perspective for the world to see and contemplate when they reported the number of American casualties suffered at the hands of the superior anti-aircraft cover and the expertise of the Iraqi pilots. There would have to be from twenty percent to fifty percent losses by the Americans.

Yes. When the losses were reported. That would be when all would see how long and bloody this struggle would become.

His own efforts had become more important than ever now that the blood had started to flow. He became angry every time he thought how he had been prevented from being in place and prepared to act as he had been ordered to do. Curses on that filthy mongrel dog, Nephi Nicholes, for thwarting such carefully laid plans. And curses on that woman, Maria, for betraying the cause.

No matter.

Soon he would teach those dogs a lesson they never would forget.

*   *   *   *

Nephi heard the announcement over his car radio. Until the first plane had dropped that first bomb, or had fired that first rocket, there had been a chance for a peaceful settlement of this dispute. It had been a slim chance—diminishing day by day with every defiant statement by Saddam Hussein, and with unrelenting demands by the United States and her allies. But it had been a chance.

That was then. Now the action taken by military forces in the Persian Gulf had eliminated all vacillation, especially on Capitol Hill. Now there was one course. There would be victory or defeat. One side would taste one, the other side would have the alternative crammed down its throat.

Nephi sensed conflicting emotions. He felt relief from the uncertainties. President Bush's resolve relieved his concerns. This would not become another Vietnam. But he could not divorce from his mind the same anxieties that Eleña had been expressing all along. There would be much blood shed. Innocent people would be harmed—women and children. Some of the perpetrators might even escape justice from an angry world. In the end it would need to be the Lord who would sort out the mess created by greed and the passion for power.

"What do you think about your old man, now?" Roy Ivars asked Maria without looking away from the television monitor.

"I don't like war," she answered. "I know my father is directly involved in all this. And I'm proud of him for his commitment and achievements. At this very moment, I don't know exactly what to say about that—how to answer your question. A lot of people are being killed right now. I don't like thinking about that."

Her response sobered the excitement Roy had experienced when he first heard the news over C-Span. He had expected Maria to simply tell him she was very proud. What she did say revealed much more than he was prepared to face. Obviously, her feelings had been shaped over a long period of time. He wasn't sure what he should say or if he should say anything at all. In the short time he had known this girl, he had found her to be very bright—definitely above average in intelligence. He figured she would be articulate enough to give him a run for his money in an argument. But arguing wasn't the answer. There were no judges here. There would not be a winner. And it was most likely that a serious debate would leave them both as losers.

Still, he felt a need to say something. There was within his mind a thought he felt needed to be expressed. Unfortunately, it was taking its own sweet time giving shape to itself. Whatever it was, it was best not to reach for it until the most strategic moment came for him to say it. She would be ready to hear it then. In the meanwhile, stick with questions, he thought.

"Have you ever asked your father how he feels about war?"

"No. We've had a great many discussions about it—arguments, really. And when we discussed it, I guess I was more interested in convincing him that I was right than I was in listening to his point of view. I just assumed he was for it or else he wouldn't have made a career out of the military."

"I see," Roy responded thoughtfully. Her answer impressed him. It revealed that he was right about her. She was intelligent. Also, she showed maturity. Not bad. But assumptions can be wrong.

"Don't be too hard on your old man, Maria. I know he's just doing what he feels is important."

"I know. But why did he choose the military for a career,

anyway? I mean, he could have been a banker, a doctor, an attorney, anything he wanted to be. So why the military?"

"He loves to fly," Roy said automatically. "I can't remember anyone in our group who loved to fly more than he did."

"He could have been an airline pilot."

"It's not the same. Believe me."

"Maybe so, but while you're up there flying around, aren't you just practicing for the day when you can go to war?"

"Maria, I can't imagine any rational person who has been close to war, as your father has been and as I have been, being anxious to rush into another war. The whole idea is to keep strong enough, to keep well enough prepared so that you don't have to go to war.

"They choose generals partly because they know what they are doing. But they also want generals who are able to avoid war and who are able to avoid as many casualties as possible. Your dad fits into both of those categories. He's a very good man."

"I know that. I just wish he had chosen another profession. I mean maybe if he had to be in the military, maybe I would have liked it better if he had been some kind of foot soldier or something. I know he would never shoot someone he knew was innocent. But from thousands of feet up, you can't tell where those bombs are going."

This was something Roy had dealt with before. So many people believed pilots were without feeling because they did not actually see the enemy. What they didn't know was that the mind frequently enhanced reality, and quiet, reflective moments were filled with sounds and sights of the destruction they had carried to the target. With some people he would be simply callous and say things that would shock them—prove to them what they had previously believed. Such people generally lacked the awareness required to understand, no matter what he would have said. To this sensitive mind he would be more accurate. He had only expressed these feelings to his wife and closest friends during very private moments. It had helped to bind his wife and him together. She was able to help his wounds to heal. Similarly, the bond between him and his real friends had fused with purpose.

"You know, Maria, when you approach your target, all you can think of is getting yourself lined up perfectly. You begin thinking of speed, of wind direction and of every possible thing that might interfere with succeeding in your mission. Right up to the last second you worry about drifting off course the slightest bit. Then when you hit that release and drop your load, the first thing you think about is whether your bombs will hit the target—whether you calculated every angle. Then you look back and when they explode, you can't help wonder for a split second what else you might have hit. But you force those thoughts from your mind. It's not easy. You just have to. Otherwise you can't do the rest of what you need to do in order to survive. If you begin worrying about those kinds of things, you can't make it through the flack or past the interceptors they throw at you. Only those thoughts don't entirely go away. You carry them with you right up to the time you look at the recon photos.

"If you hit the target, you let yourself off the hook. If you missed, they flood back into your mind. Just what did I hit? Who else did I kill? Why did they have to be there in the first place? Why didn't I see my mistake? Why am I so stupid? Sometimes it takes days to get rid of them. Sometimes you never get rid of them. But you still have to do your job. You have to put them behind you, force them down. You don't have time for them. You can't afford them. They'll kill you. And besides your own driving need to survive, there's something more. You still have your duty."

"Yes, but what makes your duty so important? I mean, if you made one mistake, wouldn't you be afraid you'd make another?"

"Sure. No question about it. But duty is real. There are responsibilities to be dealt with. I must admit there were times I almost refused to fly a mission. But I never did. You just can't refuse. Sometimes it takes the greatest courage to defeat your own fears. And the only way around all that is to keep control of yourself— hone your skills so you can fly better—become better at your job."

"What—at killing people?"

"No, Maria. The purpose of an air strike is to reduce the enemy's ability to make war—to destroy his equipment. Also it's meant to reduce the enemy's desire to resist. Now there are bound to be people killed doing that. But if I can reduce the will of an army to fight, then that's going to save lives—on both sides, but especially on ours.

"Try to keep in mind that the only reason you go to war in the first place is because people stop talking with the other side. War is simply the extension of diplomatic endeavors, by other means. If diplomacy always would work, there would be no need for war. But there are some people who simply won't negotiate. Petty tyrants, puffed up in their own self-importance. It's obvious that Saddam Hussein is that kind of leader."

"Well, how come we aren't negotiating with Saddam now? I mean, it didn't seem like we gave him a chance in all this."

"But we did. Aren't you aware that they've been negotiating with that man for about a year? He just stopped negotiating and stormed into Kuwait. He was the one to call off negotiations."

"I didn't know that."

"Unfortunately, we have to go to war over there to protect our interests. And I really believe we can do it without too much loss to our side. From what I gather, they're going to rely heavily on air strikes before sending anyone in on the ground. That means they're going to be depending a lot on your dad and men like him to get this war over quickly."

"I certainly hope so," she admitted. She was tired. She had been so much against war for such a long period of time. It saddened her to think of the suffering ahead—for both sides.

Then she thought about what Nephi had said. War had existed since before the earth was created? How sad. How terrible that people would be willing to kill and to die for anything. She had become so weary of fighting against war. It was the one issue that made sense in Germany and it made sense to her now. It was like no one seemed to understand. No one seemed to care. Her father, Roy Ivars, and even Nephi, to a certain extent—they all seemed to justify war as an acceptable thing. Nephi did seem to hold a limited point of view. He thought war was justified if it was to protect his family and way of life.

"Exactly when is it okay to go to war?" she asked bluntly.

"To protect yourself, your family, your country, your way of life, your religion—those kind of things," he said. "It gets kind of complicated in a case like this when the threat does not look like so much of a threat as it might appear to be special protection for an industry. But, believe me, if Saddam Hussein is allowed to take control of the majority of the world's oil reserves, then it will have a very direct bearing on our way of life from that moment on. We just cannot afford such a situation. It would ruin us."

She didn't ask any more questions. She just stared at the T.V. screen and the scenes of war, though not really seeing or hearing anything.

When Nephi arrived, he simply sat down beside Maria and watched too.

It was around 6 p.m. when Tina Ivars walked into the office. She had called earlier and had asked her husband to wait for her. She joined the group, but her attention span wasn't as long as the others. Her thoughts moved naturally to the practical.

"When do you want to eat?" she asked her husband in a voice loud enough that the others could hear.

"Come to think of it, I am hungry. Any time."

"You want to eat out or go home?"

"If we go home we can watch T.V.," Roy observed.

"You want to come with us?" Tina asked Maria and Nephi.

They looked at each other and agreed. Maria still was afraid of being alone, and Nephi was still afraid of being alone—with her.

"We'll have to stop at the market," Tina announced. "And as long as we are there we can pick up anything you would like to eat."

Just before they left there was a call for Nephi from Levant.

"You know anything about a benefit on Friday for the families of the United States Air Force Reserve?" the FBI man asked.

"No. I don't. Just a second," Nephi held his hand over the mouthpiece and asked Roy if he had heard of the benefit.

"Just a second," he said. And he shuffled through a pile of papers on Maria's desk. He had put them in the place where the scheduler would handle the requests for appointments and the invitations. "Here it is. Big bucks. For a worthy cause. Friday night at the International Plaza Hotel. A hundred and fifty bucks per person. Buffet. Vice president's coming. Sounds like a worthy cause."

"Yes, we know about it," Nephi finally responded. "The Congressman has an invitation to it."

"Good. Stay away from there."

"Is that the one you were looking for?"

"That's the one. The only one. It's a good lead. And I'm betting on it."

"Sounds reasonable. And we'll stay away. I can't afford that kind of money anyway."

"We'll nail him there. I've already got men on it."

"Thanks."

*   *   *   *

Kassim had left his hotel room shortly after he had checked in. He could not deal with the one-sided television reports that were being aired by the biased American press. Watching those retired generals guess about the war strategy had been interesting at first. But there were so many flaws in their thinking that it was impossible to maintain his objectivity. They did not account for the great military strategies that had held off Iran's massive army. Nor did they take into account the tough discipline of the Iraqi people.

There had been no conscious plan to leave the room then, but someone came on camera with a report of the losses experienced by the United Nations forces during the first wave of air attacks. It was too impossible for him to cope with. How could the American people believe such lies? Two planes lost. Only two. Out of a thousand sorties flown? How could that be? The anti-aircraft defenses that he knew were in place around Baghdad and other cities, and especially around military installations, were impenetrable. The world had seen how thick it was when those cursed reporters showed pictures of Baghdad. How could anyone fly through that and survive? They could not, of course. The American military was lying. Iraqi estimates of fourteen enemy planes downed had to be conservative reports. How could anyone believe only two allied planes had been destroyed?

He stomped out of his room and slammed the door. He had no idea where he was going. But he had to go somewhere. He had to deal some kind of blow against an enemy. He would decide which enemy on the way.

He carried with him his most trusted weapon—his Uzzi. It was small enough to fit in his athletic bag. And he had enough ammunition to answer any situation.

By the time he had walked to a nearby car rental agency, he had cooled enough to think about what he was doing. The motivation had not left him. He still wanted to kill someone—to hurt someone. He wished that he still had one of his prisoners to deal with. They would have been the perfect outlet for his ire against the Great Satan. He would have to settle for someone else.

He opted for a high performance car from the agency. He tested it in driving away. There was no need for him to worry about having it traced back to him. He had several sets of identification cards. This car had been rented to one Enrique Goméz. The cost of it had even been put on Mr. Goméz's credit card. The agency was not concerned. Mr. Goméz had opted for full insurance on the vehicle. It had been a profitable deal for them.

But the man who had called himself Goméz was mumbling to himself in Arabic rather than in Spanish as he drove away.

"I will find that traitor, Maria Moore. And I will deal with her as I should have done in the first place. And also the pig whose sty she now wallows in."

Kassim had no difficulty finding a parking place near the House office buildings at that time of night. He walked quickly to the entrance and entered, using the Goméz ID again. He walked to the office of Congressman Hersch and found the door open. Inside was the girl. He could see her. And she sat next to the Nicholes man. How fortunate, he thought. He had expected to find her only after making a covert inquiry about her whereabouts. But she was there. He would only have to follow her and he would have her.

It would be a bit tricky. He would have to be very careful— apply every skill. Otherwise he would lose her. Standing at the door he heard them planning to go somewhere together—a foursome. So much the better. The blood of four spilled for the cause of Allah. The man Nephi would be taking Maria in a car owned by one of the others. That car was parked on the street, not in the garage.

Kassim walked away from the door when he was certain they were coming. He pretended to enter another office as the four came out. They closed and locked the door and began walking toward him. He had to step inside the next office.

No one was there. But someone soon came.

"May I help you?" the young woman asked.

"Thank you. Is this Congressman Hersch's office?"

"I'm sorry, it's not. His office is two doors down. Same side of the hall. You can't miss it."

The terrorist smiled at the receptionist and opened the door far enough to notice that the foursome had passed his hiding place and were walking away from him.

"Thank you for your trouble."

"No trouble at all," the woman said.

If he lost the others, he just might come back for this one, al-Jarwi thought to himself. He had not brought his weapon. They would have confiscated it at the door and arrested him. But he knew many other ways to kill. That would not be necessary, he assured himself. He would do everything he could to maintain contact with his primary target. He smiled at his secondary target and stepped into the hall to follow his marks. They had gone beyond the corner. He hurried so he wouldn't lose them. He stood at the top of the stairwell and listened to them as they descended ahead of him. They were splitting up.

"You sure you won't come with us, Maria?" said the voice of the man who owned the car Nicholes was to drive.

"No, thank you. I wouldn't want to crowd you," Maria's voice answered.

"Why am I not surprised?" came the voice of the other woman. Then he heard laughter.

"Meet you at the C Street entrance to my parking garage," that new voice said. "You sure you know where Tina left the car?"

"Sure do," he heard Nicholes' voice respond.

Al-Jarwi moved carefully down the stairs and followed the couple out the door. They were heading down the street where his own car was parked. This was almost too easy. Even so, if he lost them he would be able to pick them up again at the entrance to the other man's garage.

But he didn't lose them. It was easy to follow them. They were novices at all this. So was the man in the other car. He followed the two Mercedes onto the freeway and down I-395 to King Street where they got off. For a second he lost them but found them quickly enough to know they were heading into a major shopping center. Stores had been built around a large parking lot. Al-Jarwi followed them toward the far end. He watched them park and walk toward the Giant Market.

The store's street approach and entrance faced south. The market occupied the entire end of the U-shaped shopping center. Al-Jarwi positioned his car in the fire lane on the east end of the approach. From this place he could see the entrance. And he would be in the best position to follow. If the chance presented itself he was in a position to run them down. Yes. If he could do that, he would be able to save his ammunition for another time.

He tested his engine. It had a lively sound. He could depend on it.

Inside the market the biggest problem the four of them had was deciding what they wanted to eat. First they decided to keep the meal simple so it would not interfere with watching newscasts of the war. But by the time they finished making their selections from the extensive deli counter, nothing remained of the simplicity rule. They compensated for having fractured the first rule by deciding to use paper plates and serve a buffet style supper.

The shopping cart ended up filled with delicacies and picnic supplies. A round of teasing began soon after they checked out. They all contributed jibes as if they had been friends for years. The Ivars were just that kind of people. They enjoyed life and made sure their family and friends did also.

There absolutely was no reason to expect anything other than a pleasant evening together.

They did not hear the roar of the engine and the squealing tires until they were in the middle of the street. Each face turned instantly toward the ominous sound. Each saw the car racing toward them.

Roy moved first. He had been pushing the shopping cart. He just whirled it and shoved it directly at the car. Then he shoved Nephi in one direction before yanking Tina toward him and falling away, toward the store's entrance.

Nephi froze at the sound and sight of the car's motion—until he felt Roy's hand in the middle of his back. It was the right thing to do—the right way to go. But he rushed Eleña too quickly and the two of them tripped over each other. On the ground the only thing he could do was to continue rolling away. As best he could, he rolled on his arms so he would not squash her. Then he dragged her over his own body to safety.

Kassim al-Jarwi looked back for just a second. He knew he had hit something. There had been a flurry of arms and bodies moving in front of him just as the impact occurred. Now he could see the four of them on the ground—two of them still rolling.

The car was running. It hadn't been damaged enough to abandon it. He would escape without any trouble. The attack had been successful.

He smiled, satisfied with his work.

CHAPTER 11

NEAR BAILEYS CROSSROADS, VA —

NEPHI HEARD THE CAR'S SOUND FADING AND REALIZED HE was holding Eleña as tightly as he could. He relaxed so his arms would allow her to breathe. It didn't matter. She had locked onto him with equal intensity, and she wasn't breathing anyway. He wanted to see if she was hurt but she wouldn't let go of him. Her face was forced into the corner of his neck and shoulder. Then she started sobbing. It grew into a near hysterical pattern. Her hands moved—one at a time, not completely allowing her grip on him to disengage.

"It's all right," he spoke quietly to her, smoothing her hair and gently rubbing the back of her shoulder. "It's all right."

He could feel her face nodding up and down. And she loosened her grip on him slightly. But when he moved to try and get up, she reacted by drawing him closer to her.

"I'm just going to get up," he said.

"Stay right there. Hold still," ordered a man's voice from above them. "You should not move until we know you're all right. Stay right there."

"I'm all right," Nephi argued. "I need to get up. I've got to make a phone call."

He had to rise upwards through a few bodies that were bent over them from curiosity. Some in the crowd truly wanted to help. Most were there just to gawk.

"I still think you should stay down," the first man continued. "You could have broken something."

"Nothing's broken. I'm all right. You all right, Eleña?" he spoke softly to her.

She nodded again. "I'll be all right," her voice came with the trembling quality of a person nearly in shock.

"Roy," Nephi shouted. "You all right? Tina?"

"Doing fine," Roy yelled back. "Just scratched a little and a bruised ego."

The manager pressed through the crowd. He held a clipboard and waved it in the air.

"Give them room there," he shouted. "I've already called the police. And the ambulance is on its way. Stay calm everybody. And for goodness sakes, give them room."

The manager saw Nephi help Eleña sit up. She seemed to be all right. A miracle. All of them were all right. Praise the Lord, he muttered. Since they were all moving and all appeared to be unharmed by the incident, there was little reason to worry about liability. Maybe they wouldn't need the ambulance. Maybe that's what one of the victims was doing—calling off the ambulance.

Actually, Nephi had a different kind of call to make. It was to the FBI. Levant needed to know about this.

Crazy kids, the store manager thought. Give a kid a big car and look what he does. The manager quickly assessed what he had done to prevent such foolish accidents. Speed bumps had been in place for years. No one had ever defied them before. The driver must have been crazy to do a thing like this. It was the driver who would be accountable for this. Not the store.

But what a mess it had caused. Their whole order, mostly deli food at that, was scattered all over the entrance. The shopping cart was bent and twisted in a grotesque way. He was still assessing the situation when one of his box boys rushed over.

"I got his license number," the young man told his boss in an excited, breathless voice. "I ran after him. But he didn't stop. He just kept going west on King Street. I was too far back to watch if he turned. I'm sorry."

He handed his boss the slip of paper on which he had written the license plate number. The manager praised his employee and then ordered him to clean up the mess.

"Oh," the manager thought afterwards. "Locate the sales slip and duplicate everything on it. Get that right out here as fast as you can."

"Yes, sir," the box boy yelled, not certain what his boss wanted him to do first. It didn't take him long to decide. He would look first for the sales slip. That would give him an excuse to be busy refilling the order. While he was doing that, maybe the boss would tell someone else to clean up the mess.

The patrol car arrived before the first ambulance. The two officers made the victims sit on a bench just outside the main door. One officer knelt in front of them and began taking information from them. The other officer scanned the area for evidence. Also, he began taking statements from those willing to admit having seen the incident.

The ambulance came shortly before Levant got there. The paramedics began with the women. That gave the FBI man time to speak with Nephi.

"You're sure it was al-Jarwi?"

"I only saw him for a second. But, yes, it was al-Jarwi."

On the agent's order, the senior officer requested a make on the license plate. Following up on the number, the officer found the car had been rented by one Enrique Goméz from Albuquerque, New Mexico.

A fast check on the suspect's New Mexico drivers license had proved it to be fake. The credit card probably was too. While it was a debit card with plenty of money in the account, there was no way to trace the owner. Levant had proof enough that Goméz was phony.

The agent spoke with Maria next. She hadn't seen anything but the car's grill. All Tina saw was Nephi and Maria falling in the other direction. Roy was too busy to notice who was driving.

Descriptions of the driver by witnesses differed significantly. There was nothing to tie al-Jarwi to the incident. On the other hand, there was no real evidence to exonerate him from it either.

Levant looked at the four of them and shook his head.

"Do you realize how lucky you are?"

Nephi and Maria had more reason to understand their good fortune. They had been extremely close to the edge of that cliff. "I want that man and I want him now!" the supervising agent spat out as he walked away from them. "I don't want to wait until Friday. I want him now!"

He could do nothing to accelerate al-Jarwi's capture. The terrorist had severed every existing tie he had made in the United States—except for the benefit on Friday and this act of coming after Nephi Nicholes and Maria Moore. They were his only links to the cowardly assassin. They obviously had become targets—for revenge or something that only the guy's twisted Arabian mind understood. For the moment they were safe. He would have to protect them until they caught al-Jarwi.

But these people were in no greater jeopardy than the hundreds who were hoping to attend the benefit and enjoy the social event. Levant had encouraged his superiors to order the benefit called off. But his suggestion had been denied. They would gamble on catching this guy ahead of time or in the act. Calling off the benefit would tip off the terrorist. Then they would have had to start from scratch to figure out what he would do.

Also, leadership in the Justice Department simply did not want to appear as if they were giving in to terrorist demands or threats. President Bush had set the standard. He would not be held hostage in the White House. The rest of the administration had sought their own ways to follow his lead.

That only makes my job tougher, Levant thought to himself. More than ever he wanted this killer. He had become a threat to some nice people as well as to a crowd of people who would be gathering to honor some real heroes. They deserved to have a safe place to conduct their benefit. He would see to that.

And he would see to it that these people were kept out of danger.

"I'm putting a twenty-four-hour net around you," he announced to the foursome. "I want you to follow their instructions to the letter, do you understand?"

The four willingly responded to the affirmative—although Roy felt a bit contrary. As an attorney he didn't like taking orders from a police agency. He had been under fire before. He knew the terror of it. Now was not a good time to abandon caution. He just didn't like being hemmed in. Even so, he agreed. Tina's safety meant enough for him to agree.

"The only other place I really want to go is to the hospital to visit Yussef and Sariah," Nephi said.

Levant looked intently at the young man. He tried to stare the man down. But the young man kept looking at him with those eyes. How innocent they were. Nicholes would not be good at this business. There was trust in those eyes. Too much trust to be effective as a lawman. Levant had every reason to deny the request. But he could not.

"Okay. But not until tomorrow when it's light and when we can protect you with more agents. You don't try to go alone, okay—anywhere."

"Fair enough," Nephi said.

The accident had drawn the attention of a huge crowd. The longer the police stayed the bigger the crowd got. Some thought it had been an armed robbery. While the ambulances remained, curiosity held at its peak. Clerks and customers from both sides of the massive shopping center swarmed around. By the time the FBI had arrived, someone significant had become part of the crowd. He was a tall man with dark hair and lightly tanned skin. He carried an athletic bag.

Kassim al-Jarwi had driven away and when he realized no one had followed him, he had parked the car. He would not need it. It would be the fictitious Enrique Goméz who would have to answer for the accident and for the default of contract.

What the terrorist saw from his vantage point in the crowd rekindled the ire that had once swelled within him. He had missed. He had missed terribly. How could he have missed? He had the angle on them. There had been no escape for them. He had felt something hit the car. And whatever he hit had severely damaged the front end. Blood had splattered over the front of the car. At least it looked like blood. He had never been so certain of having killed someone as he had been when he hit them. But he had missed them.

He would not miss again. He hefted his gym bag to assure himself he was still in business. They would not escape again. At least two would not. His two.

He was without wheels now. He had to watch the four of them leave. Only instead of leaving in two cars as they had come, there were three cars that left in caravan. He needed to know where they were going.

The box boy knew. He seemed to know everything. And the manager cooperated too. With a story of having found the athletic bag that had been dropped by one of the victims, the manager simply allowed the good Samaritan to take down all the names and addresses from his clipboard.

BALLSTON, VA —

In the Ivars' apartment, Levant made a series of phone calls. Methodically he organized the 24-hour security rotation. When he wasn't talking on the phone, he studied the apartment thoroughly. He checked both entrances. He checked the windows and where someone would have to be to see in—or shoot in.

"I'd keep those drapes closed. And don't stand between the window and any light source," he ordered.

As he passed the dining room table he casually latched onto some chips.

"Sorry," he said when he realized what he had done.

"No, no," Tina Ivars responded instantly out of years of being a mother and hostess to friends. "Help yourself. There's plenty."

"Thank you. But I really have to go. I need to check out what access you have in and out of here. Maybe some other time."

And he left.

In spite of Tina's urging, none of them really ate the food. They picked at it and drank the juices that Tina had mixed with a little ginger ale. But the food had lost its appeal.

Maria sat extra close to Nephi. Tina noticed that. She took it as a sure sign of romance. Maria would not have argued.

Nephi had become to her a symbol of security. He had saved her life. He had shown her—proven to her—that their relationship had a very special meaning. He had been kind to her. He had shown her respect. He had shared and had survived an attempt on their lives. But most importantly, there had developed within her a strong emotional attachment to him. That part of it began somewhere during the tour of the Capitol. But every contact she had made with him had added to her feelings. Even their discussions and disagreements had become a kind of evidence to her that she loved him. She had turned away from others who may have disagreed with her. But she had not been willing to allow any such trivia to interfere with her relationship with Nephi.

She wanted things to settle down. She wanted an apartment like this—or a home of their own. But it had to be like this—like the Ivars' home. Oh, she didn't mean *exactly* like it. She didn't mean a place with so many pictures, mementoes and memorabilia. It would take a lifetime to collect the right items to decorate their own place. But she did want a quiet, lived-in haven where the two of them could share their days and show others how to live in love and peace.

While the others watched developments in the Persian Gulf, Maria Elefia considered things that not even the war could impede. She knew they would marry. She knew there would be a home—this kind of home. She knew there would be children. She knew there would be love. And she knew all this would mature in her life in a way she had previously considered impossible.

Never before had she considered the remarkable potentials involved with sharing life. So much of her life—all of her life— had been centered upon herself. She had accepted what her parents provided without consideration for cost or responsibility. In time she wanted more than what they believed she should have and she had rebelled against them—against everything she had once held dear to her heart.

She shuddered and drew Nephi's arm closer to her, clinging more surely to his strength. She didn't like the person she had been a few days ago. She knew the residual of that person still lurked within her. But since meeting Nephi, it was almost as if that person had lived in a different world, in a different time. That life had become so opposite to the life she envisioned for herself right now, this very minute. She didn't like that other person in that other life. That person was not her. She was someone else. She was better than that person—yes, better—much better. So many times she had accused others of judging. Now she had made the judgment. It was final and irrevocable. And she had found peace, of sorts, in having made it.

But what had Nephi said? It had come in such a casual way she hardly had noticed it. She would have to repent. She would have to ask the Lord to forgive her. Okay. She was ready. Whatever it took. She was ready to begin her new life—to reach for her new dream—to find the peace she had been searching for all this time.

Funny. That other girl had thought that by being closest to the front of the peace demonstrations peace could be established.

But now she knew that girl had been dead wrong. Peace was found in the soul—it was right here, with him.

And it didn't matter what happened anywhere else. There would be peace in her world.

The first agent to knock on the Ivars' front door introduced himself as Howard Dalton. Levant had sent him because Nephi knew him and he wanted no problem of mistaken identity messing up the project. Dalton went over the same routine as his boss had done. But he willingly shared the buffet. It was easy to talk him into it. He was hungry. He was likely to be on duty for a long while. He liked being treated as a guest rather than an officer of the law. Still, he kept his professional attitude on alert.

Shortly after he had finished, he settled down to watch the progress of the war. There had been one knock at the door. It had been the home teachers. Roy explained that Mormons kept track of each other and helped each other through home teaching.

"Somehow I just don't think Brother Johnson and his companion would be able to provide much of the help we need," Roy observed of the good-hearted brethren who had come for a brief visit. Brother Johnson was a retired postal worker—an executive who once assisted in organizing work flow in various branches around the country.

Brother Johnson and Brother May had to prove to Dalton they were no threat. When the doorbell had rung, the agent jumped out of his chair and took the position he had pre-determined would offer the most strategic cover. Without knowing the harmless nature of the visitors or their purpose, the agent held tightly onto the handle of his automatic. It was partly drawn in case of any foul play.

Just before the home teachers left, Nephi began feeling edgy. He noticed the time—about 9:30. There was something he had to do, but he couldn't think what it was. Right after the home teachers excused themselves, so also did Nephi. He went to his room, made a short inquiry and anxiously sought an answer. He wanted to know what he should do. What rose in his mind was the idea he had to visit the hospital—now.

Yussef and Sariah.

That's right. He rushed to the phone. The nurse informed him that they were in critical condition but still alive. He was surprised to hear that Yussef with his gunshot wound was more likely to pull through than Sariah. They wondered if Sariah would even make it through the night.

The news shocked him. He had to get to the hospital—as soon as possible.

"What's wrong?" Elefia asked, concerned about the strange look on Nephi's face.

"I've got to go to the hospital."

"Why?"

"They said that Sariah might not make it through the night. I've got to go!"

She searched his eyes and detected a certain wildness. She had never seen him like this. It frightened her. But she could understand his concern. Had he looked this way when he was coming for her? To help her? How could she deny him this feeling?

"I'm coming with you."

He started to object but saw in her eyes that it would do no good.

"We're going to the hospital," he announced to Agent Dalton.

"What?"

"We're going to the hospital. Levant said I could go to the

hospital and visit Yussef and Sariah," Nephi said, not telling the full truth.

"You're out of your mind. You can't go out there. Someone's trying to kill you."

"Levant said I could go if I took someone."

"He didn't say anything like that to me." Dalton said. His briefing had been brief—but not that brief.

"But he *did* say I could go, just not to go out alone."

"Okay, he did tell you that. But it would be stupid to go out tonight. If al-Jarwi's out there, he'd eat us alive. You can go only *if* we have plenty of backup."

Nephi shrugged and waved his hands.

Agent Dalton reached for the phone and dialed his office. In a guarded way he engaged in a vigorous conversation with someone.

"There's only one guy in the office," Dalton explained. "He can't come for at least twenty minutes. I'm calling the Arlington Police. If they can't help—you're not going. Do you understand?"

Nephi nodded. But under his breath he told Eleña that he had to go to the hospital "with or without Agent Dalton."

"Do you really think that's a good idea?" Eleña gripped his arm and looked into his face. She could not hide the fear and concern she felt. But she knew she would not stop him if he felt so strongly about going. She had come to trust his impressions.

"I've got to," Nephi told her again. The power that had grown within his bosom had provoked him to considering actions outside the nature of his character. Obedience, he thought. He would obey his instructions, hesitating only to wait for his "keeper." But he wouldn't—couldn't wait too long.

Dalton looked back at the couple standing beside the front door. He wanted to order them away from the door, but he didn't want to sound too harsh. This was crazy. Why would Levant approve going to the hospital at this time of night? In the morning? Okay. There would be at least three agents on duty then. That would be enough to provide cover. But this was ridiculous.

"Hello," he yelled into the mouthpiece. Then he muttered an obscenity against all desk clerks. "Hello, Lieutenant? This is Agent Dalton, FBI. I'd like to request some backup tonight."

Nephi looked at the agent. Obviously Dalton was having trouble. And Nephi could imagine the agent overriding his personal desire in order to follow what he felt were his instructions. He would have to circumvent the system, he thought.

With as little movement as possible he slipped through the front door. Elefia slipped out behind him. They rushed down the hall to the stairway and headed toward the lobby.

"Oh, Jeeze!" Dalton exclaimed when he noticed the couple had vanished from the apartment. "Look, Lieutenant, I appreciate the problems you're having, but this is an emergency. The two people I'm here to protect just left the apartment. Do what you have to do to verify my status. But get someone over here right away. I need you as soon as you can get here. No more than five minutes—okay?"

He slammed down the phone and tore through the entrance after the couple. He hit the elevator button and anxiously waited for the unit to open.

"They're going to get killed," he mumbled, wondering if it would be faster to ignore the elevator and head down the stairs.

Nephi led Elefia down the flights of stairs. The physical exertion brought into his soul a new feeling. "What are you doing?" rose in his mind. But the power of the anxiety he had sensed in the apartment caused him to deny the safeguards he had learned to use when dealing with spiritual matters. Besides, there wasn't time to wait for confirmations. Dalton would be angry and would deny them their opportunity to visit Yussef and Sariah.

Nephi and Elefia were walking out the front door when Dalton's elevator finally opened onto the first floor.

"Wait! Stop!" he shouted, sprinting toward them. "Get back inside!"

Kassim raised his hands slightly from the driver's wheel in front of him when he saw his two targets coming out of the building unescorted. He could not believe what he was witnessing. Allah was being good to him this night. He would have his revenge. Now he would strike his first blow against the American infidel intruders. He slid back the Uzzi's bolt and allowed it to slam closed. The first shell was in place. He made sure the safety was off.

He began firing just as a third American stepped out onto the steps with Nephi and Eleña.

They fell. He knew he had hit one of them. Blood had stained the wall. But he was not going to be deceived this time. He would not leave until they were all dead. He started his newly rented car and moved in for the sure kill.

The first explosions sprayed bullets around the entrance to the apartment building. Agent Dalton yelled for them to get down.

He had drawn his automatic before he was hit. Falling to the sidewalk caused him to lose consciousness.

Nephi had grabbed Eleña and forced her to the ground, hiding behind a huge cement urn planter. He raised up to peek over the planter and saw the car coming. He pressed on Eleña's shoulders to keep her out of the way.

The terrorist moved closer. He had noticed the third man reaching under his coat as if to take out a gun. But that man no longer moved. His first burst obviously had taken him out. But what of the other two—the most important targets? There was someone looking over the edge of that planter.

He quickly stopped the slowly rolling sedan and pointed his Uzzi at the planter. He emptied his clip in and around it. It took him but a second to change the clip. He had two bound together. All he had to do was reverse them.

Then he emptied the new clip, firing toward the planter again.

The second burst peppered the cement around them. Nephi knew they could not be hurt by direct fire. But he worried about ricocheting bullets and glass falling from behind.

"Stay down," he urged Elefia.

But Elefia didn't need to be urged. She held her face flat against the pavement. When the second burst stopped she opened her eyes. It was then she saw Dalton's automatic almost under her face.

Then the third burst came. It was longer than either of the first two. And as it continued, emotions rose within her.

The second it was over, she raised up. She had hold of the automatic. She knew how to use it. Her father had taught her many years ago. She held the automatic with two hands in front of her, aiming at the car—her elbows locked comfortably. "You stay away from us!" she shouted. "You stay away from my husband and my home!" she continued.

And she saw it was al-Jarwi driving the car.

She didn't wait any longer. She didn't sight down the barrel. And she didn't remember what her father tried to teach her about keeping her eyes open. Instead, she remembered there would be noise—horrible noise. She squinted against that noise, forcing her eyes tightly closed. But she did remember to squeeze, not jerk, the trigger. And although the automatic jumped with each shot, she managed to fire each round in the general direction of the car and that ugly man.

She kept firing until her clip was empty.

When she opened her eyes, she found the car was gone.

And for a second the thought slipped into her mind—"What else did I hit?"

She slowly lowered the smoking weapon and a very surprised Nephi Nicholes put his arm around her and gently took the empty gun from her trembling hands.

One look at the fallen agent destroyed Nephi's composure. He dropped to his knees beside the young man who had done so much to save their lives—to prevent this very thing from happening.

"Oh no! No! Call somebody," he ordered without thinking that Elefia was the only other person nearby.

But his eyes would not lift from the FBI agent. And he would never be able to erase the sound of the groan and gasping he could hear coming from the man.

"It'll be all right," Nephi said. But it was a conditioned response. There was no way he could tell if Agent Dalton would recover or not.

The full impact of what he had done began to fill Nephi with severe anguish. He had failed. He had been deceived. And this man was paying a heavy price for his failure. In quick succession evidence that he should have recognized earlier flashed through his mind—anxiety, unbelievable, powerful anxiety—denial of the opportunity to receive confirmation—complete disregard of thoughts suggesting he analyze and evaluate the source of this instruction—finally, denial of the Spirit's attempt to prevent him from continuing on this insane attempt to leave for the hospital.

"Oh my dearest Savior. What have I done? Forgive me. Forgive me." But even his tears could not stay his torment.

CHAPTER 12

CENTRAL SAUDI ARABIA —

GENERAL ARNOLD G. MOORE GATHERED THE RECON-
naissance photographs from his desk making sure they were back
in order. He stacked them on the report folder and slipped the
whole package into a folio with CLASSIFIED written on it in
big red letters. He straightened himself and walked briskly down
the hall to his boss's office.

"General in?" he asked the sergeant typing at her desk.

"He's expecting you, sir." She stood smartly and stepped to
the door. She tapped on the door twice and opened it. "General
Moore is here, sir."

"Come on in, Arnie," came the familiar voice of Lieutenant
General Charles Horner, commanding general for air operations
in Saudi Arabia.

"Thank you," Arnold Moore said to the sergeant in a pleasant
voice.

"You're welcome, sir." The secretary closed the door.

"Thanks for coming so quickly, Arnie. You look over those
recon photos and the report I gave you?"

General Horner stood at his desk in his shirt sleeves holding
an eight by ten photograph. His desk was littered with them.

"Yes, sir."

"What do you think?"

"I think these modifications will punch any kind of a hole we want through those extra hard bunkers. The only problem I can see is carrying the ordnance to the target. If we could slim it down a tad I think it would be a lot more aerodynamic and a whole lot easier to deliver. We can cut down on the size by trying that new explosive. If it's everything they claim it to be, the rocket will be even more deadly than this report projects."

"The new explosive is not a bad idea. I like it. And you're right. It is too fat. I'm glad you caught that too. Slimming it down is exactly what we need. We don't have time to test any new configurations. You think we could use the casing from something we're already flying? Maybe something made of carbon fiber?"

"Yes, sir. That's my recommendation. It's all in here."

"Good." General Horner didn't even open the folio. "I'm so sure you've got it right, Arnie, I'll tell you what. I'm sending you back home so you can personally expedite this new missile. We only need a dozen. It shouldn't take all that long for them to be made. The per unit cost is likely to be heavy. But we've got to open up those bunkers. We could end up losing this war if they start using what's in there."

Arnie Moore didn't exactly like what he had just heard. The war had barely started. Things had gone so well. And now he was being sent home to throw his weight around and get something built. At first he wondered if he had done something wrong. That frantic moment got buried with the secure knowledge that his units had performed every bit as well as many of the regular units. In fact, three of his best reservists had scored in the top five percent of all missions flown—so far as accuracy was concerned. The only mark on his unit's record was the unopened bunkers his men had hit but had not destroyed.

"May I ask a question, sir?"

"Of course, Arnie."

"Exactly what have they got in there that's so important?"

"This is classified all the way, General. But intelligence reports are pretty conclusive. They've got a new chemical weapon and that's where they're storing the components. They say it's some kind of binary weapon. They store one chemical in one bunker and the other chemical in the other bunker."

"Binary? I had no idea they had that kind of technology."

"They do now. They picked it up from the East Germans. Of course, they did it before the Berlin Wall came down and the two Germanys merged. By the time that happened it was too late. Saddam had their trade secrets. Now we're faced with destroying that potential. And we've got to do it at the earliest possible time."

"I was hoping the general would prefer having me here to coordinate my reserve units."

"Look, Arnie. If there was anyone else I could trust to do this thing right I would send him—or her. But there isn't. You're the best man I have in this field.

"Furthermore, I know there are men on your own staff who can fill in for you while you're gone. You told me that yourself when you showed me how ready you were. Now, were you just whistling Dixie? Or are they ready?"

"They're ready, sir."

"Good. I thought so. Your men wouldn't be doing as well as they are doing if they weren't ready. Now it really should not take you all that long to get things moving. You don't have to wait for them to finish the job. Just get it on line and get your fanny back here. I want that ordnance built and loaded on your best fighter, ready to deliver down Saddam's throat within a month."

"Yes, sir. Whatever you want, sir."

"Now don't you get formal and snippy with me, Arnie. We've been friends too long. And I really need you to do this thing."

"I know. And I'm glad you trust me with the job. But I don't mind saying, sir, I'd still rather be here with my men."

"I know that. And your job will be waiting for you when you get back. But I need those missiles. Get them for me. Okay?"

"Yes, sir," Arnold Moore said, snapping a salute at his boss.

The senior general returned the salute.

"Oh, by the way, Arnie. Could you do something else for me while your back in Washington?"

"Of course."

"Wait till you hear what it is. You never struck me as one to go for these kind of things. But it is for a good cause."

"A social event, sir?"

General Horner nodded. "It's for the families of our reserve units. Your units, General. Could you put in an appearance and deliver a message from me? It's Friday night. You'll be there in time."

"Of course, sir. This one I'd be happy to make for you. Those are my men you're talking about."

"Thanks, Arnie. I'll get even with you somehow."

*   *   *   *

"Back to Washington?" Margarita Moore asked in surprise. She had a reputation for raising her voice in volume as well as tone when she made a long-distance call. This outburst reached heights much greater than normal. "Why? You haven't been replaced or anything?"

"No. Nothing like that," Arnie Moore told his wife. "It's urgent business for General Horner. He's asked me to do it personally."

"Personally?" she asked, understanding immediately it had been some kind of coup. "Oh, that's wonderful. But as long as you're going home, I've got to go with you, Arnie. You've got to swing by and pick me up."

"Why? What's the matter?"

"I've been trying to reach Maria. She doesn't answer. I tried her place. I tried ours. I've tried at all hours of the day and night. And I'm worried sick."

"I can't just swing by and pick you up. This is a very serious assignment. I have to finish it and get back as soon as I can. Why don't you just book a commercial flight from London and I'll meet you at home Friday morning."

"Oh, why didn't I think of that? My ticket won't cost me nearly as much as I've spent calling all over the place trying to find Maria."

"Now don't worry about Maria, babe," the general said in his cover-up voice. "She can take care of herself. Remember? I'm the one who taught her everything she knows." He laughed.

But the news had worried the general. He knew she had been mingling with questionable company. Those kind of reports didn't make his day any brighter. But he had to keep up the appearance of confidence for his wife's sake.

"That's exactly why I'm worried, you charmer. Besides I want to see for myself," she joked, allowing him to believe she had fallen for his "not to worry" strategy.

"Okay, babe," the general nearly signed off. "Oh, yes. We have to go to a benefit for the general too. It's an extra favor. But it'll be worth it. Friday night."

BALLSTON, VA —

Bob Levant hung up the phone.

"Well," he reported. "They found the car—abandoned three blocks from here, near the Metro station."

He looked at Maria. She looked up, directly at him. He noted something in her expression he had not seen before. Her back was straight, her eyes were steady and her lips were set firmly—not tightly—just firmly. She was a much different person than he had seen holding on to her man.

"You made a shambles of the windows in that car, Maria. They accounted for six of your nine shots. And they found a trace of blood in there too."

"I hit him?"

"Yes. But there's no way of telling how badly he's hit or whether it was a bullet or flying glass that caused the wound."

"But he's hit," she said, her body giving a brief, involuntary shudder. "Good. Now maybe he'll leave us alone."

"Don't be too sure, Maria. It might be that he's just wounded slightly—wounded just enough to be very upset at you for nicking him."

"That's all right. He started this war and if he isn't smart enough to get out of it right now, then he'll just have to take the consequences."

Nephi had to look at the woman who just said what he thought he heard. He didn't say anything. He couldn't help but smile at her. She was some feisty little gal. Much more than he had expected. But at this moment he wasn't certain he deserved someone like her—feisty or not. She had been promised to him and he had been led to her but he had sinned a great sin. He could feel the effects of having sinned—of having succumbed so easily to a false message. For it was a sin to be deceived. And now he stood to lose everything.

That the experience had humbled him was a major understatement. But the others had not understood. They thought he had been shaken by the actual shooting. Elefia had tried to comfort him. So also had Roy and Tina Ivars. But as sincere and intense as their efforts had been they had not quite reached the mark. Only One could provide him the relief he craved. There was no way they could understand—nothing they could do. He had not confessed to them what had happened and how he had failed. This was his burden to carry. The weight of it pressed upon him more than any other wrong he had carried in his life.

"Now look, Maria. You're under our protection. We'll take care of al-Jarwi."

"Fine. You do that. But do it right this time. I'm not going to be held prisoner because some terrorist thinks he can come in here and do anything he wants. Who does he think he's messing with?"

Levant could tell her voice was gaining steam in its delivery. This was an angry woman. This was a tough woman. This might even be a woman who would be hard for him to control. And while it was good to see her want to fight, his job now would be to keep her under control so she wouldn't interfere.

It had been stupid for them to leave the building. If they had stayed put, Dalton would not be in the hospital. Also, they just might have gotten al-Jarwi right then. Dalton was a great shot. He could have nailed al-Jarwi with half a chance. Given another opportunity, Levant didn't want any civilians screwing up the mission. His men would nail that terrorist. It had become a personal thing with him now. He liked Howard Dalton. He didn't like thinking of him in the hospital. He didn't like thinking of any of his men in jeopardy.

"Now look, Maria. You've got to understand. You're not safe yet. You've got to stay out of sight until we nail him."

Maria stood up. She leaned toward the FBI man and pointed her finger at him—pumping it to emphasize her point.

"No, sir. I'm not going to go crazy hiding in some apartment. I work in a Congressional office. And I'm going to that benefit tomorrow. And you're not going to stop me!"

She whirled and walked away.

Levant sagged back in his chair. He didn't need this added pressure. Nephi read the message of frustration on the FBI man's face.

"I'll talk with her."

He followed in the direction Eleña had gone. And he found her in the bathroom, leaning against the sink, pressing a washcloth tightly against her mouth.

At first she turned away from him. Then she whirled toward him and grabbed hold of him. She forced her face into her place on his shoulder. He could feel the rise and fall of her chest as she breathed. But sounds were not coming with the sobs. In a moment she released him and stepped to the side. She began wiping her face with the cloth. Then she reached for a tissue and returned to her place close to him.

"I'm not going to let him ruin our lives," she said in a tearful, but determined voice.

"He's just trying to help us, Eleña."

"Not him. Him! I'm talking about Kassim." The tearful quality dissolved from her voice. In its place came an increasing strength. "I'm not going to allow that man to interfere with us. Do you understand?"

He looked at her with a great deal of admiration for her newly discovered strength.

"I love you," Nephi said.

"Is that all you can think of? Nephi, this is serious."

"I know. You're still on the edge of that cliff."

She looked up at him and suddenly realized he had been carrying this worry all along. He had been strong for her. Now it was time she was strong for him.

"We're both on the cliff," she said calmly. But that knowledge didn't prevent her from enjoying the luxury of relaxing for a private moment in his arms.

News Brief
Thursday, January 17, 1991

CENTRAL SAUDI ARABIA The United States and its allies continued a relentless series of air attacks against strategic targets in Iraq and Kuwait following initial attacks in predawn hours this morning.

Initial reports of Allied casualties were extremely low. One American and one British fighter bomber were the only losses reported by authorities at mission headquarters. Iraqi radio claimed to have downed 14 enemy planes.

Defense Secretary Dick Cheney said the U.S. and allied planes flew 1,000 sorties. Targets included military bases and command and control centers.

President Bush said, "I think all of us are very pleased that so far the operation is going forward with great success."

Gen. Colin Powell, Chairman of the Joint Chiefs of Staff, said, "I'm comfortable that we were able to achieve control of Iraqi air space."

Late reports have indicated that Iraqi artillery had shelled an abandoned oil refinery near the coastal town of Khafji, located just a few miles from the Saudi Arabian border of Kuwait.

NEW YORK CITY—Stock prices went through the ceiling today in a euphoric reaction to the successful first stages of war. Oil prices collapsed.

BERLIN—Terrorist attacks have been reported on four U.S. facilities in Germany with further terrorist activity reported in India, Italy and Ecuador as well.

TUNISIA—At a burial service today for two top PLO aides assassinated Monday, Bassam Abu Sharif, an associate of PLO chief Yasser Arafat, said his group opposed "all acts of terrorism."

Sharif condemned the attack on Iraq by U.S.-led multinational forces, but said a call by the PLO's Executive Committee for forces to resist "American aggression" did not extend to terrorist attacks against the United States and Europe.

CRYSTAL CITY, VA —

Kassim al-Jarwi sat on the edge of one of the beds in his room, reading the Western press account of the war. He slammed it down after reading the report from Tunisia.

"Cowards!" he shouted, letting the word stretch into a groan that wrenched loose from the depth of his soul. He snatched the paper, wadded it and threw it to the floor.

"This never would have happened if that bungling fool,

Hamza, had finished the job properly. He never should have acted until they all were there!" He should have done that job himself, he chided himself slightly. No one ever would have known who the assassin had been. He would have finished them all and fled.

But the work here seemed to be of higher priority to his superiors. He forced himself to restore his disciplined stature. Besides, he needed to daub the oozing wound on his ear. He had been fortunate the bullet had not been a shade closer. Oh, well. If that is all they could do to him he would claim it as a hero's wound. With alcohol and an aerosol bandage, he had managed to stop the bleeding. By Friday night it would be nothing more than an exciting memento of his visit to the United States of America—the Great Satan.

He forced himself to think of his mission. It would not be long before the biased American press finally would have something to write about—something it could not ignore— something it would have to report correctly. Of course, he expected them to try and cover up this as well as everything else about the war.

But they could not hide an incident such as this. He would not allow it. He would inform journalists from Muslim countries to keep vigil on Friday. Surely they could be trusted to cover this event objectively.

Only a few things left to do now. Simple things. Nothing difficult, especially since he would rely on himself to do them. The bomb was built. All that remained was to set it in place and see that it reached the most people. To know exactly where to place the bomb, he would have to visit the site. There were several ways it could be done. He needed to find the very best.

BALLSTON, VA —

"You don't have to go to work today," Roy gave her one last chance.

"I'm certainly not going to sit around here wringing my hands, wondering what al-Jarwi is going to do next."

"You know, that just might be the best place for her," the FBI agent added. "Security on the Hill is very good. That reduces our load. If you folks just won't do anything unexpected, it would help considerably."

They agreed to that. All but Nephi. He was in another part of the apartment. When he joined the others, they made their move to leave. This time several agents joined the party. This time they all held their weapons at their sides, not waiting to draw them from holsters. This time the cars they used waited in the secured parking facility below the apartment building. This time they checked with the agents monitoring people coming and going from the building, its parking facility, and in the streets around the building. This time they left without an incident. This time, of course, Kassim al-Jarwi was nowhere near the apartment building. But they didn't know that. They had to deal with the situation as if he was going to attack right then. And every agent felt disappointed he had not shown up for this exercise.

Roy Ivars made sure everyone had an assignment when they arrived at the office. He even put Tina to work. It was an abnormal routine for abnormal times. Since vacations had cut down the number of staff present there was plenty for everyone to do. Roy distributed the mail. He found two items that had to be handled immediately. He took care of them personally. He contacted the Congressman to report on those issues and bring him up-to-date on what had been happening to their staff members. The rest of the mail got routed according to their topics. Soon, only the FBI men appeared idle. But they actually had their hands full, staying alert and on guard every time someone came into the office—anticipating problems.

Maria found her assignment fascinating. At first it seemed confusing. Everyone promised that she could handle it. It just took time. She was assigned the task of making appointments for the Congressman. The job really belonged to someone else. Like most everyone else, the Congressman's scheduler was on vacation. Rumors persisted that the scheduler was close to finding a new position—off the Hill. Considering that possibility, Roy felt training Maria could be a good investment in her time and his.

She soon discovered that many more people wanted to meet with the Congressman than he had time for. It didn't take long for her to know that if the job opened up and she got it permanently, she would have to develop a sense of priorities. It would be a matter of learning who and what was important.

"Just keep all these requests handy. Pencil them in. The final decisions probably won't be made until the week before," Roy instructed her. "All we do is show the Congressman what options he has and he makes the decisions. Some will be obvious. Some will be borderline. Ron will meet with as many as he can. One thing we have to point out to people is how fickle his commitments are. He could be called away at any time from an appointment that had been set in concrete weeks before. There are any number of things that could interfere with an appointment. Sometimes he has to leave in the middle of a meeting and run over to vote. Mostly people say they understand. They have no other choice. Except that one of us generally can fill in for the Congressman. We have a staff member assigned to every issue. And when you can't find the right person to fill in, you call me. I fill in when there is no one else."

She looked at him and smiled. There in front of her was the calendar and all the loose pieces of paper with notes on them. She couldn't help remembering one time when she was little. She had gone to her daddy's office and had asked him what he was doing. She remembered he had taken her behind his desk and had shown her what he was working on. She didn't understand anything her daddy had said. All she could remember was the huge amount of paper work he did in his job. What she *had* noticed in some detail had been the number of handsome young men running around in their neatly pressed uniforms.

There were no uniforms this day. The only extra people in the office were the grouchy old FBI agents who scowled every time she stepped from behind her desk or walked by the window. But she willingly ignored their scowls. She had changed. She didn't care about watching men anymore—uniformed or not. Except, she did manage a smile for Nephi whenever he walked by.

Once someone from the district called and said he was having a problem with the Internal Revenue Service. She had to stifle a giggle when the man kept calling it the "Infernal Revenue Service." He wanted to know how he could get the agency to listen to him instead of constantly demanding money. The residual elements of the rebel inside her loved tracking down that information. Nephi told her they called such things "cases." Mostly cases were handled in the district. This one she didn't want to let go of because if anyone was going to give the IRS a black eye, she wanted to be in on it. Not that she had anything against them. She hardly had dealt with them in all her life. It was just the reputation they had and the awful things she had heard they did to people.

Maria didn't like hearing stories of how government agencies, or any other big bully, picked on normal people.

Nephi took pleasure in watching Elefia plunge into her new work. He wasn't certain how things would work out with Sariah. He hoped she could return soon. Whatever time it would take her to recover would be the certain time he would have Elefia around him. And according to Roy, it was possible that time could be extended, depending on what the Congressman's new committee assignment might be—or what the current scheduler decided to do.

Nephi found it interesting to hear her hum to herself as she worked. He had never heard such a thing in an office before. But he liked it. In fact he started thinking of how it would sound in their own home.

His work had piled up. Mail seemed to have multiplied and replenished his desk in the past few days while he had been running around with Elefia. He began plowing through it, dealing roughly with items that lacked immediacy or importance. News—both papers and letters—were dispatched after a brief scanning. Constituent letters were routed out to the district if there was the slightest hint they could be dealt with out there. Dear Colleague letters were quickly relegated to the appropriate file—either under a bill's name or number, or under the issue they dealt with.

Once the sorting had been done, Nephi turned to items with the highest priority. He first selected a report he had been anxious to see for three weeks. As he read down the index, he couldn't resist thinking how good it felt to be directing his attention to an issue that could affect millions of people. His contribution probably would amount to only a tiny role in the bill's passage, but he worked at each of his issues as if his was the most important role. He figured that one day that attitude would pay off. So he simply lost himself in reading the report and he did not notice Eleña had stepped around the corner to his desk.

It startled him when she spoke. But he quickly recovered. She had a question about procedure to ask him. After he answered she started to walk away—then stopped.

"You know, this is kind of fun," she told him.

"First symptom of Potomac Fever," he teased. "Give it time, take two aspirin and maybe it'll go away."

She laughed. "You should talk. You've got it bad."

"That I do," he responded. "But it only hurts the rest of your life."

Eleña really enjoyed working in the Congressional office. "This is my new life," she told Nephi. "It's a life with so many wonderful possibilities. Do you know what I mean?"

He nodded and motioned for her to follow him. He knew where it was safe to go in the office for a little privacy. So they walked to one of those corners in a very business-like manner. When they got there he simply turned around and took her in his arms and held her.

"I love you, Maria Eleña Moore."

"Nicholes," she added. "Soon to be Nicholes."

They broke it up, mainly because they did not want to get caught, but also because they had so much work to do.

Before he could regain his prior level of concentration on the report, Nephi began to feel something building inside him. It was a powerful feeling. When this had come before, it had been a sign that something awaited him from the other side of the veil. Spiritual messages come at the convenience of the Lord and not at the recipient's. Over the years Nephi had learned that such feelings often could be counterfeits by the adversary or even something carnal like indigestion, nervousness or hidden personal desire. It had become a routine of sorts to try and find out which of the three possible sources such a feeling had come from: spiritual, carnal or evil. At work or in even more public places he had managed to find ways to conduct his analysis without looking peculiar. It was the routine he should have followed last night.

In this situation, all he had to do was turn his swivel chair so only his back could be seen from the open part of the room. He bowed his head just enough to appear as if he were reading. No one could see his eyes close. And no one could hear him speak within his heart and mind.

He simply rebuked Lucifer and his followers and all forms of evil from his body and mind and from the office. He did this by the power of the priesthood he held and in the name of Jesus Christ. Then he asked for an outpouring of the Holy Spirit and for the gift of discernment that he might know if what he was feeling had come from the Lord.

It had.

There began to build within him a kind of pressure— pressure he felt within his bosom. But it was impossible to tell if the strength of it was pressing in or pushing out. It made him feel as if his chest would burst. But not the least bit of pain accompanied it. No indication caused him concern that the pressure might have been a heart attack or anything similar. Instead, it was a warm, peaceful, yet powerful feeling.

"Father, is it permitted for me to receive the information thou hast prepared for me to receive?"

Instantly the warmth within his bosom increased. Instantly, the instruction was given to him—the words shaping within his mind—the voice, different than his own, yet familiar to him.

"Go to your own apartment. There is no danger. Your life shall be preserved. But there are instructions you need to carry out in regard to the work you are doing. Without them you could perish."

That was all.

But a strong feeling of well being remained.

So much evidence had come to him to prove that it had been a true message that he almost denied himself the right to confirm the source. But he caught himself. He had learned it was much more prudent to ask for confirmation than to risk offending the Spirit, or worse, to be deceived. It was a sin to be deceived.

"Is it permitted to ask for confirmation of this instruction?" he asked.

And before his question had been completed, there was an increase in the strength of the feeling. His mind was opened and he knew it was extremely urgent for him to receive this information. Not only was his life involved, but the lives of many others were endangered—including the life of Maria Elefia Moore.

It was a true message. He knew that as well as he knew his own name. Now all he had to do was to find some way to slip away from the air-tight security that had been wrapped around him and Elefia. The more he thought of it, the more impossible it seemed. He had to accomplish something he had been instructed to do by the Spirit. It was far more important for him to do that than for him to do anything anyone else had instructed him to do. There might be some leeway so far as time was concerned. Still it could not be put off.

Once before, in a different situation, he had been tempted to procrastinate. It took only a moment for a new experience—a new lesson—to close upon him. A dense, ominous feeling pressed upon him, weighing upon him. He repented immediately.

Sorry, he thought to himself as if he was talking to the two agents who were diligently trying to protect him from danger. But I've got to get out of here.

The question still was, how?

It turned out to be very simple.

All he had to do was to tell them he was stepping across the hall to the bathroom. That was the truth. But one of the men came with him. Nephi's opportunity came when the agent decided he would allow the Congressional aide a little privacy. After all, the room was empty and there was no other entrance or exit. So the agent stepped out into the hall.

Nephi felt very strongly that he should just wait for a moment. So he did. And after sufficient time, he felt impressed to leave. When he stepped into the hall, he could see the agent leaning through the office door. Apparently he was talking with the other agent.

Without rushing, without panic, without planning anything else, Nephi simply walked forward three large steps. That put him in the middle of the connecting corridor as it angled away from the hall where his own office was located. Three steps were all Nephi needed to be around that corner and completely beyond view of the agent's post. Then Nephi just slipped down the staircase two floors to the basement. He headed across the hall there and down two flights of escalators to the tunnel that connected with the Rayburn Building. Midway through that tunnel, he turned into another tunnel that led to another flight of stairs. Down two flights and he emerged in the parking level where his car waited for him.

He felt bad for the deception. But he had no other choice. He had been instructed to leave. The way had been opened for him to leave. So he left. And even as he approached his car he still had not considered the possible consequences of his actions. Eventually he would have to explain what had happened, why he left and what he had been doing. It would not be easy.

He unlocked the door and slipped behind the wheel. Before starting the engine there converged on him serious concerns—mental and emotional pressures obviously intended to turn him around and prevent him from meeting his appointment. Fear and dread. How could he face the embarrassment?

It would not be just Roy Ivars asking questions—Brother Roy Ivars—formerly Bishop Ivars. There would be gentiles—gentiles who wrote reports—public reports. How could he ever satisfy their queries? Even some solid members of the Church had difficulty believing spiritual things could happen to ordinary people. Nephi had learned to live with that. But he had never learned how to explain such unusual circumstances to gentiles. And he was not anxious to learn now.

He drove from the underground facility onto the street. At this time of day it was easy to connect with the freeway. He was certain no one had followed him. But he continued checking to see. When he reached his apartment he felt assured that no one would be there waiting for him. He was right.

Inside the apartment he knelt down and prayed. Then he lay down on his bed. But no answer came. He inquired about it and wondered if it all had been a mistake—if he had managed to misunderstand the message.

The only thing was, the warmth he had felt when he had received the instruction persisted. And the warmth intensified when he asked for another confirmation of his instruction.

He had learned through sad experience that forcing an answer could prove disastrous. He had no margin for error in this matter. Now was no time to fail. He had to exercise strict control of himself. Patience.

The Lord will give messages to whomever He wants to give them and whenever He wants to give them. The individual's responsibility in all this is to prepare and qualify for them. Nephi had found that the most certain way to qualify for a spiritual blessing was to get into the scriptures. Not just read them, but to plunge into them—lose himself in studying them.

He asked for direction in what topic he should study. The feeling came with great power.

Priesthood.

And he began to search the scriptures where priesthood power and authority were discussed. The topical guide listed extensive references and had broken the topic of "Priesthood" into twelve different categories. He was impressed to start with the topic of Priesthood Authority and thought he might move on to Magnifying Callings Within the Priesthood. Along the way he recognized the strong correlation between the principles of the priesthood and the principle of faith. Since a complete understanding of faith requires a complete knowledge of the character, attributes and perfections of God, he studied those things as well.

As he studied he lost track of time. He thought once about eating. But decided that what he was reading was much more important.

*   *   *   *

Kassim al-Jarwi placed his prayer rug on the hotel room floor and began one of his midday prayers. But it was hard for him to concentrate on the ritual. He felt an intense hatred within him. Everyone around him had contributed to that emotion. Even his control speaking from Paris had become a source of irritation to him. The stupid man simply could not understand why Kassim had not acted already. Explanations had fallen on insensitive ears. And the terrorist was faced with the prospects of acting now or being acted upon.

He could not read the newspaper without finding something in it that whipped his emotions. He could not watch television or listen to the radio without having something trigger his ire.

Common threads in all his passionate responses had shaped into images of the two infidels who had been able to escape his wrath. He had no time to spend destroying them now. But after he took care of his project on Friday, he would dedicate as much time as might be required to deal with both of them properly.

Such were his inner thoughts as his external mind raced through the ritual of honoring his god. It provided him little relief from the onslaught of Western coverage of the war he was trying to participate in. To be a true believer among all these unbelievers was a cursed fate.

He had been surprised to find they had armed the girl. He had not waited for the man to raise up and fire his weapon. He had not thought the authorities would allow them to protect themselves. Obviously they had provided a bodyguard. With him taking the bullets meant for Maria and Nephi, the leaders had probably already surrounded the victims with extra personnel. The most likely thing he could count on was that their assassination would require greater planning than the bombing incident at the gala event on Friday.

Still thinking of what needed to be done, he carried one of the five-gallon plastic containers to his third rental vehicle—a van this time. And he returned for the other container and the detonator.

He drove across the Potomac, across the 14th Street Bridge and headed toward town. He drove around the International

Plaza Hotel and parked as close to the target area as he could. The only thing he really had to do today was to study the area. He would need to know which would be the best way to accomplish his plan.

He started by walking up the alley and approaching the delivery platform. Before he could enter the building a security guard approached. Al-Jarwi quickly began writing in the portfolio he had brought with him.

"No problem," al-Jarwi said in a voice loud enough for the guard to hear.

"With what?" the guard asked.

"Our trucks. There will be no problem with our trucks. We will be able to get in here with no problem at all."

"Big trucks come in here all the time. What you bringing in?"

"Scenery."

"What?"

"Scenery. You know—for the big production."

"The what? No. They don't tell me nothin'."

"I know what you mean," al-Jarwi sympathized with him and waved and walked into the hotel.

One of the waiters was kind enough to tell him in which ballroom the benefit for the Air Force Reserve would be. Al-Jarwi headed there and looked around. He paid special attention to the venting system. Another waiter happened to tell him the route over which they would have to carry all the food and drinks.

"We can't take any hot food through there," the waiter said, pointing at the most convenient hallway. Even though it was a relatively direct access between the kitchen and the hall, it was not to be used.

"That hall is like a wind tunnel," he complained. "It sucks in so much air during one of those big bashes, that it's like a hurricane through there. We go around. It's better that way. Food stays hotter."

"I would hope so," al-Jarwi agreed to himself as he made a note in his portfolio.

The same waiter showed him where the locker rooms were. There would always be a stash of fresh uniforms in the locker rooms. There would be even more on Friday. Everyone had been told to expect extra hours and extra staff.

All he needed now was a table he could set up directly under the big, square grating on the wall. That had to be the intake portal for the ballroom's ventilation system. There always were tables around a hotel like this. It would be a cinch. The luckiest part was that none of the waiters would be walking in on him. The friendly waiter had told him they closed the door at both ends of the hall the minute they turned on the fans which aired out the ballroom.

Access, privacy, and a built-in delivery system. He had found the perfect way to deal the greatest blow of all against these infidel intruders. All he had left to do was arrange for the diversion.

*   *   *   *

According to plan a team of FBI agents descended upon the International Plaza Hotel. Two were assigned to the loading dock. But they did not arrive until half an hour after the terrorist left the premises. They asked the security guard if any strange deliveries had been made. He said no. It didn't occur to him to tell them about the man with the scenery.

CHAPTER 13

News Brief
Friday, January 18, 1991

SAUDI ARABIA—The second day of Operation Desert Storm was marked by increased air strikes and Tomahawk missile attacks by U.S. and allied forces on strategic military targets in Iraq and occupied Kuwait.

Iraq in turn launched SCUD missile attacks against targets in Northern Saudi Arabia and against Israel, a country not involved in the war.

The missile launched against Saudi Arabia was intercepted by a U.S. Patriot anti-missile missile and was seen during one segment of a live television broadcast.

However, according to Gen. H. Norman Schwarzkopf, commander of U.S. forces in the Gulf, the number of sorties being flown into the battle zone has increased from 1,000 the first day to a rate of 2,000 on this second day.

Gen. Charles Horner, U.S. Air Force commander in the Persian Gulf, said U.S. planes had shot down eight Iraqi aircraft in air-to-air combat.

WASHINGTON, D.C.—President Bush today praised Israeli restraint in the face of Iraq's attack against civilian targets in Tel Aviv and Haifa and promised the "darndest search-and-destroy mission that's ever been undertaken."

Iraqi SCUD missiles can be launched from mobile launchers that could be driven to different locations after each firing.

FBI officials today announced that it knew of no credible threats of terrorism in the Washington, D.C. area. It is expected that tourism to the Capitol will be curtailed significantly as a result of the Persian Gulf war and the threat of terrorist activity.

Fear of terrorist attacks have brought increased security measures across the United States, especially in airport facilities as numerous bomb threats have been reported.

BALLSTON, VA —

TINA IVARS ANSWERED THE DOOR DRESSED IN HER FAVORITE kimono. It was white with her name embroidered tastefully in Japanese characters at her left shoulder. She invited the disheveled looking FBI agent into her apartment. The early morning sun had barely given the world its newest day. And none of the people in that room were at all ready for it or for Robert Levant's report. From time to time they all had taken brief naps. But none had slept very well.

Levant shook his head and told the three very worried people that they had had no success in locating Nephi. "We've looked everywhere for him," Levant said.

"Have you looked in his apartment?" Maria asked.

"Yes."

"Out in the back? He sometimes parks his car in the visitors parking area. It's in the back."

"We searched everywhere, Miss Moore. We have not found his car. And he is not in his apartment. We had the manager accompany us. He let us in. And no one was there."

"Could you tell if anything was missing?"

Levant shook his head. "There was no way we could tell. But everything looked to be in order. I mean, there had not been a struggle or anything like that."

"Get back out there and find him!" Maria demanded.

"We're doing everything we can. Believe me," Levant pleaded.

Maria glared at him a moment longer. But she could not hold that posture forever. She had been in anguish from the moment the agent had returned from the men's room and had reported that Nephi had disappeared. She was able to control her emotions to a certain extent then, but the longer he remained missing, the more her mind captured visions of his being held and tortured by Kassim.

She strode around the modest living room for a few minutes and retreated to the guest room she had been using. When the door was closed, she could hold back the tears no longer. All she could do was to press her tissue-covered fist against her mouth to lessen the sound of her fears and concern.

Roy suspected what she was doing. He knew how she felt. Nephi had become a dear friend to him too, and he was being torn by the same emotions. In a few minutes he slipped into the guest room and sat beside her on the bed.

"I'm fond of him too," he said, having placed his hand on her shoulder. "We have to hope he is all right."

"But you don't know how horrible it was. Kassim can do some ugly things to people. Sariah knows. I know. But Levant doesn't know. Or he'd be ripping this town apart."

"I understand," Roy said to comfort her.

She turned in place and took advantage of his shoulder.

"Oh, Roy. I love him so much. What am I going to do?"

He had no idea. But he had to give one to her. Somehow he had to fill her mind with some form of hope.

"We're going to do what he would want us to do. Okay?"

She looked up at him. She didn't say anything. But the question emerged from her eyes.

"And what he would want us to do is to go on about our business as if nothing had happened—as if he was still right here with us."

"But he's not."

"I know that. But you've got to get your mind set on the idea that he will be walking through that door any minute. Look. I didn't bring it up before, but this isn't the first time he's done this."

"It isn't?"

"Oh no. He hasn't been with us very long, but he has established a pattern of sorts."

"A pattern?"

"Yes. Every once in a while, when he would be facing some particularly difficult problem, he would talk with me about it. And then, all of a sudden I would be looking for him and he would have disappeared. Just like he did yesterday. It would frustrate me to no end. Sometimes he would be gone for a couple of hours. Once he was gone all afternoon. But he always came back. And when he did he just took care of his problem as if it was the easiest thing he had been given to do."

"You think that's what he's doing now? Getting away to think or something?"

"Why don't we count on it—until we find out differently."

She looked at him to see if she could detect any deceit in what he had said. There was none there.

"All right," she said, straightening herself around. "Then we're going to go all the way. I'm going to that benefit tonight."

Her idea, presented in such an assertive way, startled Roy. She mentioned yesterday she wanted to go. But that was before Nephi had turned up missing. He had assumed circumstances had altered her thinking. But no such thing could be assumed now from her tone of voice.

At first he was against it. But planning to go to the benefit certainly would give her reason to expect Nephi to show up—in one piece. Besides, if al-Jarwi was going to do his thing there, it would be the best chance to grab him. If they could do it without killing the bugger, they might get him to reveal what he had done with Nephi—if he had Nephi.

"Good idea. Levant won't like it much. But I do. He can't do much about stopping us. I'll just arrange for four tickets. That'll be fun. Tina and I will probably run into a lot of people we haven't seen for years."

Inspector Levant strode from the Ivars' apartment. The agent with him had to hurry to keep up. It had not been a particularly good morning for the inspector. Out of respect for Maria Moore he had taken time from his oppressive schedule to report to her and assure her they were doing all they could to find Nicholes. But she had done nothing but scold him as if they had done nothing.

For the moment nothing was what they could afford to do on his case. Other agencies they had enlisted would be working to find him now. The rest of Robert Levant's day would be filled with arrangements to defend the International Plaza from a terrorist attack.

They had a solid plan. Men had been in place since yesterday. Nothing was coming into that building without their knowing about it. Specifically they would know about any soda pop bottles that someone might try to carry inside. Through the day there would be briefings for personnel assigned to the hotel from every law enforcement agency in town. Rare cooperation between the FBI, Secret Service, Capitol police, D.C. police, and Air Force Security Police had been arranged for. They couldn't use dogs to sniff out the chemicals. In spite of great arguments, the Attorney General's office had ordered that nothing be done to prevent the benefit from looking completely normal. That meant no special chemical warfare suits could be worn. A lot of the security forces would be dressed as civilians. Levant's head began to ache just thinking of what it would take to keep track of all those men.

*   *   *   *

About mid-morning, Kassim al-Jarwi drove up to the loading dock of the International Plaza Hotel. He was so worried that the guard might remember him that he shaved off his beloved goatee and darkened his skin. With luck the guard would not make the connection between yesterday's scenery and today's delivery. But he brought along a pint flask of bourbon in case the guard did recognize him.

When al-Jarwi reached the loading dock in the van he had rented, it disturbed him to see two men in suits watching everything that was going on. One of them studied the invoice Kassim had prepared. The other inspected the five-gallon containers he was unloading. Syrup base. A dozen five-gallon jugs of syrup base. Actually there were only ten jugs of base. The two others contained what al-Jarwi really wanted to get inside. With a jerk of his head the guard let him pass.

"You got a walk-in box?" he asked one of the cooks.

There was no verbal answer, just a flick of a huge butcher knife. He walked in that direction and hauled open the double sealed door by pulling on the heavy duty handle.

Inside were shelves loaded with boxes and pans and containers of all sorts. Some items had been tagged with names on them. Al-Jarwi took a roll of masking tape from his pocket, tore off two strips, slapped one on each bottle and wrote on each: "Hold for Jefferson Reception."

That was it. He hauled in the other jugs and stacked them with some other cases—outside the cold box. He waved at the guard and watched the two men in plain clothes scowl at him. Then he drove away. It was time for him to meet with Hasan.

The young firebrand had agreed to make the frontal assault. It would be all Kassim would need. With such a diversion he would easily have enough time to set the jugs in the hall, twist the tops and walk away. That would be about eight p.m. Five to ten minutes later disaster would touch the heart of the Great Satan. Then the filthy American press would have to write about something it could not ignore—something it could not change. And the world would know the power of Islam and its new Mahdi, Saddam Hussein.

Perhaps the world might also hear of its new defender, Kassim Mustafa al-Jarwi.

That was strange. Why, after all these years, had his middle name come to mind? No one knew it. His mother was the last person to call him by his full name. And he had forbidden her to use it. No matter. Then, again. Perhaps he should use it. It had a distinguished ring to it. Kassim Mustafa al-Jarwi. Yes. Almost poetic.

*   *   *   *

Tina arrived at the office around closing time. The most critical thing they allowed themselves to discuss was whether they wanted to eat first or to depend on the benefit to feed them.

"If we can't get enough to eat there, I'll take us to dinner afterwards," Roy offered.

"Sounds good to me," Tina spoke in a light-hearted way.

"The four of us," Maria added.

"Of course," Roy said.

They didn't have to leave quite yet. Roy said he still had some things to clean up. He always had things to clean up. He could have left any time. But he wanted to time their arrival. He didn't like the idea of standing around down there, wringing their hands and biting their nails. They would be better off at the office occupying their minds with something. He began calculating time, estimating when they should leave so they would not be there too early. It would be good if they arrived there about 7:30 or so. That would give them plenty of time to circulate before Vice President Quayle would arrive—just before 8:00, someone had told him.

Shortly before 6:30 p.m., Nephi completed the work he had been called away from his office to complete. Solemn instructions had been given him. Never before had they come with such power.

When he had been instructed to leave his apartment, he had been told exactly what he needed to take with him—a number of books, his new suit and some other clothes. He hopped into his car but he didn't go far. He was directed to drive south on the freeway, away from Washington. He ended up in a motel near the Springfield Mall. He checked in, paid for two days and told them he didn't want to be disturbed under any circumstance.

He had not been disturbed, not even by maid service. And he had been able to complete the work he had come to do.

His instructions had been given clearly—three times. When it came the first time his mind filled instantly with doubt. This was incredible. Never had he heard of someone doing something like this. But as his instructions were given the second time additional information was given him, reminding him of numerous instances recorded in the scriptures when such things had happened—at least they alluded to what actually had happened.

By the time his instructions had been given the third and final time he had been filled with such spiritual strength that he knew he could accomplish anything—so long as the source of that strength remained with him.

Then shortly after he had received his instructions that final time, the Spirit withdrew. He could hardly raise his arm from the bed on which he had lain. Almost immediately his doubts returned, his fears returned—fears of being questioned by gentiles—fears of being questioned and mocked by those in the Church who might not understand the workings of the Spirit.

He could be tried for his membership—by good, faithful members—those who might suspect he was trying to start his own church or usurp authority or commit some other offense against the Church's leadership.

In the next hours he fought back those feelings. Weakened by the power of what he had experienced, his total dependence upon the Lord and the priesthood he held became even more evident than ever before. How long he struggled he could not tell. But finally those serious oppressive feelings left his room. And the strength that had drained from him gradually began to return.

His first major challenge had to be the simple act of lifting himself from the bed. From then on, each movement he could convince himself to make seemed to generate further energy—greater response by his system. The shower helped. And he shaved. He groomed himself to appear as if nothing extraordinary had happened. The physical effort required to carry his things to the car helped him some. But when he finally settled into his seat to drive he still wondered if he could make it to the hotel and complete his assignment.

There was yet time, he was told in a quiet, still way. And just hearing that assurance sustained and supported him.

Driving down I-395 was easy. In fact, his mind cleared and his muscles gained more tone in the familiar acts of looking and steering, of accelerating and slowing, of planning and executing. By the time he turned onto the surface roads that led from the freeway toward the International Plaza, his coordination and strength had returned.

He knew he would have trouble finding a parking place. So he simply chose to leave his car for parking attendants to deal with. It would cost him a bundle in ransom to retrieve it later. But that wasn't important now. He had to get inside as quickly as he could. It was 7:48.

The International Plaza remained one of those marvelous anachronisms in Washington. Highly ornate, the splendor had somehow avoided the ravages of time and neglect as well as temptations for change. The doormen all wore uniforms—that fit. The car attendants had special jackets—that fit. The rugs were soft and plush as was the furniture scattered around the huge entrance.

Extending from behind the elaborate front desk was a rectangular room, its space broken up by clusters of sofas and easy chairs with coffee tables between them for convenience.

Mingled with these furnishings were well-tended palms and tropical plants. The deep greens of the foliage contrasted splendidly with light hues on the walls and the balanced textures and tones of the drapes and wall hangings.

People were moving toward the far end of the large room. That was where a goldplated sign announced the location of the Grand Ballroom.

Wasn't that the vice president? Yes. He was just entering the ballroom right now with the trail of Secret Service men around him.

At that end of the room was also where the exquisite fountain sprayed streams of colorfully lighted water into the air so it could fall gently onto the flowering water lilies in a modest pool.

Elefia stood there in the exact spot he had seen her in his dream.

They had arrived just 15 minutes before Nephi did.

And Roy had been right. He and Tina did see a great many people they had not seen in years. Maria accompanied them for a while. But she was mesmerized by the fountain at the end of the long hall. She knew it was the one Nephi had sketched.

She was still staring at it when she heard a familiar voice.

"Maria!" She turned around to see her mother coming toward her with open arms.

"Mother! What are you doing here?" she said as they embraced.

"I had to come to this thing with your father."

"I thought you were in England."

"I was. But your father had to come back on business. He won't talk about it. I just hope he hasn't been sacked."

"Daddy? Daddy's here? Where?"

"Why, Maria. What in the world has gotten over you? You look absolutely excited to see your father."

"I do—I do want to see him, Mother." Maria looked around her. Now her father's was another face she had to search for.

Then her eyes settled on an approaching figure.

"Nephi!" she shouted, forgetting everything and running to meet him. She virtually leaped into his arms.

"I thought you were . . ." she couldn't finish. In the first place, she was so relieved she had tightened her face to cut off the tears. And in the second place, she had been taught not to cry in public. Of course, her mother also had taught her not to make a spectacle of herself. But somehow that was one rule she had no intention of following at the moment.

"Nephi, this is my mother," she said, gathering her composure after a moment. "Mother, I want you to meet Nephi Nicholes."

Nephi accepted her hand to shake it. And he liked the strength and tone of it. Like daughter, like mother. Pretty good stock. Great beginning.

"I'm so happy to meet you, Mrs. Moore. I have a lot to talk with you about. But I also have some urgent business I must attend to right now. Would you please excuse me for a few minutes. I'll be right back. And then we can talk. I'm very much in love with your daughter and I'd like to ask your blessings. We'd like to get married."

He slipped away from Maria's grasp and began walking away.

"Nephi! Where are you going?"

"It's all right. I'll only be a minute."

"Maria?" the stunned Rita Moore said. "Maria, who was that? What's going on?"

"He's the man I'm going to marry, Mother. He's a wonderful man. You'll love him." She started after him.

But her mother held onto her arm. "The man you're going to marry? Why, that's wonderful. Wait a minute. Come back. Your father's coming. He's just parking the car. Can't you just wait a minute? I need to talk with you."

"Mother, please let me go. I'll explain later. I have to go with him. I'll be right back."

She followed Nephi. But he was walking very fast—too fast for her to keep up through the crowd of people. She sensed he was heading for the edge of the cliff—and he was going there alone.

"Maria," Roy shouted. "Was that Nephi I saw?"

"Yes. He's all right."

"Where's he going?"

"I don't know."

* * * *

Kassim had arrived before any of them. He spent a great deal of time in the locker room where the tailored uniforms hung on a plain pipe rack. The waiter with whom he had talked the day before had been correct. There were a great many uniforms hanging there to accommodate the extra help required for the benefit. Selecting one that fit, he simply blended in with the other new faces.

He carried trays to the Grand Ballroom and he carried trays of drinks through the crowd.

A light-hearted, almost festive mood grew within him. He was actually serving these people their last meal. How wonderful to see them enjoy it so.

But he kept close track of time. He had one complication he could not have known before the event started. They had stationed one man on the kitchen side of the hall he had to use. He smiled at the guard, walking past to note his size, the equipment he carried and the moves he could expect.

The plan shaped within his mind. He located a small table and carried it to the door. Mumbling and complaining he asked the guard why he always was given the stupid, out of the ordinary jobs. He couldn't make any tips working in the hall. The guard just smiled at him and helped him by opening the door.

Al-Jarwi set the table in place under the intake grating. He did that about the same time Roy escorted Tina and Maria through the front entrance. By then the doors were closed and the draft through the hall had become quite severe. Kassim could sense victory as he felt the air rush past his face. His mission would prove highly successful. He praised Allah for the great gift and for the foresight of the architect.

With the table in place, all he had to do was retrieve the two containers from the walk-in box and set them in place. A simple twist would complete preparations and he would just walk away. The mission would complete itself.

No one noticed or cared when he entered the walk-in box. No one noticed or cared when he lugged the two containers from it and let the heavy door slam behind him.

The guard even opened the hall door for him again. No one

had said anything about containers that size. The directive warned about two-liter bottles.

Nephi entered the ballroom by showing his Congressional Staff ID. He told them he had an urgent message for his boss.

They let him in.

He looked around the room until he spotted the door he had been told to look for—there at the far end. A sense of urgency continued within him—bordering on fear. He fought against the fear part of it by reciting a principle he had read the night before: *Fear and faith cannot exist in the same person at the same time.* He needed to generate more faith right now than he ever before had done.

That same intense pressure from the Spirit continued to wrap about him, strengthening him as it had done for many hours. It was as if he had been encased in it. So long as he was on this errand, it would linger with him. It would sustain him no matter what happened.

The Spirit swelled when he first had seen the door. He showed his ID to the three agents guarding the door. They were not concerned with who went out as much as they were with who might want to come inside the room—the room where the vice president was being introduced.

Nephi took hold of the doorknob. He hesitated for a moment. Then he heard a voice as if it had come from right over his shoulder. *Open it. Walk in.*

Behind him he heard another voice. It was Levant's voice.

"Nephi!"

But Nephi did not respond. He had more important things to do.

When Robert Levant spotted Nephi at the side door he felt a surge of excitement. What an incredible thing. It pleased him to know Nephi was safe. He started to move in Nephi's direction, but his radio sounded with its short burst of static.

Someone had tried to enter the building carrying three two liter bottles of soda pop. The young man tried to run away. He had knocked down an old dowager and had jumped over the hood of a limosine. They were chasing him.

"Be careful of those bottles," Levant ordered. "Stick'em inside the sealed crates. I'm on my way."

Nephi would have to wait.

As Levant moved toward the ballroom entrance he asked for a description of the kid who tried to infiltrate the building with the bottles.

"That's not al-Jarwi," Levant shouted into his radio. "Keep on your toes—all stations—stay with it. Al-Jarwi's still on the loose."

Nephi entered through the door and allowed it to close behind him. At the far end of the hall he could see the form of a man—an agent, probably—collapsed in a heap on the floor. Midway through the short hall was a table. On that table was a large tray with deep sides—the kind used to stack dirty dishes. In the tray were stacked two containers.

Al-Jarwi had just placed the second container in the tray. Nephi could see him give the top a twist. The terrorist reached for the top of the other container.

"Stop!" Nephi ordered.

The voice startled al-Jarwi. But he recovered quickly and reached for his automatic—the end of it extended with a silencer.

"I will not stop. And you will not interfere. You have meddled in my affairs once too often. There is nothing you can do to stop me now."

"Yes, there is." Nephi swallowed as the words he had been given to speak flowed into his mind. "Your bullets will not harm me. I have not yet finished the work I was sent to do."

"And I have not yet finished the work I came to do," al-Jarwi interrupted.

"You will stop immediately. Or you will pay the consequences."

"What consequences? What will you do?"

The terrorist looked away to make sure he turned the right top in the right way.

"Kassim Mustafa al-Jarwi!"

Hearing his full name startled the terrorist. When he looked back at the meddler, he saw not one but three. Two others had flanked the infidel who had his right arm raised. They were dressed in curious costumes. But they had swords and the swords were drawn.

"In the name of Jesus Christ and by the power of the Holy Priesthood that I hold, I rebuke you and curse you and call down the condemnation of the Lord God of Israel upon your head. You will leave this hall immediately! Or you will be struck down where you stand." Nephi let his arm move out of the square position but held it outward, pointing to the door behind him—the one through which he had come—not the one nearest al-Jarwi.

Al-Jarwi remained frozen in place. His cocky assurance had been replaced with sheer terror. He did not move until he saw one of the men behind Nephi gesture with his sword in the direction of the same door.

But that meant he would have to pass by them. Blocked from his mind was any recollection that there was another way out. He walked slowly toward the three of them and when he was close enough, he side-stepped along the wall—as close to the wall as he could get.

When he was barely past them, he saw one of the swordsmen raise his weapon as if to strike.

"The condemnation of God," echoed within his mind.

He screamed and ran, bursting through the double doors.

Near the doorway a stream of Nephi's friends worked toward it. "He went in there," Levant shouted. "I think he went in there."

"You mean you aren't sure?" Roy responded. "Find him. Get your men to find him! They're all over the place. Can't they keep track of one person?"

"Could he have gone through that door?" Maria asked.

Before they could answer, al-Jarwi came screaming out.

A path cleared for the crazy man to run through. No one wanted any part of this lunatic. "He's got a gun!" shouted one of Levant's men.

And Levant headed after him, his own weapon drawn and ready to fire. But he couldn't fire. Too many people around. All he could do was follow the terrorist. He shouted into his radio:

"Al-Jarwi is heading for the main entrance. Stop him!"

They tried but failed.

*   *   *   *

Parking was full. No one expected this big of a crowd. The attendants tried their best to accommodate the mass of people who wanted to leave their cars. General Arnold Moore would have preferred to leave his car. But the place was a madhouse. He appraised the situation and decided he simply would find parking on his own. He had commandeered an Air Force staff car for the evening. He had refused the use of a driver. That had been a mistake. Now he had to take his chances parking on the street.

His plan was to leave it on the street somewhere—red zone, purple zone, whatever—and hope for the best. Under the circumstances, with the war and all, it would be hard for a policeman to tag it wherever he left it, he thought.

It took him precious minutes just to work his way through the maze of abandoned cars. Finally a space opened in front of him—with all the instincts of his fighter pilot mentality, he jammed his foot on the gas.

He accelerated so fast that he hardly saw the man run in front of him. The impact jolted the man, sending him flying into the front quarter of an army staff car that had been parked askew.

"I didn't see him," General Moore shouted when he stopped and bailed out of his car. "He just ran right in front of me."

A man carrying an automatic was jogging toward them. He stooped over to look at the victim. Then for some reason he looked up at the General.

He smiled—but more at a thought than at the General. He would not have to tell the ambulance driver to drive slowly.

"Thank you, General," Levant said. "They just might give you another medal for this."

CHAPTER 14
Epilogue

News Brief
Sunday, January 20, 1991

SAUDI ARABIA—Operation Desert Storm continued this morning with relentless air strikes against strategic targets in Baghdad, southern Iraq, and Kuwait.

For a day and a half bad weather has been Iraq's best defense in this intense, albeit one-sided war. But with skies clearing on Saturday, pilots were able to drop their bombs on targets.

Saturday also saw an air-sea assault on anti-aircraft platforms in the Persian Gulf off the coast of Kuwait. The lightning raid resulted in the capture of the war's first prisoners of war. Five Iraqis were reported killed.

JERUSALEM—Negotiations continue between the United States and Israel to convince the Jewish state to back away from its eye-for-an-eye military policies.

After two successive nights of attacks by Iraqi Scud missiles, U.S. diplomats are urging continued restraint by Israel in the face of mounting pressure to seek revenge against the common foe.

U.S. spokesmen have reported offers to defend Israel with U.S. Patriot anti-missile missiles and have pledged to seek out and destroy Iraqi Scud missile launchers.

ALEXANDRIA, VA —

SOMEBODY HAD THE AUDACITY TO CALL NEPHI VERY EARLY in the morning. The Congressional aide had been so tense for so long that once given the chance to relax he had fallen into a deep sleep. When some part of his mind finally recognized the telephone's ring, Nephi slipped his uncoordinated, mostly dormant body out of bed. His legs hit the floor just a second before his torso. Now upright, he became more alert. But his body still remained uncoordinated and uncooperative. He crashed into a protruding doorjamb and bounced from it into the half-wall that set his kitchenette apart from the hallway. He staggered in the general direction of the phone and dropped his frame onto the couch beside it. He picked it up and managed to speak.

"Hullo."

Nephi was greeted by a bright, cheery voice but remained unmoved. He heard the words of the speaker on the other end but wasn't really listening. His own replies took more the form of grunts and throat clearing than spoken English. Only when he replaced the phone on its cradle did he fully realize he had just agreed to meet with his bishop within an hour.

Nephi sat on the bench outside the bishop's office. His body still ached from everything that had happened over the past week—had it been that long? Longer? It had been 10 days. No, nine—whatever. The last three or four days had seemed to him not much more than a whole month. He wondered how he might have felt if he had not been required to endure such a prolonged series of interviews with various law enforcement agencies involved with the incident. Much more rested, for sure.

They couldn't understand what happened. So they persisted in their pursuit of answers—answers beyond what he already had given them. Where did he go when he disappeared from the office? He simply had to get away and think things through. What happened in the hall at the Gala? He had no idea. He thought he saw someone go into the hall who looked like al-Jarwi. He had no idea what made the man rush from there screaming like a madman. Maybe the chemicals affected him. How should he know?

No one needed to know anything about his spiritual experience. And he truly had nothing more he could tell them about what happened in the hall. He had seen only the agent on the floor and al-Jarwi with the chemicals.

Repetition had created intense stress within him. And stress had drained his body of strength—strength he really didn't have in great abundance. They finally finished with him at around three o'clock Saturday afternoon. He rallied enough energy to call Eleña before going home. The call from the bishop's executive secretary had been the first measure of consciousness he had experienced since falling onto his bed when he finally got home.

Rushing to get ready for his appointment with the bishop had wakened him some. But he had been running on reserves for so long he wondered when they would run dry. What did the bishop want anyway? Was he in some sort of trouble for all that he had been involved in? Had he found out about the night he had spent with Eleña alone in Williamsburg? How would he explain it all?

Bishop Garner opened the door and bid goodbye to the couple with whom he had been meeting. When they began to walk away, he turned his full attention to his next appointment.

Nephi stood and looked the tall, slender leader in the eyes. And they grasped hands in a solid expression of appreciation and brotherhood. The bishop's soft, steady voice invited Nephi inside.

Seated with the bishop's desk between them they first talked about a variety of things—things friends would want to know about each other. Gradually, Nephi felt his disposition turn more positive and his strength return.

The bishop even asked him about the reception—but as a friend, not as an investigator. He accepted Nephi's brief account of the incident.

"Nephi," Bishop Garner began after a few more incidental items had been discussed. "There's a position in this ward I believe the Lord would like you to fill. Would you give it some thought and prayer? Take as much time as you need, but I would appreciate a response as soon as possible."

"Okay," Nephi answered. He had never turned down a Church calling and had wondered when one would be given him out here.

"We need you to teach the twelve and thirteen year olds."

"Sunday School?"

"Yes."

"I've never taught anyone that young before," Nephi explained.

"This can be a tough age, Brother Nicholes. Some people do very well in teaching this age group. Others have problems. The only thing I can tell you is that I sincerely believe the Lord wants you to have this experience."

"I'm willing to give it a try. But I've got to tell you, right now I don't feel qualified to take on something like this."

The bishop smiled. "None of us are ever truly qualified for the positions we're called to fill. The Lord gives us these opportunities so we can grow in them. I know it's a tough age group. But I have a good feeling about you. You have a lot to offer. You could make a big difference in their lives. They need all the help you can give them."

Nephi looked at the bishop and nodded.

"Great," the bishop said. "Just keep in mind this one thing. It's like the stake president told me when he called me to be bishop. 'Two people can do anything, so long as one of them is the Lord.'"

The bishop's words reached deeply into Nephi's soul and for a moment his heart and mind rehearsed the peaks and valleys of the emotional and spiritual roller coaster he had been riding since he first saw Eleña in the Metro Station less that ten days ago. He had found her, lost her, found her again and almost had lost her forever. The terrorist had sought their lives and had come terribly close to succeeding on three occasions.

Only one thing had remained constant—the power and willingness of a loving Father to guide and direct, to shield and protect, even in the most precarious moments. After what he had been through Nephi saw himself clearly. How weak and fickle he had been—driven too often by his carnal mind—reacting to critical circumstances as if his own judgement could possibly prevail against such a powerful and cunning adversary. He realized how close he had come to losing everything he loved when he put himself in a compromising position with Eleña.

Nephi looked into his bishop's eyes. "Yes," he answered simply. "I know."

First thing Monday morning Nephi measured the moments until things settled into the more normal routines. Without calling attention to his intent, he slipped over to the legislative side and stood quietly beside Janice Fielding, Congressman Hersch's Senior Legislative Assistant. She looked at him as she had done so often before—a touch of boredom mixed with irritation. She allowed her toe to tap on the floor in a rhythm that seemed to be keeping track of the seconds she had to endure his presence.

"Welcome back," he began. "How was your vacation?"

She shrugged. She had taken a trip home and had enjoyed it tremendously. She even had interviewed for a job and felt she had the inside track in getting it. Better pay—less work. But she wouldn't let Nephi know. Why should she? Such items of news were strictly for friends.

"It was okay," she said without feeling.

"That's too bad. People who work as hard as you do deserve a vacation that's more than 'okay.'"

She looked at him and managed a smile.

"But what I came over here to tell you was that I don't think I ever thanked you for all I learned from you when I first came here. I just wanted you to know how much I appreciate you and all you did back then when I was just learning—and how good you are at what you do. If there is anything I can do to help you, I would appreciate the opportunity to do so."

She had looked away, as she always did when he began to speak. But something in his voice caused her to look up at him. He was smiling at her—a warm smile—not at all forced. She thought about saying something sarcastic. But she stopped. She couldn't. Then she nodded. That seemed to satisfy him. He just stepped away, raising his hand in a casual wave at her.

Quickly she gathered up a couple of files and followed him through the narrow passageway to the front office. She stepped into Roy Ivars' area—just a step or two away from Nephi's—and invited the administrative assistant to walk down the hall with her.

"What on earth happened to Nephi?" she asked as soon as they cleared the doorway.

The attorney looked at her and shrugged. He had no idea how else to respond to her.

"I mean, he's changed. He's actually acting like a human being. Haven't you noticed?"

The administrative assistant smiled at her and nodded. "Yes. I have noticed." He shrugged his shoulders again.

"He just came back and said some nice things," she admitted. "I really think he meant it. He really has changed. I think he might make it after all. I kind of like him this way."

Roy stopped and they stood by the windows looking into the bland inner courtyard of the Longworth Building. And for the first time, without his having to pump her for information, she briefed him on two pieces of legislation their boss would need to deal with in the coming weeks. She even asked for his advice on strategy.

One Saturday morning, shortly after the incident at the International Plaza, Maria Elefia Moore was baptized a member of the Chruch of Jesus Christ of Latter-day Saints. In the early afternoon of that same day she stood beside the man who had immersed her in the waters of the small font at the Mount Vernon LDS Stake Center and became Mrs. Nephi Nicholes.

It startled Margarita Moore to hear Bishop Garner refer to her daughter as Elefia instead of Maria. But Rita had always liked the name and quickly adjusted to the change. Unfortunately that was not the only thing Rita was forced to adjust to that day. For one thing her daughter was not being married in a magnificent Catholic cathedral. That had been Rita's dream for her daughter from the day she was born. Instead this was just a plain old wedding. The bishop didn't even wear special robes. And the chapel was decorated only with a few flowers. What a drag.

Oh, it was a nice enough church. Actually the building did have a certain charm—stately colonial lines with impressive columns in front and a well-designed steeple. And Rita had to admit the church did look picturesque with so many tall trees placed all around the massive lawn. And there was a splendid view of the Potomac River. But it just wasn't like a cathedral.

And it mortified her to think that her daughter actually had agreed to be baptized—not just seen by her fiancé but touched by him as well—on her wedding day—before the wedding! Highly inappropriate! Bad luck for certain.

For a whole year she expected the marriage to fold. It didn't console her much to be invited to Provo, Utah, where they were going to be "sealed" to each other for time and eternity. Rita didn't mind going all that way. It really was more practical for the general to take her out there than for all of her son-in-law's family to migrate out to Washington. It just seemed so unnecessary, especially since they weren't going to let her and the general inside their temple to witness the ceremony.

To make everything worse, Eleña woke up the very morning of the big event with contractions! That made Rita plead more aggressively with everyone to let her accompany her daughter inside. All she got for her trouble was assurance they would take good care of her and move things along as quickly as they could.

So Rita and the general had to watch their very expectant daughter waddle inside that beautiful white building. They smiled at her and waved. But as soon as she disappeared inside they began venting their feelings of frustration to each other about the whole fiasco. The longer Rita spent cooling her heels, waiting for her daughter to come out, the more items Rita added to her list of complaints. She even practiced reciting her list to the general. Her son-in-law was going to hear about this for a long time.

But when they came out there was no time to talk with anyone. Eleña was in a wheelchair and Nephi was rushing her from the building. She still had on her wedding dress—modified to accommodate her bulging tummy. Between contractions they helped her into one of the Nicholes' cars. But before they could leave, the ambulance came and they transferred her.

Everyone else piled into cars as best they could and trailed after the ambulance to the hospital

Once they got there it didn't take long for the child to be born. Out of resptect, Rita Moore was given first chance to hold her granddaughter. She looked down into the priceless little face and began to cry.

"She looks a lot like you did when you were born, Eleña," Rita said, her voice tightened with emotion and tears blurring her vision.

After that, her list of complaints didn't seem so important. When Rita came to visit at the hospital the next morning, she felt far more like listening and talking than scolding.

"The ceremony was really beautiful, Mother."

"I'm glad. I was so worried about you. I wanted to be with you."

"That would have been nice, Mother. But it really wasn't like a big church wedding, you know."

"It wasn't?" Rita was truly surprised to hear that.

"No, Mother. It was very simple. Nothing elaborate at all. Oh, the temple is beautiful inside. But what was important was what we promised to each other and to the Lord. The most beautiful part was what we felt inside, not what went on outside. You really need to know a little about the gospel before you can fully understand," Elena explained.

"You don't think I could understand?" Rita snapped, a hint of her frustrations and resentments from the day before showing in her voice.

"Oh, yes. You definitely *could* understand. But right now it probably wouldn't mean much to you. You're just not ready to hear such things. I mean they weren't talking in a foreign language or anything like that. But there's a deeper meaning to the things we heard and pledged."

Rita looked at her daughter and the precious little waif she held in her arms. She saw how happy both mother and child seemed to be. It made her think of when she had held a precious little waif of her own so many years ago. And Rita knew she could not allow her petty irritations to fester within her. All this was a done deal. She had not been there for the ceremony. But she certainly could be there for her family for the rest of her life.

As much as they tried, neither Nephi nor Elena could get the Moores to study the gospel. It took the renewed friendship and increased contact with Roy and Tina Ivars to open their minds to even listen. It was the general who decided to put the great promise to the test—the one about the Book of Mormon. He began reading it. He had a hard time praying. He wasn't all that sure there was a real God available to hear what he wanted to ask.

But he asked anyway. And when he would describe what he got back he simply would say:

"Wow!" That's all he would say—just "Wow!"

It would take several months after returning from Utah before the Moores would accept baptism. But on another Saturday morning the occasion of their baptism was made a little extra special for Rita when her daughter complained of nausea and then left the room to throw up.

"It's awful for you to find out this way," Eleña said apologetically. "Old Fertile Myrtle here is going to make you a grandmother again."

* * * *

It took Arnie Moore a long time to understand what had happened to him on that fateful night of the benefit. He was relieved to be off the hook so easily for running down that man. He had hardly seen him coming. He certainly hadn't seen the weapon al-Jarwi was carrying—even though it looked so formidable to everyone else. What he had the most difficulty in understanding was exactly what everyone else couldn't understand either.

What made that highly trained and highly experienced terrorist run out of that hallway where only this one man—his meek little son-in-law—was left standing? Nephi wasn't even holding a weapon. Every time Arnie would ask him, Nephi would give him the same answer.

"I have no idea," Nephi would say. "He was standing there and I ordered him to stop what he was doing and get out. He looked at me in the most peculiar way. Then he began to obey me. He walked toward me and when he got close to me he began side-stepping along the wall. I mean, he couldn't get closer to that wall if he was painted on it. And when he was barely past me he just screamed and started to run. Then I remembered what Levant had told me about the bomb. It was a binary bomb and neither liquid was dangerous alone. So I just lifted one jug out of the tray and took the detonating devices out of the top of both bottles."

And he would shrug.

But no one believed he had told the whole story. No one except his wife. She always believed things her husband told her —especially when she received confirmation through the Spirit that they were true.

He had been right. He hadn't seen anything else. But also she knew very well that he had not told everyone the entire story. How could he tell an FBI agent—who would be writing it in some report—that he had been told to do something by the still, small voice of the Holy Spirit? And how could he tell anyone that he knew he would be preserved by the Lord and that the Lord would fight his battles for him? She understood that, all right. She just had never known exactly how the Lord had done it.

It was best left this way, she decided.

The whole thing was dealt with by the newspapers in a rather innocuous way. Sentiment favoring the war had soared so high across the country, that even the most liberal editors played the whole incident in a very minor way.

The man obviously had gone berserk. Why not leave it at that and let the whole thing fade away?

Vice President Quayle had become an instant hit. The man had run through the hall just after he had started speaking. To settle the crowd, the speaker simply mentioned that he knew people would do most anything to avoid hearing him speak. Then he held up his notes and added, "But really it wasn't going to be all that bad."

General Moore had delivered his message from General Charles Horner, commander of the U.S. Air Force in the Persian Gulf theater. His comments, along with Vice President Quayle's comments, had been well received.

The Muslim reporters, friendly to Kassim al-Jarwi, had attended as he requested. But they never could find out what he expected to happen. They simply wrote sad stories that he had been killed before delivering a message to the Vice President. They never learned what it could have been.

Yussef and Sariah married in Washington's beautiful Islamic Mosque, shortly after they were released from the hospital. Their scars had not yet healed. But they couldn't have planned the event more perfectly. They returned from their honeymoon the very day the war ended.

During the one-hundred-hour ground war, Sariah had watched as millions did, the surrender of numerous Iraqi soldiers.

One group, briefly shown on television, showed her father. Beside him were his sons—her brothers—and one uncle.

The battered remains of the terrorist were quickly dealt with by the medical examiner's office. The State Department boxed him up in an appropriate casket and released him to the Yemeni Consulate. He had become a serious embarrassment to them. Officially they denounced his actions. But they had to accept his corpse. Once the casket had arrived in Yemen, officials quickly dispatched it to Iraq. There they dealt with it as they dealt with all who failed. He was thrown into a lonely, unmarked grave. The nice casket, however, was reserved for someone who deserved it.

It took four months of intense physical therapy before FBI Agent Howard Dalton was able to return to his duties. At least twice a week Nephi visited him and helped him with his exercises. After an initial period of coolness their relationship warmed up. Dalton received a citation for bravery. A certain congressman insisted on it. Robert Levant supported the move, but he did wish they had a way to cite stupidity too. He thought Nephi would have been the perfect candidate. Nephi would not have argued with that.

One night, before the birth of their second child, Eleña dreamed of him. She saw him grown. He had become a handsome, distinguished-looking man. He was getting out of his car—in the driveway of a lovely home. Then she saw two little girls running toward him. They threw their arms around his neck, happy he was home.

She told no one about this, not even Nephi. For a fleeting moment she wondered if she should try to sketch the scene that lingered so vividly in her mind. She preferred, however, to just nestle closer to her husband. A sense of peace descended upon her. And she smiled.